Economic Change in Asia

Since the 2008 global economic crisis, East Asian economies have faced a number of macroeconomic issues including China's new growth model, the middle-income trap in developing East Asian countries, and the growing natural fiber market and its socio-economic implications. This book addresses these key topical issues which East Asian economies are facing today. Written by international experts in the area of Asian economics and business, it presents the most recent macroeconomic outlook in the region and then goes on to analyse a number of business corporations and industry-related cases, focussing on the theme of firms' strategies.

Examining the links between environmental and financial performance, corporate social responsibility and the transfer of environmental management, financial accounting standards, the relationship between corporate sustainability activities and corporate profit, and the different cultural approaches towards business ethics, this book provides both practical strategies and new theoretical insights. As such it will appeal to students, scholars and practitioners interested in Asian business and economics.

M. Bruna Zolin is Professor of Economics of Rural Development and Commodity Markets at Ca' Foscari University of Venice, Department of Economics, Italy.

Bernadette Andreosso-O'Callaghan is Adjunct Professor of East-Asian Economics at the Fakultät für Wirtschaftswissenschaft, Ruhr Universität Bochum, Germany, and Jean Monnet Chair of Economics at the Euro-Asia Centre and Kemmy Business School, University of Limerick, Ireland.

Jacques Jaussaud is Professor of Management Sciences at the Université de Pau et des Pays de l'Adour, France.

Routledge Studies in the Growth Economies of Asia

For a full list of titles in this series, please visit www.routledge.com

Economic Change in Asia

Implication for corporate strategy
and social responsibility

**Edited by M. Bruna Zolin,
Bernadette Andreosso-O'Callaghan
and Jacques Jaussaud**

Routledge
Taylor & Francis Group

LONDON AND NEW YORK

First published 2017
by Routledge
2 Park Square, Milton Park, Abingdon, Oxon OX14 4RN

and by Routledge
711 Third Avenue, New York, NY 10017

Routledge is an imprint of the Taylor & Francis Group, an informa business

© 2017 M. Bruna Zolin, Bernadette Andreosso-O'Callaghan and Jacques Jaussaud

British Library Cataloguing in Publication Data
A catalogue record for this book is available from the British Library

Library of Congress Cataloging-in-Publication Data
Names: Zolin, M. Bruna, editor. | Andrâeosso-O'Callaghan, Bernadette, 1959– editor. | Jaussaud, Jacques, 1957– editor.
Title: Economic change in Asia : implication for corporate strategy and social responsibility / edited by M. Bruna Zolin, Bernadette Andreosso-O'Callaghan and Jacques Jaussaud.
Description: 1 Edition. | New York : Routledge, 2016. | Series: Routledge studies in the growth economies of Asia ; 13 | Includes bibliographical references and index.
Identifiers: LCCN 2016014446 | ISBN 9781138186712 (hardback) | ISBN 9781315643656 (ebook)
Subjects: LCSH: Social responsibility of business—Asia. | Corporations—Asia—Finance. | Economic development—Asia.
Classification: LCC HD60.5.A78 E36 2016 | DDC 658.4/012—dc23
LC record available at https://lccn.loc.gov/2016014446

ISBN: 978-1-138-18671-2 (hbk)
ISBN: 978-1-315-64365-6 (ebk)

Typeset in Times New Roman
by Apex CoVantage, LLC

Printed and bound in Great Britain by
TJ International Ltd, Padstow, Cornwall

Contents

Figures

Tables

Acknowledgements

Many thanks are due to the Yokohama National University for hosting the 19th Euro-Asia International Research Seminar in May to June 2014, in particular to Professor Hiroyuki Nakamura, Professor Shuji Mizoguchi and Professor Shiho Futagami, all from the Faculty of Business of that university. The editors would like to thank all the authors for their participation in this project. We are also most grateful to Carolina Gavagnin of the Università Ca' Foscari of Venice for her invaluable help in the editorial process throughout the different stages of the project, as well as to Aoife O'Callaghan from *Writing Precision* for proofreading the entire manuscript.

Contributors

Igor Alvarez is Professor at the Financial Economics I Department of the University of Basque Country, Spain. Since January 2013 he has been a member of the Environmental Management Accounting Network (EMAN) Europe.

Bernadette Andreosso-O'Callaghan holds the Jean Monnet Chair of Economic Integration at the Kemmy Business School of the University of Limerick (Ireland), and she is also Adjunct Professor of East Asian Economics at the Ruhr University Bochum (Germany). She has published extensively in the following areas: comparative Europe-Asia economic integration, and economic growth and structural change in Asian countries, with a focus on East-Asian countries.

Guilhem Fabre is Professor of Economics and Chinese Studies at the Université du Havre, Le Havre (France) and Research Associate at the China Centre (CECMC), École des Hautes Études en Sciences Sociales (EHESS), Paris. Since 2011 he has been co-responsible for the BRICS Séminaires at the Fondation Maison des Sciences de l'Homme (FMSH), Paris.

Ainhoa Garayar is Assistant Professor of the Department of Financial Economy I at the University of the Basque Country in San Sebastián (Spain). Her recent research has focused on the critical analysis of the sustainability reports concept and the adoption of United Nations Global Compact initiative. She has published her research in various international academic journals (i.e. *Sustainability*, *Journal of Cleaner Production and Spanish Accounting Review*).

Carolina Gavagnin is Research Grant Holder at the Department of Economics of Ca' Foscari University of Venice, Venice (Italy). Her current research focuses on agricultural markets, food security and climate variability.

Jörn-Carsten Gottwald is full professor in East Asian Politics at the Ruhr University Bochum, Germany, since 2011. Earlier, he held positions in Political Sciences and Chinese Studies at the Free University Berlin, the University of Trier, Germany, and the National University of Ireland, Cork. With his background in Chinese Studies and Political Economy he has published on the politics of financial services regulation, China's political economy and EU-China relations.

Sadako Inoue is Professor of Accounting at the University of Marketing and Distribution Sciences (UMDS) in Kobe, Hyogo (Japan).

Jacques Jaussaud is Professor of Management, University of Pau, France, and Director of the CREG Research team in Management of this university. His research interests are in the areas of business strategy, organization, control, and human resources management, with a particular focus on Japan, China, and other Asian countries. He has published widely in these areas, including in the following academic journals: *Management International Review, The International Journal of Human Resource Management, Journal of International Management, Asian Business and Management, Asian Pacific Business Review, Transition Studies Review*, and so on.

Ikuo Kato is Research Fellow at Yokohama National University, Center for Economic Growth Strategy in Yokohama (Japan). He was conferred the degree of Ph.D. in Business Administration from Yokohama National University. He is also Representative Director and President of Add To Science Co., Ltd., Advisor of Concord International Investment Group, LP Tokyo, and Advisor of International Development Center of Japan Inc. He has experience in marketing as director at various global investment banks.

Tatsuo Kimbara is Professor at the Faculty of Commercial Sciences at the Hiroshima Shudo University, Hiroshima (Japan).

Kazuma Murakami is Associate Professor at the School of Environmental Science at the University of Shiga Prefecture, Shiga (Japan).

Eduardo Ortas is Associate Professor in Accounting and Finance at The University of Zaragoza (Spain) and invited Researcher at the Amsterdam Business School of the University of Amsterdam, at the Groningen Faculty of Economics and Business (the Netherlands) and Kent Business School (United Kingdom). His research interests are in the area of corporate social responsibility, with particular focus on environmental management issues. His research has been mainly published in *Ecological Economics, Supply Chain Management: An International Journal, Journal of Cleaner Production, Journal of Business Ethics, Energy and Corporate Social Responsibility & Environmental Management*, among others. He is also a member of the Editorial Board of the *International Journal of Sustainable Economy*.

Tatsuyuki Ota is Guest Researcher at the Asian Cultures Research Institute of Toyo University, Tokyo (Japan). He has been Professor of Economics at the Department of Management of Toyo University and has been a Visiting Professor in several universities. He served as development consultant to various government projects and international institutions. He received Fulbright Asian Scholar-in Residence status with teaching experience in the USA.

Robert Pauls is Lecturer at the Institute of Asian Politics, Faculty of East Asian Studies of the Ruhr University Bochum (Germany). He is also coordinator of the Masters Program in East Asian Politics. His current research focuses on Chinese capitalism and aims to explain the particular features of China's political economy.

Jérôme Rive is Senior Lecturer of Management at the University of Lyon – Jean Moulin and Dean of the IAE Lyon School of Management (France), with research interests in human resources management, and cross-cultural studies. He received his Ph.D. in Business Administration from the University of Lyon.

Tetsuya Takeuchi is Managing Director at TAC Co., Ltd. He received his Ph.D. in Business Administration from Yokohama National University (Japan). He has over 20 years' experience in product development and marketing as a director at various global investment banks. His research interests are in the area of corporate accounting, finance, and banking.

Marc Valax is Senior Lecturer of Management at the University of Lyon – Jean Moulin, IAE Lyon School of Management (France), with research interests in globalization, international human resources management, and cross-cultural studies. He has served as a Visiting Professor in many Latin American universities. He has worked as an international placement consultant in London, and has consulted with and conducted training programs for organizations in Africa, Europe and Asia.

M. Bruna Zolin is Professor of Economics – Rural Development and Commodity Markets – at the Department of Economics of Ca' Foscari University of Venice (Italy). She was Deputy-Head of the School of Asian Studies and Business Management at Ca' Foscari University. She has served as an expert for the Food Agricultural Organization (FAO) in Rome and she has been a visiting Professor in several universities She has published mainly in the areas of agricultural markets and rural development policies.

Abbreviations

AcSB	Accounting Standards Board of Canada
ADB	Asian Development Bank
AIC	Akaike's information criterion
AMC	asset management company
ASC	Accounting Standards Council
ASBJ	Accounting Standards Board of Japan
ASX	Australian Securities Exchange
BIR	Bureau of Internal Revenue
BOA	Board of Accountancy
BRICS	Brazil, Russia, India, China and South Africa
CAA	Clean Air Act
CalPERS	California Public Employees' Retirement Fund
CBRC	China Banking Regulatory Commission
CC Index	Chinese Cotton Index
CCI	Cotton Council International
CCP	Chinese Communist Party
CEO	chief executive officer
CEP	company's environmental performance
CFP	corporate financial performance
CFR	cost and freight
CGP	corporate governance performance
CIRC	China Insurance Regulatory Commission
CMR	company's market return
CNCRC	China National Cotton Reserve Corporation
CNPC	China National Petroleum Corporation
CO_2	carbon dioxide
COP	Conference of the Parties
CPA	certified public accountant
CPC	Communist Party of China
CRT	credit risk transfer
CSP	company's social performance
CSR	corporate social responsibility
CSRC	China Securities Regulatory Commission

DDM	Dividend Discount Model
DTI	Department of Trade and Industry
EC	European Commission
EHESS	École des Hautes Études en Sciences Sociales
EKC	Environmental Kuznets Curve
EOI	export-oriented industrialization
ESG	environmental, social and governance
EU	European Union
FAO	Food and Agriculture Organization
FDI	foreign direct investment
FIEA	Financial Instruments and Exchange Act
FMSH	Fondation Maison des Sciences de l'Homme
FP	financial performance
FRSC	Financial Reporting Standard Council
FTZ	free trade zone
GAAP	generally accepted accounting principles
GDP	gross domestic product
GFC	global financial crisis
GFCF	gross fixed capital formation
GHG	greenhouse gas
GHQ	General Health Questionnaire
GICS	Global Industry Classification Standard
GM	genetically modified
GMO	genetically modified organism
GMP	Good Manufacturing Practice
GNI	gross national income
GPIF	Government Pension Investment Fund
GRI	Global Reporting Initiative
HIC	High-Income Countries
IAS	International Accounting Standard
IASB	International Accounting Standards Boards
IASC	International Accounting Standards Committee
ICAC	International Cotton Advisory Committee
ICBC	Industrial and Commercial Bank of China
IFRS	International Financial Reporting Standards
IMF	International Monetary Fund
ISI	import-substitution industrialization
JCCI	Japan Chamber of Commerce and Industry
JETRO	Japan External Trade Organization
JFCPTA	Japan Federation of Certified Public Tax Accountants' Association
JICPA	Japanese Institute of Certified Public Accountants
KLD	Kinder, Lydenberg and Domini
LGFV	Local Government Finance Vehicle
LIC	low-income countries
LMC	lower-middle-income countries

MIC	middle-income countries
MMF	manmade fibers
MNE	multinational enterprise
MoH	Ministry of Health
MSCI	Morgan Stanley Capital International
NAO	National Audit Office
NASDAQ	National Association of Securities Dealers Automated Quotation
NDRC	National Development and Reform Commission
NEM	nonequity mode
NGO	nongovernmental organization
NHTD	National Hospital of Tropical Diseases
NOV	notice of violation
NOx	Nitrogen Oxide
NPAE	Nonpublicly Accountable Entity
NPO	nonprofit organization
NPV	net present value
NYFE	New York Futures Exchange
OECD	Organisation for Economic Co-operation and Development
OLS	ordinary least squares
P2P	peer to peer
PAS	Philippines Accounting Standard
PBOC	People's Bank of China
PDR	People's Democratic Republic
PFRS	Philippines Financial Reporting Standard
PFRSC	Philippines Financial Reporting Standard Council
PICPA	Philippines Institute of Certified Public Accountants
PPP	purchasing power parity
PRC	People's Republic of China
PRI	Principles for Responsible Investment
PSEC	Philippines Securities and Exchange Commission
PSFAS	Philippines Statement of Financial Accounting Standards
REACH	Registration, Evaluation, Authorization and Restriction of Chemical Substances
RMB	renminbi
RMC	Revenue Memorandum Circular
ROA	returns on assets
ROHS	Restriction of Hazardous Substances
RR	Revenue Regulations
SASAC	State-Owned Assets Supervision and Administration Commission
SIC	Schwarz's information criterion
SME	small and medium enterprise
SMEAJ	Small and Medium Enterprise Agency of Japan
SO_2	sulfur dioxide
SOE	state-owned enterprise
SOx	sulfur oxide

SRC	Securities Regulations Code
SRI	socially responsible investment
TB	tuberculosis
TSE	Tokyo Stock Exchange
TVE	township and village enterprise
UMC	upper-middle-income countries
UNCTAD	United Nations Conference on Trade and Development
UNGC	United Nations Global Compact
UNGCO	United Nations Global Compact Office
USDA	United States Department of Agriculture
VINARES	Vietnam Resistance Project
WBCSD	World Business Council for Sustainable Development
WDI	World Development Indicators
WMP	wealth management product
WTO	World Trade Organization
WWF	World Wide Fund for Nature

Introduction

M. Bruna Zolin, Bernadette Andreosso-O'Callaghan and Jacques Jaussaud

Economic crises normally spur reforms that ultimately stimulate economic change. The Western-born global financial crisis (GFC) is one such major event; it invigorated a reshuffling of world economic growth, with some East Asian countries starting to gain a sense of assertiveness at the global institutional level. Countries such as China seized the opportunity of the GFC to unleash a full-blown outward direct investment policy. Due to its past experience in dealing with financial and economic crises, South Korea emerged relatively unscathed, whereas the new Abe administration was able to put the Japanese economy back on an export path, albeit at still very low growth rates. Yet, the ability of Asian, and in particular of East Asian, economies to stimulate global growth has been put to question. Economic growth at the global level remains sluggish with business organizations unwilling to invest sufficiently given the still high level of uncertainty prevailing in both the Western countries and in Asia. Relatedly, uncertainty and slow growth are conducive to sociopolitical instability and perhaps to unrest.

It is in the background of the GFC that the different chapters in this volume address the key issue of business organizations' strategies in terms of corporate and social responsibility (CSR) as a way to respond to economic change in Asia. Through their CSR strategies, business organizations become important actors in smoothing out sociopolitical tensions, particularly in times of economic uncertainty.

The first two chapters by Guilhem Fabre and Robert Pauls and colleagues inform the reader on the macroeconomic environment prevailing in the biggest Asian country, namely China, since the GFC. Fabre's chapter shows how the economic slowdown in China follows the unprecedented expansion of credit due to the 2009–10 stimulus package; this shifted growth in favor of state-owned enterprises and real estate, a sector that the author refers to as "the lion's share of the state-party system". The chapter discusses how the Chinese government is now faced with the issue of sustainable growth, which encompasses the delicate problem of income distribution. The following chapter discusses the financialization hypothesis in the case of China. Although the Chinese economy is not yet financialized, as is commonly understood, most indicators show the following: the decline of the traditional growth regime based on physical capital accumulation, the shift of the economy into nonmanufacturing activities such as real estate and financial products, and a departure from financial repression paving the way to a deeper integration of China into global finance. Chapter 3 by Tatsuyuki Ota shifts the discussion to the Environmental Kuznets Curve (EKC) as applied across a number of Asian countries during the 1990–2010 period. The findings are at odds with what is normally expected from such a comparative analysis. Also appraised at the macroeconomic level and taking also into account the changing economic conditions arising from the GFC, the chapter by Carolina Gavagnin and M. Bruna Zolin aims at investigating the main characteristics of the world cotton market. The choice of this market is motivated by the importance of a downstream industry – the textile industry – in the economic take-off of many Asian countries, including China.

The five remaining chapters in the second part of the book deal with the strategies of corporate organizations. Chapter 5 by Igor Alvarez and colleagues aims to check whether the national origin of firms influences the companies' social, environmental and corporate governance performance. Based on a neoinstitutional framework and applying regression analysis, the chapter investigates the case of the three countries with the most companies committed to the United Nations Global Compact initiative, namely Spain, France and Japan. In addition, the research tests the often-expected moderating effect of the country-specific characteristics on the relationship between financial performance and firms' social, environmental and corporate governance.

The environmental dimension is a core concept in both Chapters 6 (by Tatsuo Kimbara and Kazuma Mirakami) and 8 (by Ikuo Kato and Tetsuya Takeuchi). Chapter 6 analyzes the relationship between the CSR assessment of firms and the international transfer of environmental management by using a quantitative method in the case of Japanese firms in Vietnam. Also based on data from Japanese companies, Chapter 8 examines the relationship between corporations' sustainability activities and profitability. Real option methodology and environmental accounting are key concepts and methods in this chapter.

Chapter 7 by Sadako Inoue considers two countries with different approaches to accounting standardization for small and medium enterprises (SMEs), namely the Philippines, a country that adopted the International Financial Reporting Standards (IFRS) for SMEs, and Japan, which did not in spite of a higher degree of economic and institutional development. Analyzing the accounting standardization approaches and shortcomings in both countries, Chapter 7 calls for the need to adapt better standards to the actual characteristics of SMEs compared with larger firms. Finally, Chapter 9 by Marc Valax and Jérôme Rive casts a critical eye on an important industry from the viewpoint of CSR, namely the pharmaceutical industry. Based on primary data, the cross-case study looks at the cultural differences between French and US top manager expats in this industry in relation to business ethics.

All chapters in this volume arose from the 19th Euro-Asia International Research Seminar held at Yokohama University in 2014, and all contributions have been written by experts with an international profile. Euro-Asia International Research Seminars have been held alternatively in European and Asian countries since

1994. In-depth exchanges between researchers from Europe and Asia within the framework of the seminar help blend varied approaches and analyses. Following a number of other publications drawn from previous Seminars, including Dzever and Jaussaud (1997, 1999, 2001), and Andreosso-O'Callaghan *et al.* (2001, 2007, 2008, 2012, 2014), we hope that this book will provide readers with useful insights into current economic and corporate issues in Asia.

References

Andreosso-O'Callaghan B., Bassino J.P., Dzever S. and Jaussaud J. (Eds) (2007) *The Economic Relations between Asia and Europe: Trade and Investment*, Chandos Publishing, Oxford.

Andreosso-O'Callaghan B., Bassino J.P. and Jaussaud J. (Eds) (2001) *Changing Economic Environment in Asia and Business Strategies*, Palgrave, London.

Andreosso-O'Callaghan B., Dzever S. and Jaussaud J. (Eds) (2008) *Evolving Corporate Structures and Cultures in Asia*, ISTE Publishing, London.

Andreosso-O'Callaghan B. and Jaussaud J. (Eds) (2012) The Evolving Nature of Corprate Social Responsibility: Asian and European Perspectives, Special Issue of *Asian Business and Management*, 11(3), pp. 247–2479.

Andreosso-O'Callaghan B., Jaussaud J. and Zolin M.B. (Eds) (2014) *Economic Integration in Asia – Towards the Delineation of a Sustainable Path*, New York: Palgrave.

Dzever S. and Jaussaud J. (Eds) (1997) *Perspectives on Economic Integration and Business Strategy in the Asia-Pacific Region*, Macmillan, London.

Dzever S. and Jaussaud J. (Eds) (1999) *China & India, Economic Performance and Business Strategies of Firms in the Mid 90s'*, Macmillan, London. Ouvrage collectif rédigé à partir d'une sélection des meilleures contributions au troisième séminaire international de recherche Euro-Asie.

Dzever S. and Jaussaud J. (Eds) (2001) Issues in the Europe–Asia Pacific Economy: Introduction, Special issue of the *Journal of the Asia Pacific Economy*, 6(2), pp. 155–157.

Part I

Global macroeconomic slowdown and East Asian economies

1   The lion's share

What's behind China's economic slowdown?

Guilhem Fabre

1.1   The end of the commodity supercycle

Because China accounts for 40 percent of the emerging-market GDP, its slowdown has already had large repercussions on commodity producer countries, especially Australia, where exports to China stand at 5 percent of GDP (Goldman Sachs, 2013), and Brazil and Russia, where it is around 2 percent (Lemoine, 2014).

China accounts for 12 percent of global demand for commodities, 60 to 70 percent for iron ore and soybeans, and 40 percent for copper (Coates and Luu, 2012; Pettis, 2013). As for crude oil, China imports at least 6 percent of the global supply to satisfy 60 percent of its consumption.

China's economic slowdown is already affecting worldwide commodity prices. Australian Prime Minister Kevin Rudd said that 2013 marks the end of the Chinese-purchased commodities boom, because the prices for commodities have fallen by almost 25 percent and may well fall further (Li, 2013). At the St Petersburg International Economic Forum in June 2013, Russian president Vladimir Putin explained the abrupt fall in Russia's growth rate by the fall in prices of its main exports.

The dramatic expansion of the Chinese economy in 2001 after its admittance to the World Trade Organization (WTO) was threatened by the global crisis of 2008, which reduced its main export markets in North America and Europe. It rebounded with a 4-trillion yuan (US$575 billion) stimulus package at the end of 2008, which boosted infrastructure construction and the importation of commodities and raw materials. The commodity 'supercycle' where accelerating demand and rising commodity prices stimulated growth in at least three of the five BRICS (Brazil, Russia, India, China and South Africa) countries that are commodity exporters (Brazil, Russia and South Africa), reached its peak in 2011, with copper prices six times higher than in 2003, before dropping by 30 percent in 2013, along with iron ore (Yergin, 2013).

An analysis of the determinants of China's growth is thus essential to understand its cycles of expansion and slowdown, which have worldwide repercussions. The gigantic stimulus package of 2008, equivalent to 13 points of GDP, represented a forced transition from investment and export-led growth to a model focused mainly on investment, which seeks to rebalance growth in favour of consumption.

Following the global crisis, the evolution of capital formation and investment is crucial to China's growth and prospects. Official figures show that the contribution of exports to GDP growth was diminishing since the beginning of the global crisis, whereas fixed asset investment rose to extraordinary levels (48 percent of GDP) for four consecutive years (2009–12), a trend that would have driven any other nation to overcapacity and crisis.

Although capital accumulation had contributed around half of China's economic growth since the reforms in 1979, outweighing the contribution of total factor productivity especially since 1993, such a high level of investment has a flip side in terms of low consumption. The convergence of high savings and low consumption is a long-term trend of the Chinese economy since the economic reforms and opening-up policy were relaunched in 1992. Household savings have averaged 19 percent of GDP since then, with a strong increase to 22 percent at the onset of the global financial crisis. Corporate savings averaged 15 percent of GDP from 1992 to 2007, but similarly rose to 22 percent by the mid-2000s. The rest of the savings stem from government, with a rate of around 5 percent of GDP since 1992, which more than doubled in the 2000s to 10.8 percent of GDP in 2007. All told, China's saving rate increased from 38 percent of GDP in the 1990s to around 52 percent of GDP by the late 2000s. As savings rose, household consumption fell as a share of GDP from 50 percent in the early 1990s to 35 percent since 2007, whereas government consumption varied just between 13.5 and 15 to 16 percent of GDP during the same period. There are those, however, who contest the accuracy of these figures (Yueh, 2013).

1.2   China's growth and the black hole of official statistics

In 2009, the National Bureau of Statistics released an article by one of its experts criticising the quality of the consumption estimates. Subsequently, Wang Xiaolu and Wing Thye Woo suggested that China's urban household income might be underreported by 66 percent. Unidentified 'grey income' totalled 6.2 trillion yuan, or 12 percent of GDP. Of the underreported income, 63 percent went to the wealthiest 10 percent of households, whose income is really 65 times higher than that of the poorest 10 percent, and not 23 times as indicated by official data. Household income inequality is certainly much higher than suggested by the reported Gini coefficient (0.47). Second, expenditure on housing, if the housing is for personal use, is not entirely for investment, and rental equivalent costs should be treated as consumption expenditure (Wang and Wing, 2011; Wang, 2013). Zhang Jun and Zhu Tian estimate that housing consumption standing at 6 percent of GDP is unrealistic in view of exorbitant property prices, and is more likely to represent around 10 percent of GDP. They also consider that a part of business costs or investment expenditures paid for by companies corresponds to private consumption. A large share of imported luxury cars and other goods fall into this category as well (Zhang and Zhu, 2012).

The same is true for the management costs of central and local public administrative agencies, an important component of government consumption, which rose from less than 5 percent of budgeted expenditures in 1978 to 18.7 percent in 2006. The growth of these expenses has increased by over 21 percent for the whole period, twice that of the GDP (Aglietta and Bai, 2012). Beginning in 2010 and thereafter, before the new leadership of Xi Jingping/Li Keqiang decided to react by setting new standards for public management expenditures, 40 percent of the turnover of the Galeries Lafayette, Paris' biggest luxury department store, was made by Chinese clients travelling abroad.[1]

The Penn World Tables provide an adjusted estimate for Chinese household consumption in terms of purchasing power parity (PPP) by comparing the prices of a basket of goods in different countries. This adjustment raises the household consumption rate to around 44.2 percent of GDP, an increase of ten points, but this percentage remains much lower than in other Asian countries (51.9 percent for Malaysia, around 53 percent for Taiwan and Korea, nearly 60 percent for Thailand, 61 percent for India and 66 percent for Japan).

The PPP and the bottom-up surveys change the general picture of consumption in favour of the top decile of wealthiest households, but not necessarily the downward trend of household consumption in GDP, which is better reflected by the share of labour compensation and household income in national income, which declined from 66.8 percent in 1996 to 50.6 percent in 2007. This amount lost by wages went towards capital's share and a depreciation of state assets, as shown by Simarro (Huang and Tao, 2011; Simarro, 2011; Rutkowski, 2013). Whatever the rate of household consumption in GDP (35 percent in the official figures or around 45 percent for the adjusted estimate), it remains practically identical, despite the gigantic stimulus package of 2008, which was supposed to rebalance growth in favour of consumption. To understand the reasons for these inefficiencies, we must first understand the growth dynamic before the global crisis of 2008.

1.3 Pre-crisis growth, or the height of 'cheap China': the underpricing of the factor markets

The most convincing explanation for China's dramatic growth and export performance from 2001 to 2008 has been developed by Huang Yiping of Beijing University (Huang and Tao, 2011). There is a strong asymmetry between trade liberalisation for goods and services, where free markets determine the prices of more than 95 percent of products, and factor markets for labour, capital, land, energy and the environment, which remain under government control.

The underpricing of labour, which explains partly the performance of labour-intensive manufacturing and exports, is the result of the 'household registration system' (*hukou*) which segments the rural and urban labour market and feeds the flows of migrants (*mingong*) not covered by the social welfare system. Were urban employers to make social welfare contributions for their migrant workers, their payrolls would rise by about 35 to 40 percent (Huang and Tao, 2011). This impact is particularly significant on labour since in 2005, 46 percent of the Chinese workforce was employed in the informal sector, and half of these workers were excluded from the social protection system (Park and Cai, 2011).[2] According to a study by the Research Office of the China State Council, the migrant workers from the countryside worked an average of 11 hours a day, six or seven days a week, or nearly 50 percent more than formal employees, but received only 60 percent of the pay, without counting the difference in social protection. Philippe Huang underlined that if one adds to the migrants the urban workforce in small private enterprises and the self-employed, the total employed in the informal economy comes to more than 60 percent of the urban workforce (Huang, 2011).

The cost of capital has been fixed artificially low by the domination of four state commercial banks (Industrial and Commercial Bank of China [ICBC], Bank of China, Construction Bank and Agricultural Bank), which allocate 60 percent of credit in China. Their managers are nominated by the state, and they follow its priorities by lending to the state-owned enterprises (SOEs), which get more than half of all bank loans and account for less than 30 percent of industrial output. The financial penalties induced by the spread between low deposit rates fixed by the People's Bank of China (PBOC) (2 to 4 percent), which are negative in view of inflation, and lending rates (5.5 to 7.5 percent) has cost Chinese households about 255 billion yuan (US$36 billion) or 4 percent of GDP in 2008 (Yueh, 2013). Cheap credit given to SOEs has favoured a capital-intensive regime with a high investment rate in the priority sectors defined by the government, to the detriment of labour- intensive small and medium enterprises (SMEs) and the private sector. In the Wenzhou region, where private credit was authorised on an experimental basis, the lending rates varied between 13 and 17 percent over the period 2003–10. The one-year interest rate to private credit agencies was around 20 percent (Aglietta and Bai, 2012).

Land is the main factor of production in the countryside and functions as a rural safety net for 250 million rural households. It is the property of the state in cities and of local authorities in the countryside, whereas user rights belong to the peasants, pending state approval when used for development purposes. Since the 1990s, the economic gain derived from transferring land-use rights has been considerable, because 'land and natural resources assets; are valued at renminbi (RMB) 44.3 trillion in 2010 (US$6.54 trillion at the 2010 exchange rate), whereas nonfinancial state-owned enterprises have a book value of RMB 59.1 trillion (US$8.72 trillion) (Yang *et al.*, 2012; Zhang and Chen, 2013). Since the mid-1990s, the main impetus for development has shifted from township and village enterprises (TVEs) to local government projects conducted in collaboration with outside and domestic enterprises. This trend must be understood in the context of the surge of cross-border nonequity modes (NEMs) of production as a form of governance of transnational corporations' global value chain.

The United Nations Conference on Trade and Development (UNCTAD) estimates that the direct local value-added impact of cross-border NEMs was roughly US$400 to 500 billion a year in 2010, with contract manufacturing and services outsourcing accounting for more than US$200 billion. China has served as the 'world's factory' in international joint production projects where it has played the role of assembler of manufactured products and the top importer of intermediate goods. It is these forms of processing activities that have led to its trade surpluses (UNCTAD, 2011; WTO, IDE-JETRO, 2013).

A horizontal competition developed between locations to attract businesses and investment by providing land and infrastructure for industrial use below cost. According to official statistics, the average fees for the negotiated granting of land-use rights, generally used for industrial projects, were only about 30 percent of those collected through auctions in 2003 (1.69 million yuan/hectare versus 5.67 million). Despite this huge price advantage, public auctions accounted for 15 percent of all land leasing deals in 1999, and rose to less than a third (27 percent) in 2003, following the central government's policies enforcing greater transparency.

These subsidies were granted because of the expected rewards in terms of growth, its multiplier effects on employment through services to enterprises and the revenues from taxes and especially housing and real estate development, the value of which tends to appreciate. In the Yangzi delta, for instance, local governments could sell the land to real estate developers at a price ranging from 4 to 14 times the average compensation paid to farmers, and the developed land could be resold at a price that was, on average, five times as high. Thus, the sale price of developed land could yield anywhere from 30 to 50 times the original land requisition price paid to the peasants, thereby contributing to a rising share of local government revenues (Huang, 2011; Huang and Tao, 2011; Tao, 2012).

As for energy and environment, prices of oil, gas and electricity have been regulated by the state under the National Development and Reform Commission (NDRC), which since the end of the 1990s has tried to raise low domestic prices closer to international levels. However, the strong rise in crude oil prices from 2000 to 2008 (where a barrel was close to US$150 in 2008) led the NDRC to maintain the domestic price at around US$80 a barrel. Fan Gang estimates that Chinese enterprises pay around 660 yuan (83 dollars) less than foreign multinationals for the extraction of one ton of crude oil, which means that in 2007 alone, the Chinese government received RMB 117.81 billion (US$15.5 billion) less on crude oil production than they would have at international prices (Aglietta and Bai, 2012).

Low domestic prices of oil, gas and electricity have exacerbated waste, despite environmental laws and regulations neglected at central and local levels, to meet the clear priority of economic growth. Pollution of air, water and land has reached alarming proportions to the point of threatening productivity and the health of the population. Such environmental degradation, the partial cost of which came to 3.05 percent of GDP in 2004, has already affected climate change as evidenced by the rapid melting of ice in the Himalayas, the accentuation of droughts in the North and floods in the South (Huang and Tao, 2011).

The underpricing of factor markets is equivalent to a huge producer subsidy, which Huang Yiping evaluates from 2000 to 2008 at between 8.5 and more than 12 percent of GDP at its peak years in 2006 and 2007. His main finding is that the underpricing of capital contributes, on average, to about 40 percent of the total subsidy to producers.

As for labour, migrant workers' pay grew at only half the rate of the national average; their pay gap with urban workers widened from 30 to 50 percent, and their number rose from 88 million in 2000 to 140 million in 2008. Thus, the labour cost distortion rose from only 0.1 percent of GDP in 2000 to 3.6 percent of GDP in

2008, when it bypassed capital to become the largest cost distortion item. Because this crude evaluation does not take into account the underdeveloped social welfare system, Huang Yiping suggests that it is underestimated. So the underpricing of labour represents certainly more than the average 25 percent of the producer subsidy linked with factor market distortions between 2004 and 2008.

The land issue is more complex because the nonmarket prices, through negotiation between users and local governments, are generally reserved for industrial activities, and auctioning at market prices – on average six times higher than the off-market negotiations – are reserved for real estate developers. But as the property boom surged since 2005, the differential between market and nonmarket prices may be artificial, and according to Huang Yiping, a better approach would be to look at the gap between the actual rental costs paid by industrial firms compared with potential market rates. Between 2000 and 2008, land may account for approximately 10 percent of the producer subsidy.

The same proportion may be true for the energy subsidy (10 percent) in the years where it was significant, between 2004 and 2008. But the producer subsidy on environmental degradation is more problematic, because its externalities are not taken up by enterprises, and the whole estimation is based on the official cost of environmental degradation.

Thus, in the pre–global crisis years of 2000–08, the extraordinary expansion of China has nothing to do with a 'miracle' and much to do with the underpricing of labour, capital, land and energy, which was equivalent to a gigantic transfer of resources from workers, households, and partly consumers to producers (especially SOEs) and governments. This annuity, in the sense that it is not linked to efficiency, productivity, and innovation, but derives mainly from the capacity to manipulate the allocation of the main factors of production through the command structure of the state, is basically the reward of power, as long as it is able to implement the conditions for strong economic growth, which may alleviate employment constraints and favour *social mobility*, its main tool of legitimisation.

At the same time, the liberalisation of prices for goods and services, coupled with the underpricing of the factors of production and the exchange rate of the RMB is a powerful tool of *competition* during the 2000–08 period, when China has gained privileged access to the two main world markets, the United States and Europe. The strong interactions of the US finance–led growth model and the Chinese investment and export-led growth model explain, in part, why these two countries were responsible for half of the world's economic growth between 2002 and 2008, and why this growth, based on strong income inequalities, led to the world financial crisis (Fabre, 2010).

1.4   Post-crisis growth: the role of SOEs and local governments

Although the stimulus package, launched in late 2008, helped China avert a recession with the abrupt drop in demand for its main export products from North America and Europe, the steady growth of credit, the priority of SOEs in its allocation and the way it was financed raised doubts about the sustainability of the rebound in macroeconomic growth.

Since then, China has depended on a much faster expansion of credit to generate growth. Official fixed asset investment jumped by 32 percent in 2009 alone. Total leverage, including through shadow banking, has risen from 150 percent of GDP in 2008 to an estimated 219 percent in the first half of 2013 – an increase of 69 points of GDP, one of the highest shares in the world, compared to the United States (+46 percent of GDP between 2002 and 2007) or Thailand (+66 percent) before the Asian crisis of 1997–98. This level of credit depends on national savings and is not from foreign countries, as in Japan, where total leverage is equal to 392 percent of GDP. In this sense, China's credit is manageable on a sovereign basis and not subject to capital outflows and exit strategies by institutional investors, which accelerated the Asian crisis, or to interactions with global financial markets, which spread the US subprime crisis of 2007 to the rest of the world.

China's high ratio of leverage, which has grown 18 percent year after year, twice the average growth of GDP, is comparable to the euro zone (259 percent of GDP) or the United States (253 percent of GDP), but much higher than the other BRICS countries, for example, 105 percent of GDP in India, 103 percent in Brazil and 71 percent in Russia (Goldman Sachs, 2013; Bulletin Économique Chine, 2013a). The risks do not concern consumer loans (23 percent of GDP) or central government leverage (22 percent of GDP), but the leverage of the corporate sector (151 percent of GDP) and of the Local Government Finance Vehicles (LGFVs).

According to Guo Shuying, chairman of the China Securities Regulatory Commission (CSRC), 40 percent of fixed asset investment has gone to industry since the beginning of the stimulus package. None of the manufacturing businesses with mature technologies have had a shortage of production capacity, whereas, as early as 2009, 21 out of 24 industrial sectors had excess production capacities. That may explain why the use of industrial capacities is relatively low – around 60 percent in 2011 according to the International Monetary Fund (IMF), 70 percent for traditional industries (steel, cement, aluminium) according to the NDRC, and around 50 percent or much less for equipment industries in 2013 (Bulletin Économique Chine, 2013a).

In short, the stimulus package has exacerbated the traditional supply-based growth model, which assumes that new industrial capacities and infrastructure lead automatically to demand growth (Sheng and Geng, 2013b). The SOEs are a typical illustration of this logic. They dominate the Chinese economy under the supervision of the state party. The 117 largest SOEs in critical sectors such as commodity production, construction, rail and air transportation, shipbuilding, electronics, telecommunications, coal and electricity generation, oil, automobiles and tobacco, are supervised by the State-Owned Assets Supervision and Administration Commission (SASAC), a government body. In addition, the state banks and insurance companies are regulated by the China Banking Regulatory Commission (CBRC), the China Insurance Regulatory Commission (CIRC) and other entities. The highest-level executives in the state banks, as well as the strategic SOEs, are directly nominated by the Organisation Department of the Chinese Communist

Party (CCP), which is one of the main tools of the CCP's top-down structure dealing with promotions.

SOEs, which used to employ between 60 and 75 percent of the urban population in the 1980s, were drastically reformed in the 1990s. Their number fell from 10 million in 1994 to 7.9 million in 1997 and 165,000 in 1998. Although their share of output has remained at around 30 percent of GDP since then, their share of urban employment has declined to less than 10 percent, reflecting their transition from labour- to capital-intensive entities, as well as the end of their pivotal role in terms of income redistribution and social protection whose cost was massively transferred to households (Yueh, 2013). SOEs, and especially the largest ones under SASAC's supervision, were the largest beneficiaries of the 2008 stimulus package. Total net profit of SOEs continued to rise in 2009, to RMB 4,057.7 billion, 4.37 times that of 2001 and 12 percent of GDP. What is more, total profits of the central SOEs administered by SASAC accounted for 67.5 percent of total profit in 2010. Only ten companies accounted for 70 percent of all the profits made by the central SOEs in 2009, including China Telecom, China Unicom and China Mobile, the three companies that shared a 900 million mobile subscribers market, China National Petroleum Corporation (CNPC), and Sinopec. CNPC and China Mobile alone accounted for more than one-third of the profits. This impressive performance by SOEs is not a reflection of their return on investment, which is lower than that of the nonstate sector (8.5 percent versus 12.9 percent), but the result of their market power, monopolistic or oligopolistic, and of preferential state policies (Sheng and Zhao, 2012).

First, large corporations enjoy a large profit margin through the artificially low cost of capital, which is linked, as we have seen, to a resource transfer from the captive household savers, whereas SMEs pay higher interest rates, as they must obtain capital from the nonbank or shadow banking system, where risk is higher. According to an IMF working paper, the total resource transfer by this two-tier financial sector depends on the size and spread between administrative and market interest rates and the extent of credit allocated through the nonbank financial sector. From 2001 to 2008, the preferential financing cost on loans accounted for 47 percent of total nominal profits of SOEs, whereas from 2001 to 2011, the subsidy to SOEs through the underpricing of capital was estimated at around 4 percent of GDP (Lee, Syed and Xueyan, 2012), a continuation of the trend observed by Huang Yiping during the first decade of 2000. Were this bias toward SOEs redressed, China's investment rate would fall by 5 percent of GDP without an adverse effect on economic growth (Dollar and Wei, 2007).

The subsidy on land is even larger for SOEs than the underpricing of capital. From 2001 to 2009, on the basis of industrial land rents set at 3 percent of the purchase price, SOEs should have paid rents equal to 67.2 percent of their total nominal profits.

As for energy, the government takes less than 2 percent of the price of oil in China, far below the 12 percent which is imposed on joint ventures. Combined with coal, natural gas and other resources, the SOEs underpaid by more than 8 percent of their total nominal profits during the period from 2001 to 2009 (Sheng and Zhao, 2012). Because they are capital intensive, in contrast to SMEs, SOEs have the capacity to pay higher wages without jeopardizing their profits. In 2008, average compensation for their labour was 63 percent higher than that of private enterprises and 36 percent higher than that of non-SOEs. In monopolistic industries, the average income per year of employees could even reach RMB 128,000, about seven times the national average. Furthermore, a large number of SOEs and government institutions provided housing at low prices to their staff.

Despite all these subsidies and huge profits, the contribution of SOEs to the state coffers was nonexistent between 1994 and 2007 and negligible afterwards (6 percent of their profits in 2009, and 2.2 percent in 2010), whereas the tax burden on private enterprises was fixed at 25 percent. Most of their profits are reinvested or managed for central SOEs by SASAC.

In essence, SOEs may be viewed as the lion's share of the state-party system, concentrating the flows between power and capital, in a revolving door system of mixed loyalty; SOE executives enter government to promote policies and orient the allocation of resources, and officials enter SOEs to pursue economic gains (Sheng and Zhao, 2012).

The reform of SOEs according to the principle *zhuada fangxiao* (save the large, let go of the small), which privatised the small and medium-sized SOEs and created 'national champions', was enacted in 1994, the same year as an important fiscal recentralisation, the Tax Sharing Reform, to increase the fiscal revenue to GDP ratio, which rose from 12.3 percent in 1993 to 20.7 percent in 2007 (Yueh, 2013).[3] Before 1994, most fiscal revenues (78 percent), as well as expenditures (71.7 percent), went to local governments. From 1994 to at least 2010, the central government collected most fiscal revenues (52.6 percent on average), whereas its share of expenditures compared with local governments was basically unchanged (27 percent on average).

In summary, the tax-sharing reform of 1994 resulted in a gigantic transfer of resources to the central government. Along with the reform of state enterprises, the creation of a strong top-down economic structure, local governments (at the provincial; prefectural; or prefectural-city, district, township and village levels) were responsible for economic development and the provision of public services. Their total resources could not keep up with their financial obligations, which included supporting retirees and laid-off workers from former SOEs in the 1990s. In 2012, local governments still accounted, on average, for 70 percent of local expenditures, 90 percent of general public service expenditures, 76 percent of public security, 84 percent of education, 68 percent of social security and employment, 78 percent of health care, 59 percent of environmental protection and 49 percent of science and technology expenditures (Hu, 2013).

This centralisation of revenue collection and decentralisation of expenditure responsibilities led to a mismatch between revenues and expenditures at the local level, partly covered by transfer payments subject to government discretion, and mainly covered by the income of the land-use rights transactions for a period of 40 to 70 years (Feng, 2012; Xing and Man, 2012). Whereas the 1994 tax sharing reform corresponded to a fiscal recentralisation, revenue-sharing arrangements for land leasing moved in the opposite direction. Following the generalisation of land leasing as public policy and local practice in 1992, the State Auditing Office found that 80 percent of the land-leasing revenues was concealed from local fiscal authorities and that 90 percent of the remaining amount was allocated to local discretionary budgets instead of being shared (60 to 40 percent) between the central government and the local authorities. Consequently, the central government decided to assign all land-leasing revenues to municipal governments as a part of the 1994 tax-sharing reform.

As local governments assumed full responsibility for urban construction, they soon became infrastructure and real estate developers. Land leasing was used to finance the bulk of infrastructure construction, with the rest being borrowed from state-owned banks and generally secured by municipally owned land. According to Peterson, debt service often is paid by selling off the leasing rights to parcels of land whose value has been enhanced by the debt–finance infrastructure projects (Peterson, 2006).

Clearly, risks are associated with such land-use development policies: if the proceeds of asset sales are not exclusively used for long-term infrastructure investments but become part of the municipal operating budget, local governments become dependent upon asset sales to cover their expenditures. The situation may be viable as long as asset prices rise, which tends to create a real estate bubble, but may become problematic when land prices go down. Because land has been used massively, like in Japan in the 1980s, as a collateral for loans, this affects not only the fiscal balance of local governments that assume most of the public burden, but also the financial health of the state-owned banks and other financial entities. As we shall see, these risks have been exacerbated by the stimulus package of 2008.

1.5   Land leasing as the main vehicle to finance the stimulus package and its consequences

Because the bulk of the stimulus package in 2009–10 (around 70 percent) had to be financed by the state companies and local authorities, the sale of land-use rights became a part not only of the investments, but also of the operating budgets of local governments. Land sales had long been used as an important tool of government intervention, either by underpricing land for industrial projects (80 to 85 percent of land transfers) in a horizontal competition between local governments, which encourages overinvestment, or by pursuing high prices for real estate projects, which generate short-term taxable incomes for local authorities, particularly for house sales, leading to high business taxes. In the Pearl River Delta Region, often known as the world's factory, local governments (city, district and township) even offered 'zero land price' in the late 1990s and early years of 2000 to compete for industrial development projects (Aglietta and Bai, 2012; Tao, 2012).

From 2001 to 2008, the proceeds from land-use rights represented, on average, 40.5 percent of local government income, but they jumped to 61 percent of income during the two years of the stimulus package (48.8 percent in 2009 and 74.1 percent in 2010), before remaining flat in 2011 and 2012 at around RMB 2.9 trillion

(5 to 6 percent of GDP) (Deng, Gyourko and Wu, 2012; Sheng and Geng, 2013b). This dramatic leap is linked to the strong injection of credit. According to CBRC statistics, by the end of 2009, the local government loan balance was RMB 7.38 trillion, an annual growth of 70 percent (Feng, 2012).

The reliance on asset sales is especially risky because land prices are volatile. Recent research based on land auction sales in 35 major cities between 2003 and 2011 has shown that, despite significant heterogeneity, there is a large reversion to the mean on their annual price growth (on the order of 35 percent). Land price volatility is three to five times above house price volatility. Construction costs are flat, and construction workers' wages grow strongly but with relatively low variation, so the volatility of housing prices is driven by the land market and not by other factors of production (Deng, Gyourko and Wu, 2012).

The volatility of land prices is not so much due to a fall in demand by private or parapublic developers, but to the periodic intervention of the central government on land supply in order to restrict credit growth and overinvestment. In 2004, for instance, central regulation prohibited municipal land purchases for urban development, partly as a fiscal measure to restrain excessive local investment. The race for land reserves led to the establishment of 6,015 development zones, of which only 20 percent had received the requisite approval of the State Council or provincial governments (Peterson, 2006).

The same thing happened during the stimulus package. The LGFVs created for the first fiscal stimulus plan after the 1998 Asian financial crisis boomed in order to borrow from the banks (He and Man, 2012) because leverage was forbidden at the local level, and SOEs, with the aid of easier credit policies, invested more and more in the growing real estate sector. Under SASAC administration, 70 percent of SOEs were engaged in real estate operations and managed some 2,500 hotels throughout the country, not to mention local-level SOEs. More than 30 percent of fixed asset investment was directed in 2010 towards the real estate sector, both residential and nonresidential (Aveline-Dubach, 2013; Gaulard, 2013). Since 2011, the central government has tried to rein in the credit growth by raising the one-year interest lending rate and the reserve requirements of banks from 14 percent in 2009 to 21.5 percent in 2011, but the reduction of the square footage permitted to be sold in land auctions (−16 percent in 2011 in 35 major cities, confirmed in 2012) also served as a dissuasive tool.

The consequences of this real estate bubble are, above all, social: before the stimulus package in 2007, a research report estimated that there were 40 million dispossessed farmers due to urban expansion and infrastructure projects, and land-related incidents were already the top cause of rural grievances and protests, as the municipalities' sale price for leasing land for urban use often exceeded the purchase price paid to farmers by a factor of 100 (Peterson, 2006; Tao, 2012). Yu Jianrong, a researcher on rural China, calculated in 2010 that the government had expropriated 6.7 million hectares of rural land over a 20-year period, paying farmers 2 trillion yuan (US$326 billion) less than market value (Yu, 2013).

In cities, the high price paid for land by real estate developers shifted to housing prices, which have become less and less affordable for average-income households.

The ratio between the price of residential housing and the yearly average household income at the end of the stimulus package (2010) has bypassed 8, the level observed in Spain and the United States at the highest level of their real estate booms, and even exceeds 15 in the coastal cities. Since 2010, more than a quarter of foreign direct investment in China has been directed to real estate, and the value of real estate assets owned by foreign investors in China has grown to US$1.1 trillion, the second regional position behind Japan, and is valued at about 10 percent of global real estate investments (Aveline-Dubach, 2013; Gaulard, 2013). Recent research has shown that from 2004 to 2009, property prices rose by 250 percent in 25 major Chinese cities (Deng, Gyourko and Wu, 2012). Access to property is more and more denied to urban average-income households, except in suburban areas, close to the informal 50,000 urban villages and small-property-rights housing where half of the 160 million interprovincial migrant workers live (Tao, 2012).

On the other side of the social spectrum, the number of Chinese billionaires in the real estate sector rose from 18 percent in 2008 to 27 percent in 2010, which indicates the magnitude of wealth concentration generated by the stimulus package (Gaulard, 2013). But apart from this strong social polarisation effect (the main losers from this form of economic growth – landless peasants and low-income urban citizens – have more difficulty in achieving upward mobility), the conditions of economic growth have changed since the 2010 peak.

1.6   The end of cheap China and the expansion of shadow banking

In 2010, workers' strikes in the giant Taiwanese Foxconn factory in Shenzhen, the number one assembler of consumer electronic products for well-known brands, attracted world attention to the labour conditions of migrants, underpaid and deprived of social protection. But the end of cheap Chinese labour really began with the stimulus package, which confirmed labour shortages in China's coastal areas such as the Pearl River Delta and the Yangzi River Delta. In addition, the shortages pointed to the higher education and qualification of workers and the propensity of potential migrants to remain closer to home and to work off farms, sometimes in factories moving from coastal areas inland because of rising production costs.[4]

In 2010 the annual wage of a Chinese urban worker reached 37,147 yuan (or US$5,487), about the same as in the Philippines and Thailand (Li *et al.*, 2012). International comparisons give a better idea of this catch-up phenomenon: the average wage in China was about twice that in Indonesia in 2000, but it rose to 3.5 times by 2011. From 2000 to 2011, cumulative wage growth in China was 473 percent, much higher than the 238 percent in Indonesia, 137 percent in India and 46 percent in Mexico. On the currency side, from 2005 to 2012, the RMB appreciated by 57.4 percent and 56.8 percent, respectively, against the Indian rupee and the Mexican peso (Zhang and Chen, 2013).

By easing credit, the stimulus package appreciated land prices not only for real estate projects, but also for industrial projects, especially in the largest cities of coastal areas where land reserves were diminishing, despite the constant extension of urban areas. According to official statistics, the average price per square metre of land on sale rose from RMB 573 in 2003 to RMB 3,393 in 2012, a 492 percent rise over ten years (Zhang and Chen, 2013). The appreciation of land and labour costs led a lot of foreign and domestic enterprises to relocate labour-intensive activities in inland regions.

With the rise of land and labour prices, the credit effects on growth tended to diminish (Sheng and Geng, 2013a)[5] at the time (2011) when the central government tried to rein it in by raising repeatedly the one-year lending rate and the obligatory reserve ratio of banks. But these traditional tools became less and less efficient, with the dramatic expansion of the two-tier financial system, or 'shadow banking', to finance not only the SMEs but the LGFVs, which can no longer rely on cheap bank loans. According to the CBRC, shadow banking, which refers to all lines of credit not regulated by the same standards as conventional bank loans, increased from RMB 800 billion (US$130 billion) in 2008 to RMB 7.6 trillion (US$1.2 trillion) in 2012, around 15 percent of GDP. Total off-balance-sheet activity in China, composed of credit to property developers (30 to 40 percent), LGFVs (20–30 percent) and SMEs and individual and bridge loan borrowers, is estimated at around RMB 17 trillion (US$2.69 trillion), a third of GDP (Hu, 2011; Sheng and Geng, 2013b).

Although regulators have been keeping control over risks in the banking sector, they have tolerated the boom in shadow banking to maintain fast growth by meeting the financing needs of local governments and property developers. This inherent contradiction in policy objectives explains the shadow banking boom. Investors tend to believe that there is an implicit government guarantee, since the borrowers are tied to the local governments. The moral hazard may aggravate financial risks and inequality. Because many shadow banking products are reserved for high-net-worth investors (the minimum subscription is usually RMB 1 to 3 million), as in the US hedge fund industry, this implies that only the wealthy can take advantage of the government guarantee, whereas the eventual losses of LGFVs would be socialised. Bank of China Chief Executive Officer (CEO) Xiao Gang criticised the common practice of relying on a nontransparent capital pool to manage wealth management products (WMPs), reserved for individuals with certain minimum deposit balances (Gang, 2012).

Shadow banking would appear to be a positive force in a system dominated by state-owned banks lending to SOEs because it provides access to credit for labour-intensive SMEs that have difficulties getting bank loans. However, Charlene Chu, who has followed Chinese banks for a long time, considers that its expansion in 2013 to cover about half of all new credit is worrisome, as many of the credit decisions are driven by relationships with heavy political influence in the context of tremendous confidence in the ability and the willingness of the CCP to bail everyone out (Goldman Sachs, 2013). As for real estate, a range of industrial companies from shipbuilders to oil majors also engage in shadow banking as side businesses (Rabinovitch, 2012b).

At the end of 2012, banks had an exposure of 14 percent of their loans to LGFVs and 6 percent to property developers, which is manageable, because their nonperforming loan ratio is only 1.2 percent. But the problem comes from WMPs, apparently inspired by the US credit risk transfer products (CRTs), that banks sell to retail investors. According to CBRC, the amount of these short-term instruments (with an average maturity period of less than one year) soared to RMB 7.1 trillion at the end of 2012 – 7.4 percent of bank deposits. Some of these funds are used in long-term projects such as infrastructure and property operations. And new WMPs are now issued to fill the gap left by expiring ones, as underlined by Xiao Gang, which is equivalent to financial cavalry. The maturity duration mismatch is not an issue so long as the demand for WMPs is strong and the bank can repay maturing products with money flowing in to buy new ones, but if the asset pool stopped growing someday, it might explode, according to some traders (Rabinovitch, 2012a). Many WMPs are linked to stocks, bonds and exchange rates, and about 36 percent of them are related to trusts. With the tightening of bank lending control at the end of 2010, property developers and LGFVs turned to the bond market and trust companies opened to high-net-worth individuals and professional investors. Trust companies quickly became the second largest group of nonbank financial institutions. Their assets under management rose sixfold to RMB 7 trillion from 2008 to 2012, bypassing the insurance (6.9 trillion) and the mutual funds (2.9 trillion) sectors. In other words, the low nonperforming loans of banks are linked to the capacity of WMPs and trust companies to provide new loans to LGFVs and property developers, which are largely used to pay off old debts (Zhang and Chen, 2013).

The exact amount of local government and LGVFs debt has led to different estimates, ranging in 2010 from RMB 10.7 trillion (National Audit Office [NAO]) to 14.7 trillion (Central Bank). In December 2013, another NAO report estimated the local government public debt at the end of the first semester to be RMB 17,891 trillion (33. 2 percent of GDP), and the central government debt would be at RMB 12,384 trillion (23 percent of GDP). China's total public debt would be RMB 30,275 trillion (US$4,900 billion), or 56.2 percent of GDP. Debt sustainability analysis and stress tests illustrate that this level is still manageable, according to the IMF, which excludes contingent liabilities as well as liabilities of the SOEs and the public financial sector. But local governments have recently diversified their credit sources to trusts and bonds, further eroding the capabilities for lending to the private sector, according to Zhou Xiaochuan, the Central Bank's governor (IMF, 2013; Bulletin Économique Chine, 2013b; Zhang and Barnett, 2014). Former chairman of the CBRC, Liu Mingkang, estimated the local government debt at RMB 21 trillion at the end of 2013 (37 percent of GDP), and the highest risk to China's macroeconomy in his view is that some local governments may fail to meet the standards on transparency that are necessary to justify borrowing (Hornby, 2014).

In June to July 2013 and again in December, the central bank decided to tighten short-term credit on the interbank market to control the expansion of credit in shadow banking. This move revealed the determination of the central government as well as the stresses in the financial system, since without intervention from the PBOC, the seven-day interbank rate had risen as high as 20 to 30 percent before the PBOC stated its intention to maintain sufficient liquidity, thereby calming the markets. The fragility of the financial system is clearly linked to shadow banking, LGFVs and developers' balance sheets.

In fact, as early as 2009, in more than nine provinces, the interest-bearing debt of LGFVs was twice that of local governments' revenues, notably in Beijing, Tianjin and Chongqing. But since these liabilities are off the balance sheet, local governments have had to resort to off-budget revenues to pay for them. And because the land transfer fees are the most important off-budget revenues of local governments – just sufficient to cover their annual interest payments – the liquidity and solvency of local government finances, and more generally the financial stability of China, are directly linked to fluctuations in land markets (He and Man, 2012). LGFVs are directly tied to real estate developers. If the real estate market cools, developers are going to shy away from land sales and LGFVs will face financing problems (Zhang and Chen, 2013).

1.7 Finance-led growth and capital accumulation: China's economy as a hostage of real estate investment

As the two cash crunches of June and December 2013 have shown, financial stability has become the priority of government policy. The State Council is perfectly aware that the link between money supply measures and GDP has broken down. As Ruchir Sharma put it: "Five years ago, it took just US$1 of debt to generate US$1 of economic growth in China. In 2013, it took nearly US$4 – and one third of the new debt now goes to pay off old debt" (Rabinovitch, 2014). This investment inefficiency is not only the result of 'the end of cheap China' where all the main factors of production (land, labour, energy and capital) were undervalued, but also of the implicit adoption of a finance-led growth model, where most investment projects are de facto guaranteed by the local and central governments, and where the allocation of resources is partly diverted towards loss making or speculative activities. This situation is risky, as China's debt is growing much higher than its debt-service capacity, and is socially untenable in terms of inequality.

The real estate sector is the best illustration of this dynamic. In 2013 alone, real estate investment accounted for 15 percent of GDP. Home sales surged 27 percent year on year to US$1.1 trillion, the same amount as was spent in all home sales in the United States in 2012, and house prices rose 19 percent in top-tier cities (Rabinovitch, 2014). As the housing prices–to–income ratio has reached world records, between 10 and 25 for top-tier cities, speculative purchase of housing by high-net-worth individuals is stimulating the price boom (Randall and Liu, 2014). According to the Hurun Report (2013), property is still the key personal investment for more than 60 percent of Chinese millionaires (Hurun Report, 2013). But apart from the millionaires, Chinese officials make up the bulk of real estate property buyers. As the economist He Qinglian explained in her blog, the officials involved in real estate or any kind of decision making at the local level are "presented with special offers. Based on developers' estimate of the flats' values, these officials got 30 percent to 50 percent off – they were actually taking bribes in disguise" (He, 2013).

At the same time, the rise of house prices has pushed saving deposits out from the banks into the shadow banking sector to seek higher returns, and this creates a vicious circle which feeds the speculative demand in real estate as buyers access these funds (Randall and Liu, 2014). Some cities continue to enact measures to prevent speculative real estate purchases, such as raising the minimum down payment for second homes, but these restrictions have had little impact on purchases by the wealthy urban elites with multiple homes, which account for 20 percent of the housing stock according to real estate professionals (Rabinovitch, 2014).

Despite the hastened pace of real estate development in urban expansion, with about three out of five of city-dwelling Chinese owning their own homes, the value of real estate investment is primarily determined by the capacity to valorise it, or the rent generated from leasing it. And rents, as dividends from owning real estate as investment assets, have not increased in tandem with housing prices. According to Zhu Ning, the bias may result in a major understatement of the housing market appreciation (Zhu, 2014). A potential decline in land and real estate value would inevitably reduce investments and the borrowing capacity of LGFVs (Lu and Tao, 2013). But the lessons of the US real estate bubble seem so distant (Follain and Giertz, 2013).

In these conditions, growth slowdown due to the tightening of credit and the desire to deleverage is imperative to reduce financial risks. As Yu Yongding put it, China's economy is being held hostage by real estate investment.[6] Given persistent reports of excess housing stock, it is clear that the race for land and the real estate bubble continue and serve to clear the intertwined debts of the shadow banking system, LGFVs and property developers. In 2013, China land sales hit RMB 4.1 trillion (US$672 billion), growing 17 percent from the previous record of 2011 (RMB 3.5 trillion), and land reserved for real estate use, which accounts for about one-quarter of zone land sales, rose by nearly 27 percent year on year (Hornby, 2014). Land sales alone represented 33 percent of the national and local fiscal revenue in 2013 (RMB 12.1 trillion). In short, China's rapid urbanisation policy is now diverted to pursue the traditional supply-side growth model, which assumes that infrastructure investment leads automatically to demand growth, without taking into account its social as well as economic costs (Pettis, 2013) stemming from rising discontent over property prices for citizens and forceful requisition of land for peasants. The NDRC estimated that each urban resident required RMB 100,000 (US$16,000) in additional government spending. With a target of 400 million new urban residents over the next decade, including migrant workers, this implies new expenditures of RMB 40 trillion (US$6,500 billion), equivalent to China's GDP in 2010 (Borst and Rutkowski, 2013).

Maintaining high rates of growth to improve social mobility is no longer a necessity because the labour market remains tight and employment is no longer a big issue. But the deleveraging process, which may cyclically further the slowdown process, cannot be efficient if is not backed up by a package of institutional and economic reforms aiming at the main beneficiaries of credit growth – high-leverage local governments, well-connected real estate developers and SOEs, especially at the central level, under SASAC.

As Minxin Pei emphasises, in a high-growth environment, each group or individual could count on getting a lucrative contract or project. When growth falters, the food fight among party members will become vicious (Pei, 2013). Viewed in other terms, the capacity of the Xi Jinping/ Li Keqiang tandem to redistribute the lion's share and to resist powerful lobbies by launching a much-needed structural reform package will decide their political future after the Third Plenary Session of the 18th CPC Central Committee in November 2013.

The structural reform package as defined by President Xi Jinping concerns the decisive role to be played by the market in resource allocation, the improvement of the state asset management system in favour of social security funds, public finances and people's well-being, the boosting of the nonpublic ownership economy, a fiscal and tax system reform that matches clarification of the respective responsibilities and resources of the central and local governments, a rural and urban integration through farmers' better land-use rights and migrants' access to the urban housing and social security system and an integrated regulation of natural resource assets in order to face environmental degradation.

1.8 Slower growth and rising financial risks: the narrow space policy of the new direction

It is clear that the restructuration of debt implies a redefinition of the power relations and respective functions of the central and local governments (Zhao, 2013), as well as the relations between the central government and the state sector. The pyramidal structure of debts is linked to the power structure. SOEs under SASAC, as well as local government leaders, are appointed centrally, and until recently their promotion has been based largely on the ability to generate high profits or GDP growth at their respective levels, which are themselves funded on access to credit and state assets, without consideration for efficiency, overcapacity or overinvestment.

These considerations are delegated to the central government, which is supposed to regulate macroeconomic management, deal with financial stability and bail everyone out in case of problems. China's national balance sheet was estimated in 2010 at RMB 142.3 trillion for assets and RMB 69.6 trillion for liabilities (Yang *et al.*, 2012). In essence, this system where power provides access to credit, local authorities manage most public expenditures and the central government is supposed to cover all risks is based on a shared irresponsibility.

However, the central government has the ability to manœuvre. At the beginning of 2014, it gave local governments the go-ahead to issue bonds as a way of rolling over their debt to avoid defaults. This massive debt-refinancing operation is underway (Rabinovitch, 2014). As a sovereign currency issuer, China has the policy space which dispenses it just like the United States, the United Kingdom and Japan, from the fiscal austerity which has been failing in Europe. The danger faced by excessive sovereign government budget deficits is inflation, not insolvency (Randall and Liu, 2014).

Although local government debt is sustainable at the 2018 horizon, according to different scenarios calculated by the IMF, the fragmentation of debts at the local level tends to raise the borrowing costs because LGFVs borrow from the market – banks, the corporate bond market and trust companies – on commercial terms and generally without an explicit government guarantee (Zhang and Barnett, 2014). Besides, local governments might easily hide deficits and debts or engage in short-run policies to obtain financing that are not sound for the long run. For these reasons, some stress that the fiscal reform package should put more of the spending and responsibilities at the central level, precisely because that is the level at which policy makers should be on guard against inflation (Randall and Liu, 2014).

Although national and local government deficits and debt are relatively limited, China's corporate debt stands at a world record as a percentage of GDP (150 percent). If much of this debt has been issued by SOEs and the national government will come to the rescue of these firms, potential liabilities could be as high as 100 percent of GDP, perhaps even more if we take into account the impact of this bailout on banks' policies (Randall and Liu, 2014). Past experience has shown that the four asset management companies (AMCs) have efficiently managed since 1999 the huge (40 to 50 percent) nonperforming loans made by the banking system.[7]

Tighter credit and the rise of financing costs will produce a slowdown on real estate transactions, which may affect, along with the industrial overcapacity, the public finance resources, at the same time as expenditures are growing, not only to cover the foreseeable losses of the financial system, but also to meet the social targets of the new leadership.

Because income redistribution and inclusive development depend largely on the state financial capacity, fiscal policy will be, with the state-sector restructuration, the key part of the structural reform package. It seems no longer feasible that the central government should receive the largest share of tax revenue, leaving local government dependent on discretionary transfers, tax rebates and land sales. China's tax system is biased in favour of manufacturing over services and is regressive in the sense that it relies largely on value-added tax. Total social spending on social security, education and health care equals just over a third of government revenue, or 9 percent of GDP, versus 50 percent of expenditure for other middle-income countries, and 15 percent of GDP in Brazil and Russia (Bulletin Économique Chine, 2009). Measures such as the levy of a property tax, which accounts for a third of total tax revenues for state and local governments in the United States in 2011, can also be the solution to lighten the financial burden of local governments while taxing capital accumulation which has benefited a small elite (Hu, 2013).

All these structural reforms, which are essential in the long term, necessarily hurt a lot of interests as they imply a redistribution of income in favour of the working population. They depend on the political legitimacy of the present leadership, in and outside the state-party system, and its capacity to forge a social coalition stronger than the rent-seeking lobbies in the state party. Apart from the anti-Japanese rhetoric, the main tool of this coalition has been the apparent unity of the leadership and the fight against corruption, aiming not only at the 'flies' of ordinary bureaucracy but also at the 'tigers' of the elite.

Because the CCP's legitimacy in urban areas is largely dependent on continued improvement in living standards, a halt to or even a strong slowdown in this dynamic could seriously erode it (Zhong and Chen, 2013). The challenge of the deleveraging process is to reconcile growth slowdown with sufficient employment and rising household income in order to restructure the economy in favour of consumption. But in the short term, the necessary reduction of investment will put pressure on employment and household income growth, unless there is a significant transfer of resources from the state and real estate sectors to households (Pettis, 2013). This income redistribution will necessarily affect the lion's share of China's economic and political elite. A supply-side policy to ensure full competition in the private game preserve of SOEs, especially in the petroleum, telecommunications, banking and automobile sectors, will take time and hardly defuse the time bomb of inequality.

China is thus at a crucial turning point for the next few years, as the postponement of problems by the real estate bubble has done nothing but worsen the situation. Between slower growth and rising financial risks, the new political leadership still has a policy space to prevent a house of cards scenario, but everything will depend on the lion's reaction, which is not easily tameable.

Notes

1 Personal interview by the author, Shanghai, November 2012.
2 In 2012, according to Wang Xiaolu (2013), only 16.9 percent of migrant workers had medical coverage.
3 From 2000 to 2010 the average government expenditure to GDP was 19.4 percent, a relatively small share compared with other developing economies, as these figures do not take into account the ownership of state enterprises.
4 In 2012, 160 million migrants left their provinces and 100 million left their local jurisdictions but remained within their respective provinces, which results in an estimate of 260 million migrants in China, according to the State Statistics Bureau.
5 Total factor productivity, which measures economic efficiency, grew 4 percent from the admission of China to the WTO in 2001 to 2007, but has fallen by almost half since the stimulus package of 2008.
6 According to Yu (2013) "with per capita income at less than US$6,000, homeownership in China is roughly 90 percent, compared to less than 70 percent in the United States . . . five of the ten tallest skyscrapers under construction worldwide are in China . . . China's economy is being held hostage by real estate investment".
7 The AMCs have well managed the nonperforming loans ratio of state banks, which fell from 40 to 50 percent in 1997 to 1.8 percent in 2009 (Bulletin Économique Chine, 2009).

References

Aglietta M. and Bai G. (2012) *La voie chinoise: capitalisme et Empire*, Odile Jacob, Paris.
Aveline-Dubach N. (2013) Finance Capital Launches an Assault on Chinese Real Estate, *China Perspectives*, Special Feature: Real Estate Speculation and its Social

Consequences, No.2013/2, French Centre for Research on Contemporary China (CEFC), Hong Kong.

Borst N. and Rutkowski R. (2013) China's New Populist Urbanization, *China Economic Watch*, Peterson Institute of International Economics (PIIE), 19 March 2013. Available from: www.piie.com/blogs/china/?p=2376 [Accessed: 8 July 2015].

Bulletin Économique Chine (2009) No.16, Aout 2009, Direction Générale Trésor, Ambassade de France en Chine, Beijing.

Bulletin Économique Chine (2013a) No.58, Juillet 2013, Direction Générale Trésor, Ambassade de France en Chine, Beijing.

Bulletin Économique Chine (2013b) No.61, Décembre 2013, Direction Générale Trésor, Ambassade de France en Chine, Beijing.

Coates B. and Luu N. (2012) China's Emergence in Global Commodity Markets, *Economic Roundup*, 1, pp. 1–30.

Deng Y., Gyourko J. and Wu J. (2012) *Land and House Price Measurement in China*, Working Paper No.18403, National Bureau of Economic Research, Cambridge, MA.

Dollar D. and Wei S.J. (2007) *Das (Wasted) Capital: Firm Ownership and Investment Efficiency in China*, Working Paper No.07/9, International Monetary Fund.

Fabre G. (2010) The Twilight of Chimerica? China and the Collapse of the American Model, in *Current Issues in Economic Integration, Can Asia Inspire the West?*, (eds) Andreosso-O'Callaghan B. and Zolin M.B., Ashgate Publishing, Farnham, pp. 53–74.

Feng X. (2012) *Features, Problems and Reform of County and Township Fiscal Administration System in China*, Working Paper, Lincoln Institute of Land Policy, Washington.

Follain J.R. and Giertz S.H. (2013) *Preventing House Price Bubbles: Lessons from the 2006–2012 Bust*, Lincoln Institute of Land Policy, Washington.

Gang X. (2012) Regulating Shadow Banking, *China Daily*, 12 October 2012. Available from: www.chinadaily.com.cn/opinion/2012–10/12/content_15812305.htm [Accessed: 3 June 2015].

Gaulard M. (2013) Changes in the Chinese Property Market: An Indicator of the Difficulties Faced by Local Authorities, *China Perspectives*, Special Feature: Real Estate Speculation and Its Social Consequences, No.2013/2, French Centre for Research on Contemporary China (CEFC), Hong Kong.

Goldman Sachs (2013) *Top of Mind: Global Economics, Commodities, and Strategy Research*, Issue 15, 5 August 2013, New York: The Goldman Sachs Group Inc.

He Q. (2013) *When All That's Left in China's Economy Is Real Property*, September 2013. Available from: http://hqlenglish.blogspot.com/2013/09/when-all-thats-left-in-chinas-economy.html [Accessed: 21 June 2015].

He Y. and Man J.Y. (2012) *The Debt Magnitude and Insolvency Risk of Local Financing Platforms in China*, Working Paper, Lincoln Institute of Land Policy, Washington.

Hornby L. (2014) China Land Sales Pull in Record $672bn, *Financial Times*, 12 February 2014.

Hu A. (2011) *China in 2020: A New Type of Superpower*, Brooking Institution, Washington.

Hu Y. (2013) China's Local Government Debt: Saving for a Rainy Day, *China Economic Watch*, Peterson Institute of International Economics (PIIE), 3 September 2013. Available from: http://blogs.piie.com/china/?p=3193 [Accessed: 1 October 2015].

Huang P.C.C. (2011) The Theoretical and Practical Implications of China's Development Experience: The Role of Informal Economic Practices, *Modern China*, 37(1), pp. 3–43.

Huang Y. and Tao K. (2011) *Causes of and Remedies for the People's Republic of China's External Imbalances: The Role of Factor Market Distortion*, ADBI Working Paper Series 279, Asian Development Bank Institute, Tokyo.

Hurun Report (2013) *The Chinese Millionaire Wealth Report 2013*. Available from: www.hurun.net/usen/NewsShow.aspx?nid=408 [Accessed: 24 July 2015]

IMF (2013) *Country Report: People's Republic of China*, No.13/211, International Monetary Fund, Washington, DC.

Lee I.H., Syed M. and Xueyan L. (2012) *Is China Over-Investing and Does It Matter?*, International Monetary Fund (IMF) Working Paper, No.12/277, November 2012.

Lemoine F. (2014) *L'économie des BRIC*, in BRICS et économies émergentes séminaire, FMSH/EHESS, 27 January 2014.

Li H., Li L., Wu B. and Xiong Y. (2012) The End of Cheap Chinese Labor, *Journal of Economic Perspectives*, 26(4), pp. 57–74.

Li J. (2013) Commodity Suppliers Hurt by China Demand, *China Daily*, 12 July 2013. Available from: http://usa.chinadaily.com.cn/business/2013–07/12/content_16766307.htm [Accessed: 17 May 2015].

Lu Y. and Tao S. (2013) *Local Government Financing Platforms in China: A Fortune or Misfortune?*, International Monetary Fund (IMF) Working Paper, No.13/243, October 2013.

Park A. and Cai F. (2011) The Informalization of the Chinese Labor Market, in *From Iron Rice Bowl to Informalization: Markets, State and Workers in a Changing China*, (eds) Kuruvilla S., Lee C.K. and Gallagher's M., Cornell University Press, Ithaca, pp. 17–35.

Pei M. (2013) The Politics of a Slowing China, *Project Syndicate*, 6 July 2013.

Peterson G.E. (2006) *Land leasing and Land Sale as an Infrastructure-Financing Option*, World Bank, Policy Research Working Paper 4043, November 2006.

Pettis M. (2013) *China Financial Markets: The Urbanization Fallacy*, 16 August 2013. Available from: http://blog.mpettis.com/2013/08/the-urbanization-fallacy/ [Accessed: 3 November 2015].

Rabinovitch S. (2012a) China RRR: Wrong Focus, *Financial Times*, 1 February 2012. Available from: http://blogs.ft.com/beyond-brics/2012/02/01/china-rrr-wrong-focus/ [Accessed: 21 March 2015].

Rabinovitch S. (2012b) China Urbanisation: Lords of the Ring, *Financial Times*, 5 December 2012. Available from: http://blogs.ft.com/beyond-brics/2012/12/05/china-urbanisation-lords-of-the-ring/ [Accessed: 21 March 2015].

Rabinovitch S. (2014) China Gives Local Governments Go-Ahead to Roll over Debt, *Financial Times*, 2 January 2014. Available from: www.ft.com/intl/cms/s/0/055e48f8–7371–11e3-a0c0–00144feabdc0.html#axzz42PsOSphz [Accessed: 27 August 2015].

Randall W.L. and Liu X. (2014) *Options for China in a Dollar Standard World: A Sovereign Currency Approach*, Working Paper No.783, Levy Economics Institute of Bard College.

Rutkowski R. (2013) *Ignore the Noise: Why Chinese Household Consumption Is Still Too Low*, Peterson Institute for International Economics (PIIE), 12 August 2013.

Sheng A. and Geng X. (2013a) China Grows Down, *Project Syndicate*, 15 July 2013.

Sheng A. and Geng X. (2013b) China's New Growth Order, *Project Syndicate*, 19 August 2013.

Sheng H. and Zhao N. (2012) *China's State-Owned Enterprises: Nature, Performance and Reform*, UNIRULE Institute of Economics, Beijing.

Simarro R. (2011) *Functional Distribution of Growth and Income and Economic Growth in the Chinese Economy*, Department of Economics Working Papers No.168, School of Oriental and African Studies, University of London.

Tao R. (2012) *The Issue of Land in China's Transition and Urbanization*, Working Paper, Lincoln Institute of Land Policy, Beijing.

UNCTAD (2011) *World Investment Report 2011: Non-equity Modes of International Production and Development*, New York and Geneva: United Nations Conference on Trade and Development, United Nations.

Wang X. (2013) Measuring the Width of the Wealth Gap, *Caixin Online*, 23 September 2013. Available from: http://english.caixin.com/2013–09–23/100585181.html?p1 [Accessed: 22 September 2015].

Wang X. and Wing T.W. (2011) The Size and Distribution of Hidden Household Income in China, *Asian Economic Papers*, 10(1), pp. 1–26.

WTO and IDE-JETRO (2013) *Trade Patterns and Global Value Chains in East Asia: From Trade in Goods to Trade in Tasks*, Geneva: World Trade Organization and Institute of Developing Economies.

Xing W. and Man J.Y. (2012) *Regional Tax Transfer and Horizontal Tax Assignment in China*, Working Paper, Lincoln Institute of Land Policy, Beijing.

Yang L., Xiaojing Z., Xin C., Duoduo T. and Cheng L. (2012) China's Sovereign Balance Sheet and Its Risk Assessment, *Economic Research Journal*, 47(6), pp. 4–19.

Yergin D. (2013) China's Big Commodity Chill, *The Wall Street Journal*, 8 August 2013. Available from: www.wsj.com/articles/SB10001424127887323477604579000423245331040 [Accessed: 24 April 2015].

Yu Y. (2013) China's Investment Addiction, *Project Syndicate*, 7 October 2013.

Yueh L. (2013) *China's Growth: The Making of an Economic Superpower*, Oxford: Oxford University Press.

Zhang J. and Zhu T. (2012) China's Consumption Rate Is Too Low? *Financial Times: Chinese Economy*, 31 December 2012.

Zhang Y.S. and Barnett S. (2014) *Fiscal Vulnerabilities and Risks from Local Government Finance in China*, International Monetary Fund (IMF), Working Paper, No.14/4, January 2014.

Zhang Z. and Chen W. (2013) *China: Rising Risks of Financial Crisis*, Asia Special Report, Nomura Global Economics, Hong Kong.

Zhao S. (2013) *Zhongxing jieding zhongyang difang quanli guanxi* (Let Us Define the Power Relations between the Central and the Local Governments), Zhongguo jingji baogao (China Economic Report), n°9, Beijing: State Council Development Research Centre.

Zhong Y. and Chen Y. (2013) Regime Support in Urban China, *Asian Survey*, 53(2), pp. 369–392.

Zhu N. (2014) Keeping the Lid on Housing Prices, *China Daily*, 31 January 2014. Available from: http://europe.chinadaily.com.cn/business/2014–01/31/content_17267156.htm [Accessed: 10 October 2015].

2 On a path towards financialization?

The expanding role of finance in China's growth regime

Robert Pauls, Bernadette Andreosso-O'Callaghan, and Jörn-Carsten Gottwald

2.1 Introduction

Since the 1990s, China's economic growth has been characterized by rapid extensive accumulation, based on an investment-led and export-oriented growth regime maximized by the underpricing of factor prices (Fabre, 2013). As an export-oriented economy, China was highly vulnerable to the fallout of the global financial crisis (GFC) and the global contraction of demand it caused, but government policy, including a large-scale stimulus program, has managed to cushion the expected severe impact of the crisis. Thus, ironically, in the aftermath of the GFC, 'communism saved capitalism' in the eyes of Chinese observers through the decisive implementation of a huge macroeconomic stimulus program; this provided the People's Republic of China (PRC) and the global economy – through the PRC's prominent role in global trade and global chains of production – with urgently needed demand. Since 2010, however, the formerly exceptional GDP growth rates produced by the Chinese economy have been in constant decline, revealing not only a possibly lasting impact of the GFC on global demand, but also fundamental weaknesses and contradictions within the Chinese growth model itself.

The investment-led extensive growth regime, relying on cheap migrant labour, created overcapacities and substantial imbalances, with the latter expressed in a strong increase in the profit share of national income to the detriment of wages. Accordingly, household consumption as a share of final demand has been declining, compensated for by exports (Zhu and Kotz, 2011; Molero-Simarro, 2015). At the same time, however, relentless accumulation in the labor-intensive industries has, as early as 2005, led to the appearance of labor shortages in the eastern and southern coastal manufacturing centres, which opened the way for a sustained increase in real wages in subsequent years. Because the labor-intensive private sector operates in an environment of cutthroat competition and restricted access to long-term financing, investments have not provided sufficient increases in productivity to compensate for the increase in wages. Thus, overproduction/insufficient demand, as well as a looming productivity crisis, are signalling the end of the artificially 'cheap China' model.[1]

Since Deng Xiaoping's policies of 'reform and opening', economic growth has become a central element of a new social contract between the Leninist cadre party and the population: the Communist Party of China (CPC) stayed at the apex of China's political and economic order, delivering a constant improvement of living conditions and promising the return of the Middle Kingdom to its old international standing. In this regard, growth policies have an even clearer connection to fundamental issues of the political order than in most advanced economies. They are crucially linked with the legitimacy and stability of China's authoritarian political regime. In terms of economic policy, the current conjuncture of unfavourable economic developments presents a number of formidable challenges to the CPC, illustrated, for example, by a policy turnover apparently replacing policies for boosting demand advocated by Prime Minister Li Keqiang at the 2012 Central Economic Works Conference, with new supply-side policies, advanced since late 2015 by President and Party Chairman Xi Jinping.

Aside from such oscillations, reforming finance and financial regulation has continued to be a core concern in the CPC's recent economic policies, in the hope that the development of the financial sector will facilitate the transition to what may become a new 'epochal' growth (Kuznets, 1973). In part driven by the stimulus program, Chinese finance and real estate have already expanded rapidly, although the nature and quality of this development are yet unclear. Relying on financial instruments to sustain China's economic growth that in turn lies at the heart of the political order raises substantial issues. China's leadership had carefully avoided premature liberalization and opening of its financial sector in spite of its WTO commitments (Andreosso-O'Callaghan and Gottwald, 2013), arguably also to avoid the potentially negative impact of a liberalized financial sector on economic stability. But financial repression within the Chinese system led to the emergence of a multilayer system of financial services outside the official banking sector. This process, which had long gone unnoticed by the powers-that-be, may now pose a threat to economic and possibly political order in China, as banks and companies expand their shadow banking activities. The 'financialization' of China's economy, promising to facilitate economic reform and risking economic stability, thus presents a double-edged sword for the CPC.

Before this background, based on a survey of the theoretical discussion on financialization, this chapter surveys the evidence for financialization of the Chinese economy looking at micro- and macro-level economic developments and innovations in regulatory policy.

2.2   The study of financialization and its significance to China

2.2.1   *The phenomenon of financialization*

The phenomenon of financialization has recently drawn increased attention in economic and social science research (Engelen, 2008). Although there is some consensus in the literature about the empirical phenomena that financialization entails, perspectives on the conceptual and theoretical foundations of financialization differ (Zwan, 2014). In its most basic meaning, financialization refers to the growing importance of financial markets and financial institutions in the economy (Orhangazi, 2008: 863), and it can be linked to a number of developments, such as

> ... the deregulation of the financial sector and the development of new financial instruments, the liberalisation of international capital flows, and increasing exchange rate volatility; the creation of powerful institutional investors; shareholder-value orientation and changes in corporate governance; facilitated access to credit for social groups previously described as 'underbanked' [...]
>
> (Stockhammer, 2014: 34, authors' translation)

Financialization is thus closely linked to the emergence of global financial markets, including their underlying principles and ideologies. Processes of financialization have first been identified in the advanced economies of the United States and Europe, but the global integration of financial and investment activities merits a closer look at comparable developments in the emerging economies of Brazil, China, and India.

So far, existing research on financialization can broadly be divided into two distinctive approaches: the first research perspective focuses on the effects of financialization on the micro- and meso-levels of the economy, namely on firms and industries in the financial as well as nonfinancial sectors. The second perspective approaches financialization from a macro perspective and is concerned with structural changes in the capitalist political economy that have occurred since the end of the 1960s and accompanying developments in the regulation of financial activities.[2]

2.2.2   Financialization in the financial and nonfinancial sectors of the economy

In the financial sector itself, which comprises financial institutions including insurance companies and real estate firms, financialization has been marked by intense competition leading to processes of rapid concentration, at least in the case of the United States. At the same time, profits of the financial sector have grown extraordinarily fast, which Crotty (2008) explains by the very high growth in demand for financial products, over-the-counter trading, and increased risk in financial investments.

Growing profits can also be explained by the growing importance of the unregulated or underregulated shadow banking sector. Shadow banking can be defined as "a complex credit intermediation network operating outside of the regulated banking sector" (Lysandrou and Nesvetailova, 2015: 1). Lysandrou and Nesvetailova identify two arguments in the literature regarding the explosive growth of shadow banking since the end of the 1990s. The first argument explains the rise of shadow banking through factors endogenous to the banking sector. According to this view, banks increasingly conduct financial activities off-balance to fully profit from regulatory arbitrage and financial innovation outside the existing regulatory framework. The second argument explains the rise of shadow banking by factors exogenous to the banking system, such as the rise of new financial institutions, including hedge funds, investment funds, money market funds, and private-equity funds, competing for profitable investments (Stockhammer, 2014: 40). Given the low profitability of traditional investment opportunities, shadow banking developed in response to demand for new and more profitable investment opportunities, which grew exponentially during a decade of very low interest rates in many advanced economies.

In the nonfinancial sector, financialization describes changes in corporate governance and management strategies, as well as a shift in investment activities and profit sources away from core businesses towards finance. Here, the rise of the concept of shareholder value has emphasized the distribution of profits to shareholders as a corporation's primary objective, de-emphasizing the earlier focus on investment. Grounded in agency theory and the principal–agent problem of firm ownership and control, the emphasis on shareholder value has been the pretext to wide-ranging shifts in the distribution of wealth and power between shareholders, management, and labor at the firm level (Zwan, 2014). In this context, the behavior of management has shifted away from the objective of achieving long-term growth towards the objective of satisfying the short-term motives of (institutional) shareholders (Crotty, 2005).

Consequently, at the level of the firm, financialization can also be described as a process of wide-ranging changes in firm behavior regarding investment and profit strategies, as has been demonstrated by a number of studies on the US economy (Aglietta and Breton, 2001). On the one hand, with financialization, nonfinancial corporations derive a greater share of their income from financial sources and divert more income to financial markets. Consequently, and on the other hand, investment of firm income in productive assets has relatively declined. These changes in firm behavior may, since the 1980s, have led to the decoupling of the development of firm profits and investment spending (Van Treeck, 2009: 923).

These shifts in investment strategies and profit sources of firms lead some researchers to suggest that financialization can be understood "as a pattern of accumulation in which profits accrue primarily through financial channels rather than through trade and commodity production" (Krippner, 2005: 174), reflecting the trend that for nonfinancial firms, profits from investments in trade and production have declined in favor of profits from investment in financial products and subsidiaries.

2.2.3   *The macroeconomic perspective on financialization*

At the macro level, financialization has been predominantly researched by scholars located in heterodox economics, the *régulation* school, economic sociology, and critical and Marxist political economy, where financialization is interpreted as a substantial structural shift in the patterns of accumulation and circulation with respect to investment and consumption in the capitalist political economy. In this view, financialization has emerged in the wake of the crisis of productivity and profitability of postwar capitalism. It represents the shift to a new kind, or even to multiple kinds, of growth or accumulation regimes (Aglietta, 2000). The finance-led accumulation regime constitutes a turn away from earlier Fordist modes of regulation that were based on a capital–labor compromise characterized by strong ties between productivity growth and wage-led demand growth within a predominantly nationally regulated political economy. Stockhammer (2014) shows that since the 1970s the financial sector and financial dealings in the United States have grown dramatically faster than the commodity-producing economy.

The decoupling of profits and investments observed as a result of changes in firm behavior, as described in the previous section, corresponds to wider shifts in macroeconomic cohesion. For the US case, Van Treeck (2009) argues that the process of financialization has enabled firms' profit income to increase despite a decline in investment expenditure since the 1970s because of an increase in household consumption expenditure for financial products. This increase in household expenditure has been facilitated by the redistribution of firms' profits as dividends to households, a decline of household savings, and an expansion of credit to households. Furthermore, government debt and foreign capital inflows were also predominantly used to increase consumption.

Boyer (2000) develops a hypothetical model of a 'fully developed' finance-led accumulation regime, which can help to relate several observable phenomena of financialization. In this model, firm governance and competition between firms are dominated by the shareholder value principle, emphasizing profits over investment, and shifting the field of competition between firms from product to financial markets. The wage–labor nexus is decoupled from investment and productivity and instead subordinated to the profit expectations of shareholders and financial markets, requiring the flexible adjustment of the wage bill, affecting wages, working hours and employment. Households whose employment and income are adversely affected by changes in the wage relation procure additional income through extended access to financial products and credit, sustaining or even spurring the level of consumption. The state's ability to incur debt is restrained by the financial markets' willingness to lend as household investments in government bonds are reduced. The tax base shrinks as it shifts away from mobile capital to labor and fixed assets. The task of monetary policy moves from coordinating growth and inflation to regulating finance and especially preventing the growth of financial bubbles (Boyer, 2000: 118).

Following a more international perspective and informed by an analysis of causes and consequences of the financial crisis, Stockhammer (2014) argues that financialization in predominantly Anglo-Saxon economies has led to the creation of two growth strategies that are to a certain degree complementary, one debt led, mostly in Anglo-American countries, and the other export led, as, for example, in China, Japan, and Germany. Thus, on the level of the international economy, the phenomenon of financialization can be connected to capital account liberalization and subsequent increased financial flows between countries, which, it can be argued, served as a significant precondition for the emergence of debt-led and export-led accumulation regimes. The sustainability of this accumulation regime has been put to question by the global financial crisis. It is important to note that current account liberalization has been one of the factors contributing to a number of earlier currency and financial crises in emerging economies such as the Asian crisis or the Latin American debt crisis, among others (Stockhammer, 2014).

2.2.4 Financialization as a framework for understanding China

The phenomenon of financialization has spurred research in a number of disciplines. Due to the diversity and novelty of this research, financialization is still a predominantly descriptive concept with fuzzy boundaries rather than a coherent theoretical framework.

Research on financialization has predominantly focused on developments in the US economy and to a lesser extent on other developed economies. The question thus remains whether financialization as a concept can explain developments in emerging economies such as China. Following Engelen (2008), the research would have to be careful to test the empirical applicability of the concept to new cases and find out if it can provide meaningful explanations that other concepts cannot. Research on emerging economies such as China may provide insights into the interconnectedness of financialized and financializing or nonfinancialized economies (as, for example, in Froud *et al.*, 2014). Little research on financialization has been done in political science; hence only limited attention has been paid to the politics of financialization, that is, the role of political actors in financial governance and regulation (Heires and Nölke, 2014), with the notable exception of Krippner (2011).

In view of this theoretical discussion, the following sections will analyze economic and political developments in China through the lens of financialization, exploring the extent to which it can be meaningfully applied to the Chinese case.

2.3 Financialization in China: the economic trend

2.3.1 Macroeconomic indicators

Macroeconomic data on post-GFC economic growth reveal the extent to which the export- and investment-led growth model of China has been brought into question. Figure 2.1 shows how the reliance on the Western (essentially US) markets has led to a downward trend of Chinese exports since 2007 and how investment (gross fixed capital formation) has plateaued after the effects of the November 2008 stimulus package have waned.

Of specific relevance is the way total investment has evolved vis-à-vis total savings[3] in the recent past and specifically before the crisis so as to infer some preliminary conclusions relating to the issue of financialization. Also shown in Figure 2.1, savings and investment have tended to be decoupled between 2004 and 2011, with total investment flat when savings were rising at the beginning of the period and total investment rising sharply during the two years preceding the crisis, whereas savings were declining during that time.

Turning to profit rates, Figure 2.2 shows profit rates (as defined by the returns on assets [ROA]) of state-owned enterprises (SOEs) and other manufacturing firms

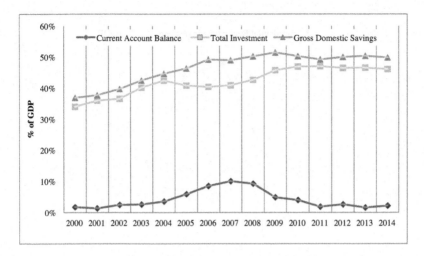

Figure 2.1 China: current account balance, investment, and savings

Source: Derived from World Bank DataBank (http://databank.worldbank.org) and CEIC Data China Premium Database (www.ceicdata.com), last accessed March 6, 2016.

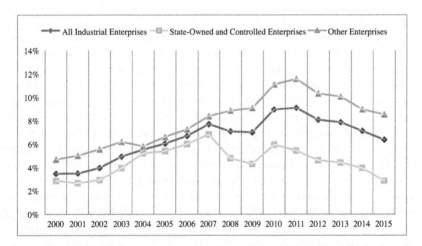

Figure 2.2 China: profitability of industrial SOEs and non-SOEs (profits as a share of assets)

Source: Derived from CEIC Data China Premium Database (www.ceicdata.com), last accessed March 6, 2016.

in China. As can be seen from this figure, the profitability of industrial SOEs in China as a whole was largely in line with that of non-SOEs, only 1 to 2 percentage points lower, before the crisis. Other similar profitability indicators show roughly the same picture. The gap has nevertheless quickly widened since 2008. Although

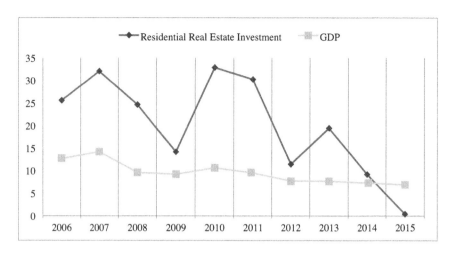

Figure 2.3 Residential real estate investment and GDP growth rates (%)

Source: Derived from CEIC Data China Premium Database (www.ceicdata.com), last accessed March 6, 2016.

industrial SOEs as a whole show reasonable performance relative to non-SOEs, there is substantial variety at the sectoral level. SOEs in all control 44 percent of total assets in industry, but across different industrial sectors this share varies significantly (Fabre, 2013). Moreover, there is a positive correlation between the performance of SOEs and their market shares in individual sectors, a result which might suggest that SOEs profit from their monopoly power (Lardy, 2014: 98).

Declining opportunities for profitable industrial investment (gross fixed capital formation [GFCF]) might signal an incentive to turn to property investment or other financial investment. Regarding the former, the main evidence shown by Figure 2.3 is that over the period 2007–14 (and particularly during 2010–11) the increase in residential real estate investment has generally surpassed the growth rate of the economy. The figure shows that the adjustment brought about by the global financial crisis in terms of investment in residential real estate has been erratic. The decline of growth rates from 2007 onwards has been paralleled with declining real estate investment rates. Again, the short-term effect of the 2008 stimulus package can be seen (with an upward trend in the GDP growth rate after March 2009). Subsequent developments, however, show that this trend has been unsustainable, as real estate investment growth rates drop below GDP growth rates.

2.3.2   *The growing importance of China's capital and financial markets*

The growing importance of China's capital and financial markets can be appraised through an analysis of both stock market capitalization and its more dynamic development compared with the nonfinancial sector.

Table 2.1 and Figure 2.4 show the formidable increase of market capitalization in China's stock exchanges over a 11-year and a 14-year time span, respectively. Although much of the evolution is due to a catching-up phenomenon,
given China's underdeveloped stock markets, the increase (from US$512 billion
in 2003 to the current US$6 trillion in 2014, Table 2.1) is quite impressive. When
relative figures are used (Table 2.2 and Figure 2.4), it appears that the extent of
market capitalization in China accounts only for a fraction of that of the United
States. However, the figures of both Table 2.1 and Figure 2.4 also clearly show
that in spite of having stock markets still very much in their infancy, China has
caught up extremely rapidly with Western countries in only a few years. In 2004,
the China–US ratio of the stock traded as a percentage of GDP was 24.2 per cent;
in 2012, this ratio grew to 53.4 per cent, implying that the gap between China and
the United States is narrowing or that China's stock market trading as a percentage of GDP is more and more in line with that of the United States.

In addition to the formidable increase in stock market capitalization, the traditionally strong reliance of the Chinese economy on bank financing has grown in
importance since the GFC, also shown in Figure 2.4. Although the Chinese insurance and stock markets are still relatively underdeveloped compared with those of
the United States, data in Figure 2.4 show that bank credit has grown in importance
in China since the GFC.

A comparison of listed firms in the financial and nonfinancial sectors shows that
profits and fixed asset investment in the financial sector of the economy have been

Table 2.1 Market capitalization and stocks traded: United States and China compared

	Market capitalization of listed companies (current mn. US$)		Stocks traded (total value of GDP in %)	
	United States	*China*	*United States*	*China*
2003	14,266,265.65	512,978.77	148.8	23.5
2004	16,323,726.33	447,720.26	168.6	26.3
2005	17,000,864.47	401,852.25	211.3	17.3
2006	19,568,972.5	1,145,454.87	238.8	42.5
2007	19,922,279.82	4,478,866.53	300.8	179.0
2008	11,590,277.78	1,778,784.04	353.7	85.7
2009	15,077,285.74	3,573,152.46	215.9	154.8
2010	17,283,451.68	4,027,840.3	203.5	136.7
2011	15,640,707.04	3,412,108.29	282.9	89.1
2012	18,668,333.21	3,697,376.04	211.6	59.4
2013	24,034,853.52	3,949,143.49	208.7	81.1
2014	26,330,589.19	6,004,947.67	236.9	115.5

Source: Derived from World Bank DataBank (http://databank.worldbank.org), last accessed
March 6, 2016.

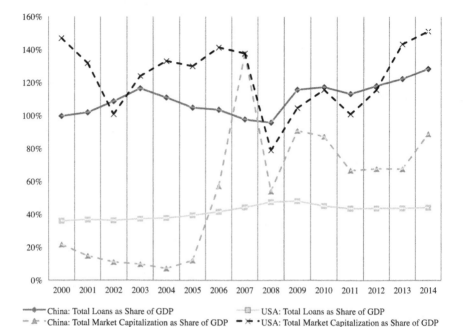

Figure 2.4 Loans and stock market capitalization in China and the United States compared (% share of GDP)

Source: Derived from CEIC Data China Premium Database (www.ceicdata.com), last accessed March 06 2016.

Table 2.2 Various estimates of the extent of shadow banking in China

Source	Year	USD trillions	% of 2012 GDP	% of bank assets, end-2012
GF Securities	2012	4.8	57%	31%
Citi Research	2013	4.5	54%	29%
Barclays	2012	4.1	49%	27%
Hua Tai Securities	2012	4.0	48%	26%
UBS	2012	2.2–3.9	26–46%	14–25%
ANZ Bank	2012	2.4–2.7	29–33%	16–18%
Bank of America/Merrill Lynch	2012	2.3	28%	15%

Source: Li (2014: 199).

growing faster than in the manufacturing sector between 2000 and 2011 (Zhang *et al.*, 2013). It can thus be shown that the financial sector has not only grown in size, but has acquired a more privileged position in terms of wealth accumulation and generation in recent years within the Chinese political economy.

2.3.3 Shadow banking and financialization of nonfinancial corporations

Shadow banking activities have expanded greatly, especially in conjunction with the post-GFC stimulus package, between 2008 and 2010. Various estimates of the size of shadow banking in China are given in Table 2.2. According to the different estimates, shadow banking represents between a quarter and more than half of China's GDP in 2012. In the United Kingdom and United States it accounted for 363 and 180 percent, respectively, in 2012, with a global average share of shadow banking in GDP of 117 per cent (Li, 2014). These preliminary figures suggest that although shadow banking has expanded quickly in the Chinese economy, its size relative to GDP is still low when compared with other more advanced economies. However, some other sources put the Chinese figure at around the size of GDP (Wei, Davies and Shen, 2014).

Undoubtedly, shadow banking played an important role in the extension of debt in the Chinese economy, which – based on data by Fitch – could rise from 128 per cent of GDP in 2010 to 216 per cent in 2013 and further on to 271 per cent in 2017 without proper political measures. Moreover, 43 per cent of local government debts of 17.9 trillion RMB (June 2013) were channelled by nonbanks, with 11 per cent by shadow banks, according to the China National Audit Office (Wei, Davies and Shen, 2014).

Contrary to experiences in the West, the expansion of shadow banking is not a result of deregulation, but a response to a further tightening of lending regulation, such as stricter reserve requirements and interest rate controls, which were put into place to ensure that the intended expansion of lending activities caused by the stimulus package would conform to certain quality standards (Li, 2014). As a reaction to tightened regulations on lending, commercial banks, local government entities, and state-controlled corporations, all entities with relatively easy access to the formal credit system, expanded their shadow banking activities to channel stimulus resources into less regulated and more lucrative lending, and especially to private borrowers.

For example, local government finance vehicles used the original 4-trillion RMB government stimulus package to raise 12 trillion RMB in credit funds to invest in real estate, infrastructure, and other capital-intensive projects. Furthermore, state-controlled enterprises and local state entities have utilized their facilitated access to formal credit to provide loan guarantees for private businesses and real estate developers, guarantees which were in turn collateralized as wealth-management products.

A further rapidly expanding field of informal finance is that of internet-based P2P (peer-to-peer) lending (Tsai, 2015). Early concerns regarding the risk of P2P development in China (Wang, Liu and Yang, 2014) were substantiated in 2016 when 21 people were detained over the breakdown of the Ezubo platform in 2016 (Han, 2016).

As the previous discussion has already indicated, the expansion of shadow banking activities has created new financialized uses of capital predominantly for the capital-intensive, state-controlled sector and has created new financial sources for the labor-intensive private sector, which is notoriously underbanked, with the former now lending to the latter outside the regulated commercial banking sector.

These developments can be interpreted as initial steps into the financialization of nonfinancial corporations with access to formal finance.

Research into corporate financialization in the nonfinancial sector in China is still uncommon (Cai and Ren, 2014). One of the most comprehensive studies in this regard is by Zhang and Zhuge (2013), who apply Milberg's (2008) criteria for studying financialization in the United States to the Chinese case. Looking at nonfinancial listed firms, they find that, contrary to a clear upward trend in the United States, income from securities as a share of total profits has been fluctuating widely among different nonfinancial industries, showing no clear trend towards financialization, which would require that financial sources of income in the non-financial sector grow at least as fast as in the financial sector.

As such, there appears to be little evidence for a general trend towards financialization of nonfinancial firms in China to an extent witnessed in the United States and other advanced economies. Nevertheless, as the Chinese manufacturing industry has in recent years suffered from a shrinking general demand, overcapacity, rising costs, and a lack of technical innovation, which have led to a sharp decline in profit margins in the core business of nonfinancial firms (cf. Figure 2.3), some large listed companies have started to test the waters for financial investments, so that corporate financial assets are showing a gradual upward trend (Xie *et al.*, 2014), possibly linked to the development of shadow banking described earlier.

2.4   The politics of financialization and financial regulation

Financial markets constitute an extremely sensitive policy field for the Chinese leadership. They are closely interconnected with some of the most important aspects of China's socialist market economy. It is therefore important to keep in mind that various generations of Chinese leaders have postponed full-blown reforms of the financial area. Whereas other sectors of the economy were targeted earlier on in the reform process, banking, insurance, and securities were only addressed in the late 1990s following the Asian financial crisis and in preparation for China's admission into the WTO in 2001 (Naughton, 2009; Gottwald and Collins, 2014). Obviously, control of the key pillars of the economy was and continues to be of great significance for the Chinese leadership, eager to promote a stable financial system to safeguard economic and ultimately social stability. This might help explain why China's financial sector developed into a premature, multilayered financial system with a specific regulatory setup that seeks to balance party–state influence with local funding needs and requirements resulting from gradual and partial integration into global markets.

2.4.1   *Key drivers of financial reforms in China: a path towards more financialization?*

Two dynamics have characterized China's economic reforms since 1978: reforms that were implemented without explicit formal encouragement of the central authorities but that proved successful and beneficial, and reforms initiated by the central authorities. The first group of reform initiatives took place in various localities and established an impetus for policy changes – if successful – or for political measures against it – if considered either threatening or disadvantageous by the authorities (Nee and Opper, 2012). In addition to these 'bottom-up' reforms, central authorities embarked on various 'top-down' reform initiatives either allowing experiments in various sorts of special zones or granting special rights to specific institutions. In the area of financial services, top-down reforms include the restructuring of China's supervisory structure, as well as the encouragement of the biggest banks to take an active role in the go-global strategy (Gottwald, 2011).

Several crises provided important critical junctures for the central authorities to rethink their policies and test alternative approaches: the fiscal crisis of 1992–93 led to a thorough reform of China's tax system and the role of the central bank (Yang, 2005); the Asian financial crisis of 1997–98 offered first-class insights into the risks of prematurely opening up the financial sectors and the need for a strong and efficient regulatory regime; the 2008 GFC now calls for various reform measures, ranging from the gradual liberalization of the RMB via the commitment to allow 'private banks' on a level playing field, to the reform of local finance. Following a well-established pattern, a new special zone has been set up: the China (Shanghai) pilot free trade zone (FTZ) to create new insights into the privatization and liberalization of finance. "The zone is considered an integral part of China's economic and foreign exchange reform under Xi's leadership" (Chen and Ren, 2014). Top-level support helped to push through contentious plans to allow for (nearly) free convertible accounts in Shanghai, the so-called offshore accounts, within days after an announcement on May 25. Xi Jinping expressed his support by calling Shanghai a "trailblazer" for reforms (*paitoubing*) and the pilot free trade zone an important new measure (Xinhua, 2014). Three more FTZs were established in 2015.

Another key driver that stimulated intensive rounds of regulatory and corporate reforms was China's accession to the WTO in 2001. Achieved against major reservations, particularly in the state-owned sector of China's economy, WTO membership technically required an opening of the well-shielded banking and securities sectors (Schlichting, 2008; Martin, 2012). Early steps to increase the role of foreign companies and international experts, however, did not lead to a full liberalization of China's financial markets. Yet, increased internationalization of the dominant domestic players allowed for the incorporation of China's big five banks into the go-global strategy of the Chinese government, including the successive listing of all of them abroad. A prominent role was taken up by China Development Bank, technically a governmental development bank that reinvented itself into one of the most innovative and politically astute financial services providers in China (Forsythe and Sanderson, 2013).

The China Development Bank had a significant role in supporting China's big companies to establish themselves abroad. It supported the Chinese leadership in its drive to secure access to resources and markets in Africa and Latin America. It became the largest provider of development finance in the world, and it changed dramatically the landscape of local finance in China itself by introducing cash-starved local authorities to the more creative ways of leveraging the income from land sales and setting up Local Government Finance Vehicles (LGFVs) (Forsythe and Sanderson, 2013). Local authorities needed additional income, not only to cater to particular interests among local elites, but also to provide essential social services to their communities. With official sources of income severely restricted and with local bonds banned by the central authorities, leveraged income from rezoning of land, which was repackaged into semi-legal private wealth products, became a key driver of financialization in the late 2000s as some of the statistical analysis earlier suggests. Because the sale of land that was bought off farmers, then rezoned into developmental sites and sold at a massive profit lay at the heart of this development, it linked two severe threats to the legitimacy and the stability of the party-state: the issues of land rights and their abuse by the local authorities with the exponential growth of shadow banking.

In the recent past, the main driver for Chinese financial innovation, however, seems to have been the need to access a broader variety of financial products than offered by the official banking system. All relevant groups of actors – local authorities, the big banks, large SOEs, SMEs, and private customers – have turned to the shadow banking sector. The provision of credit, as well as more attractive returns on savings, have both contributed to the development of new products, which more often than not have been accepted by the legal authorities even if they were deliberately kept outside the official regulatory system (Elliot, Kroeber and Yu, 2015). Silent acquiescence on behalf of the regulatory authorities indicates a willingness to let the financial sector increase its significance for the Chinese economy, even in the face of political problems and a growing number of scandals.

2.4.2   *China's system of regulation in the face of financialization pressures*

These trends continue to exert substantial pressure on China's regulation of financial services. Since the 1990s, the PRC had established a regulatory regime for financial services that sought to combine elements of state-of-the-art technocratic regulatory agencies with pillars of the party-state. This 'Chinese model of regulatory capitalism' (Gottwald and Collins, 2014) preserved features of the developmental state that seemed to be in stark contrast with the idea of independent bodies, transparency, and independent intermediaries usually associated with the regulatory state (Heilmann, 2005; Pearson, 2005, 2007). Yet it was successful in creating a framework for market activities that seemed compatible with Anglo-Saxon and European institutional setups and provided a basis for processes of experimentation and learning (Heep, 2014). Built around a central bank with limited independence yet increasingly influenced by macroeconomic policies, the regulatory regime has specialized agencies for banking (China Banking Regulatory Commission), securities (China Securities Regulatory Commission or CSRS), and insurance (China Insurance Regulatory Commission). With the help of business associations, asset companies, and the state's sovereign wealth funds, which are all actively involved in the domestic banking sector, the system allows for control of personnel and access to credit by the party-state (Andreosso-O'Callaghan and Gottwald, 2013). The occasional direct interference by cadres, however, is mitigated by turf wars among competing bureaucratic systems (*xitong*) and conflicting policy imperatives for financial reforms.

Thus, despite far-reaching venues for interference, actual control by the party-state is occasionally piecemeal and limited. It came as a shock to both the wider public and apparently the Chinese leadership when the amount of losses inflicted to Chinese investment vehicles due to their involvement with US institutions became known in 2008–09 and, again, when a report by the Chinese Academy of Social Sciences highlighted the volume of debts by local authorities and their LGFVs in 2011–12. With direct central control of – or as a result of recent reforms – substantial political leverage over interest rates, credit allocation, and foreign exchange, the biggest banks still enjoy a built-in cushion against market pressures. Yet even the big banks are actively seeking to benefit from financial innovation through their links with the shadow banking sector.

In summary, many characteristics generally found in economic policy making in China can also be found in the policy fields of finance and financial regulation and in the dialectics of 'bottom-up' innovation and 'top-down' regulation, which in some respects may present initial steps to a more comprehensive process of financialization.

Below the central level, a magnitude of provincial banks, local banks, and investment vehicles have flourished. De facto barred from direct business with the largest SOEs and often well linked with local political authorities, they have become a major player in creating new ways to provide funding for local governments and enterprises in creating new investment mechanisms. Equally innovative has been the move of some leading Chinese enterprises into the area of consumer credit and P2P lending. Although the activities of local banks might have taken place below the radar of the central authorities, the increased activity of a company like Alibaba in the credit business was developed in consultation with the relevant state authorities. Thus, on the one hand financial innovation – private capital, Internet banking – further increases the challenges for regulators and the government, yet on the other hand it provides the leadership with room for experiments with new products, marketplaces, and businesses without committing to a complete liberalization of its financial system. This underscores the willingness of the Chinese leadership to intensify the role of financial products and financial innovation in the Chinese economy, even if the current macroeconomic indicators do not yet portray levels of financialization in line with those of Western economies.

2.5 Conclusions

Financialization is a concept with fuzzy boundaries that has been appraised from different disciplines primarily to study the case of Western economies such as the United States or the United Kingdom. This chapter has attempted to evaluate whether this concept can meaningfully be applied to the case of China, observing economic developments and bearing in mind the role of political actors in financial governance and regulation. The use of a number of macroeconomic indicators shows that investment (gross fixed capital formation) has tended to move away from savings before the GFC and has plateaued during the crisis; that profit rates of SOEs have declined sharply with the crisis; that the growth rate of residential real estate investment has, until very recently, surpassed the growth rate of the economy; that the stock market capitalization has soared, in spite of underdeveloped stock exchange markets; that there has been a substantial upward trend in corporate financial investment; and that the size of shadow banking could be as large as the Chinese GDP. Overall, investments and profits in the financial sector have been growing faster than in other sectors of the economy. Concerning its size as a share of the economy as a whole, all the measures do not put China in the league of the most financialized economies in the world, but they do show that regulated and unregulated finance in the past 10 to 15 years have gained in proportion, even if the developments in certain subsectors such as real estate have been unsteady.

Whereas the financial sector has been expanding in relative terms, there exists, as of yet, no systematic research or evidence showing that financial sources of income have become widely and systematically integrated into the core businesses of nonfinancial firms until 2013, constituting a process of financialization in the nonfinancial corporate sector. More recently, however, firm-level, bottom-up financial 'innovation' has contributed to a surge of shadow banking. Local state entities and mostly state-controlled corporations with access to formal finance, channelling these resources into unregulated financial products, may in hindsight prove to be forerunners of a wider trend of corporate financialization.

The discussion has suggested that the politics of regulation in China are not sufficiently described as a cat-and-mouse game between financial innovators regularly outpacing regulators. Indeed, on the political level, financial developments in the aftermath of the GFC may be built upon to achieve some wider reform objectives, such as the move away from the now-faltering extensive investment-led and export-oriented growth model towards a model emphasizing innovation-driven productivity gains and domestic consumption, by creating a deeper and more systematic role for finance in investment and consumption patterns. Such developments would confirm a general pattern of experimental policy making defined by the relationship of central and local actors and their competing or colluding interests in China's party-state. Whether local practice will be turned into official policies and whether they can be reconciled with a control-oriented regulatory financial system remains to be seen, depending in part upon how the 2013 Third Plenum reforms will be implemented.

In some ways, financialization, as an important approach to better understand China's political economy today, has very much been and is still an 'ad hoc' type or coincidental financialization, tied to various crisis dynamics currently observable. This could suggest therefore that uncertainty is paramount with regard to the question of how finance can be integrated systematically or even sustainably into a new and reformed growth regime. It will remain to be seen whether the many phenomena of financialization observable in China will provide the nuclei of a future fully developed financialized growth regime in the theoretical sense, of which there is currently no evidence. Just as likely, current developments may provide the basis of potential economic (and political) instability arising from 'disordered' financialization in China.

Notes

1 Views differ as to whether these years constitute a Lewis turning point, including the issue of whether the Lewis turning point is a valuable indicator due to institutional distortions of the Chinese labour market like the *hukou* system (cf. Cai and Du, 2011; Golley and Meng, 2011).
2 A third research perspective that will be of lesser importance to this chapter focuses on the financialization of everyday life and is located in the fields of social accounting and cultural economics (cf. Zwan, 2014).
3 Total national savings comprise government savings, corporate savings, and household savings (the largest component).

References

Aglietta M. (2000) Shareholder Value and Corporate Governance: Some Tricky Questions, *Economy and Society*, 29(1), pp. 146–159.

Aglietta M. and Breton R. (2001) Financial Systems, Corporate Control and Capital Accumulation, *Economy and Society*, 30(4), pp. 433–466.

Andreosso-O'Callaghan B. and Gottwald J.C. (2013) How Red is China's Red Capitalism? Continuity and Change in China's Financial Services Sector during the Global Crisis, *Asia Pacific Business Review*, Special Issue 'Demystifying Chinese Management: Issues and Challenges', 19(4), pp. 444–460.

Boyer R. (2000) Is a Finance-led Growth Regime a Viable Alternative to Fordism? A Preliminary Analysis, *Economy and Society*, 29(1), pp. 111–145.

Cai F. and Du Y. (2011) Wage Increases, Wage Convergence, and the Lewis Turning Point in China, *China Economic Review*, 22(4), pp. 601–610.

Cai M. and Ren S. (2014) Qiye jinrong hua: Yi xiang yanjiu zongshu (Corporate Financialization – A Literature Review), *Caijing Kexue*, 7, pp. 41–51.

Chen G. and Ren D. (2014) Xi Jinping Shows Support for Shanghai Free-Trade Zone in Whistle-Stop Visit, *South China Morning Post*, 23 May 2014. Available from: www.scmp.com/article/1518829/xi-jinping-shows-support-shanghai-free-trade-zone-whistle-stop-visit [Accessed: 01 March 2016].

Crotty J. (2005) The Neoliberal Paradox: The Impact of Destructive Product Market Competition and 'Modern' Financial Markets on Nonfinancial Corporation Performance in the Neoliberal Era, in *Financialization and the World Economy*, (ed) Epstein G.A., Edward Elgar, Northampton, pp. 77–110.

Crotty J. (2008) If Financial Market Competition Is Intense, Why Are Financial Firm Profits So High? Reflections on the Current 'Golden Age' of Finance, *Competition & Change*, 12(2), pp. 167–183.

Elliot D., Kroeber A. and Yu Q. (2015) Shadow Banking in China – A Primer, *Economic Studies at Brookings*, March 2015. Available from: www.brookings.edu/~/media/research/files/papers/2015/04/01-shadow-banking-china-primer/shadow_banking_china_elliott_kroeber_yu.pdf [Accessed 4 February 2016].

Engelen E. (2008) The Case for Financialization, *Competition & Change*, 12(2), pp. 111–119.

Fabre G. (2013) *The Lion's Share: What's Behind China's Economic Slowdown*, Fondation Maison des Sciences de l'Homme, Working Paper Series, 53.

Forsythe M. and Sanderson H. (2013) *China's Superbank. Debt, Oil, and Influence: How China Development Bank Is Rewriting the Rules of Finance*, John Wiley, New York/Singapore.

Froud J., Johal S., Leaver A. and Williams K. (2014) Financialization Across the Pacific: Manufacturing Cost Ratios, Supply Chains and Power, *Critical Perspectives on Accounting*, 25(1), pp. 46–57.

Golley J. and Meng X. (2011) Has China Run Out of Surplus Labour?, *China Economic Review*, 22(4), pp. 555–572.

Gottwald J.C. (2011) Cadre Capitalism Goes Global: Financial Market Reforms and the New Role of the People's Republic of China in World Markets, in *The Emergence of Southern Multinationals and their Impact on Europe*, (ed) Brennan L., Palgrave Macmillan, Basingstoke, pp. 283–300.

Gottwald J.C. and Collins N. (2014) Market Creation by Leninist Means: The Regulation of Financial Services in the People's Republic of China, *Asian Studies Review*, 38(4), pp. 620–638.

Han Y. (2016) Executives among Those Held over 50bln Yuan Scam, Xinhua Says, *Caixin Online*, 2 February 2016. Available from: http://english.caixin.com/2016-02-02/100906456.html [Accessed 9 February 2016].

Heep S. (2014) *China in Global Finance: Domestic Financial Repression and International Financial Power*, Cham, Switzerland: Springer Science & Business Media.

Heilmann S. (2005) Regulatory Innovation by Leninist Means: Communist Party Supervision in China's Financial Industry, *The China Quarterly*, 181, pp. 1–21.

Heires M. and Nölke A. (2014) Die Politische Ökonomie der Finanzialisierung. Einleitung, in *Politische Ökonomie der Finanzialisierung*, (eds) Heires M. and Nölke A., Springer VS, Wiesbaden, pp. 19–32.

Krippner G.R. (2005) The Financialization of the American Economy, *Socio-Economic Review*, 3(2), pp. 173–208.

Krippner G.R. (2011) *Capitalizing on Crisis – The Political Foundations of the Rise of Finance*, Harvard University Press, Harvard.

Kuznets S. (1973) Modern Economic Growth: Findings and Reflections, *The American Economic Review*, 63(3), pp. 247–258.

Lardy N. (2014) *Markets over Mao: The Rise of Private Business in China*, Peterson Institute for International Economics (PIIE), Washington, DC.

Li T. (2014) Shadow Banking in China: Expanding Scale, Evolving Structure, *Journal of Financial Economic Policy*, 6(3), pp. 198–211.

Lysandrou P. and Nesvetailova A. (2015) The Role of Shadow Banking Entities in the Financial Crisis: A Disaggregated View, *Review of International Political Economy*, 22(2), pp. 257–279.

Martin M.F. (2012) *China's Banking System: Issues for Congress*, Congress Research Service. Available from: www.fas.org/sgp/crs/row/R42380.pdf [Accessed: 1 March 2016].

Milberg W. (2008) Shifting Sources and Uses of Profits: Sustaining US Financialization with Global Value Chains, *Economy and Society*, 37(3), pp. 420–451.

Molero-Simarro R. (2015) Functional Distribution of Income, Aggregate Demand, and Economic Growth in the Chinese Economy 1978–2007, *International Review of Applied Economics*, 28(4), pp. 1–20.

Naughton B. (2009) *The Chinese Economy: Transition and Growth*, MIT Press, London

Nee V.G. and Opper S. (2012) *Capitalism from Below – Markets and Institutional Change in China*, Cambridge University Press, Cambridge.

Orhangazi O. (2008) Financialisation and Capital Accumulation in the Non-Financial Corporate Sector: A Theoretical and Empirical Investigation on the US Economy: 1973–2003, *Cambridge Journal of Economics*, 32(6), pp. 863–886.

Pearson M.M. (2005) The Business of Governing Business in China: Institutions and Norms of the Emerging Regulatory State, *World Politics*, 57(2), pp. 296–325.

Pearson M.M. (2007) Governing the Chinese Economy: Regulatory Reform in the Service of the State, *Public Administration Review*, 67(4), pp. 718–730.

Schlichting S. (2008) *Internationalising China's Financial Markets*, Palgrave Macmillan, Basingstoke.

Stockhammer E. (2014) Entstehung und Krise des finanz-dominierten Akkumulationsregimes – Eine postkeynesianische Perspektive auf Finanzialisierung, in *Die Politische Ökonomie der Finanzialisierung*, (eds) Heires M. and Nölke A., Springer VS, Wiesbaden, pp. 33–48.

Tsai K. (2015) The Political Economy of State Capitalism and Shadow Banking in China, *Issues & Studies*, 51(1), pp. 55–97.

Van Treeck T. (2009) The Political Economy Debate on 'Financialization' – A Macroeconomic Perspective, *Review of International Political Economy*, 16(5), pp. 907–944.

Wang S., Liu R. and Yang L. (2014) P2P Lender Heading Into Dangerous Waters, Critics Say, *Caixin Online*, 18 April 2014. Available from: http://english.caixin.com/2014–04–18/100667283.html [Accessed: 8 February 2016].

Wei L., Davies B. and Shen H. (2014) China Tightens Grip on Shadow Banks, *The Wall Street Journal*, 6 January 2014. Available from: http://online.wsj.com/news/articles/SB1 0001424052702304887104579303732528192434 [Accessed: 14 February 2014].

Xie, Jiazhi/Jiang and Yuan/Wang, Wentao (2014) Shenme qudongle zhizao ye jinrong hua touzi xingwei – jiyu A gu shangshi gongsi de jingyan zhengjiu (What Motivates Manufacturing Companies' Financialized Investment Behavior? Empirical Evidence from Listed A-Share Manufacturing Companies), *Hunan Daxue Xuebao (Shehui Kexue Ban)*, 28(4), pp. 23–29.

Xinhua (2014) Xi Jinping: zouhao keji chaunxin xianshou qi jiu neng zhanling xian jiying de youshi, *Xinhua*, 26 May 2014. Available from: http://news.xinhuanet.com/politics/2014–05/24/c_1110843342.htm [Accessed: 16 May 2014].

Yang D. (2005) *Remaking the Chinese Leviathan: Market Transition and the Politics of Governance in China*, Stanford University Press, Stanford.

Zhang, Mubin/Zhuge, Hengzhong (2013) Quanqiu hua beijing xia Zhongguo jingji de jinrong hua: Hanyi yu shizheng jianyan (Financialization of the Chinese Economy before the Background of Globalization: Meaning and Empirical Findings), Nanjing, China: Shijie Jingji yu Zhengzhi Luntan, 1, pp. 122–138.

Zhu A. and Kotz D.M. (2011) The Dependence of China's Economic Growth on Exports and Investment, *Review of Radical Political Economics*, 43(1), pp. 9–32.

Zwan N. (2014) Making Sense of Financialization, *Socio-Economic Review*, 12(1), pp. 99–129.

3 Reappraisal of the environmental Kuznets Curve in East Asian developing countries falling into middle-income traps

Tatsuyuki Ota

3.1 Introduction

Having achieved the highest growth rate of all regions in recent decades, the East Asian region has entered a new stage facing emerging challenges: above all, the middle-income trap and environmental degradation. Although some countries have successfully developed to become higher-income countries, others stagnated at lower or middle income levels. Rapid economic growth resulted in substantial shifts in the classification of economies by the World Bank between the low-income, middle-income, and high-income groups in which each country has been classified since 1990, and due attention has not been paid to environmental protection, generating widespread environmental threats in the East Asian region, especially in China, where GDP growth rates began to slow down recently. A typical example indicating the serious side effects of rapid economic growth is tersely depicted by a *Financial Times*' article (Anderlini, 2013) titled "Beijing 'airpocalypse' drives expatriates exodus".[1] Extreme air pollution is not only driving away expatriates, but causing foreign investors to refrain from investing, with investment being much in demand for growth. Middle-income China may have fallen into the middle-income trap, hitting the peak of the inverted Environmental Kuznets Curve (EKC) as postulated by Grossman and Krueger (1995).

Although more than a hundred papers had already been published by the mid-2000s on the middle-income trap and the EKC[2] since the introduction of the EKC hypothesis, the relationship between income level and pollution still remains to be tackled for empirical validation, particularly in middle-income countries (MICs). Middle-income countries have significantly increased their share to 30 per cent of global GDP,[3] while they accounted for 40 per cent of global CO_2 emissions.[4] Among six developing regions in the world, the East Asian and Pacific region has expanded the most in terms of global output, doubling its regional share to over 10 per cent by absorbing the largest inflow of foreign direct investment (FDI). It has also increased CO_2 emissions at the fastest rate in the six regions over the last two decades.[5]

This chapter investigates the controversial middle-income trap and the EKC in the East Asian region by empirically analyzing the regional and income level, with World Bank and Asian Development Bank (ADB) data. We aim to represent a characteristic pattern of the East Asian EKC. Our tentative empirical analysis suggests that the EKC is rather distorted and the turning point has not yet been reached, even in high-income countries. The underlying factors for this rather unique and unorthodox curve of the Asian EKC will be examined so as to explore the eventual escape from the middle-income trap.

3.2 Middle-income countries and the middle-income trap

3.2.1 Classification of economies by the World Bank

During the first decade of the twenty-first century, the East Asian and Southeast Asian regions have undergone drastic changes in their economic performance. Some countries developed from low-income to middle-income status, but some remained underdeveloped with little increase in income, failing to shift to the middle-income status.

As of 1990, the East Asia and Pacific region includes six low-income countries (China, Cambodia, Indonesia, Lao People's Democratic Republic (PDR), Solomon Islands, Vietnam), eleven lower-middle-income countries (Fiji, Kiribati, North Korea, Malaysia, Mongolia, Papua New Guinea, Philippines, Thailand, Tonga, Vanuatu, Western Samoa), five upper-middle-income countries (American Samoa, Guam, South Korea, New Caledonia, Pacific Islands Trust Territories) and six high-income countries (Japan, Brunei, French Polynesia, Hong Kong, Singapore, Taiwan).[6] In 2000, there were seven low-income countries (Cambodia, Indonesia, North Korea, Lao PDR, Mongolia, Myanmar, Vietnam), five middle-income countries out of which three were lower-middle-income countries (China, Philippines, Thailand) and two were upper-middle-income countries (South Korea, Malaysia). In the group of Asian high-income countries, there were two Organisation for Economic Co-operation and Development (OECD) members (Japan, South Korea), as well as Hong Kong, Singapore, Taiwan, Macao and Brunei Darussalam (Izvorski, 2011).[7] Small island countries in the Pacific are excluded for the intended purpose of this study since the economies of small islands are rather unique and irrelevant for this comparative analysis; thus, the rest of the countries in the East Asia and Pacific region that are ADB members are listed in Table 3.1.

3.2.2 Shift of income group in the process of economic development

Here we take a look at the economic development of 20 countries in East Asia and the Pacific, focusing on income shift within four income groups (i.e., low-income countries [LICs], lower-middle-income countries [LMCs], upper-middle-income countries [UMCs] and high-income countries [HICs]),[8] with a view to investigating the challenges such as economic stagnation facing the middle-income countries that is often coined the middle-income trap.

Income shift
The overall tendency of the income shift shows that the number of low-income countries decreased, whereas middle-income and high-income countries

increased during the 20-year period (1990–2010) as follows (Tables 3.1, 3.3 and 3.4):

1   The six LICs in the 1990 classification of economies dwindled to only three countries in the 2010 classification.
2   The number of MICs (i.e., six lower-middle-income countries and one upper-middle-income country) increased from seven in the 1990 classification to nine in the 2010 classification.
3   The seven HIC countries in 1990 increased to eight in 2010.
4   The countries that stayed in the same classification of economies during the period are as follows: in the case of the LIC status, two countries – namely Cambodia and Myanmar; in the case of the MIC status, four countries – namely Papua New Guinea, Philippines, Malaysia and Thailand; in the case of the HIC status, seven countries – namely Japan, Australia, Brunei, New Zealand, Hong Kong, Singapore and Taiwan.

Table 3.1 Classification of economies by income group in the East Asia and Pacific region (1990, 2000 and 2010)

	1990	*2000*	*2010*
Low-Income Group Low-Income Countries (LICs)	China, Cambodia, Indonesia, Myanmar Lao PDR, Vietnam (6)	Cambodia, Indonesia, N. Korea, Lao PDR, Mongolia, Myanmar, Vietnam (7)	Cambodia, N. Korea, Myanmar (3)
Middle-Income Group	N. Korea Malaysia, Mongolia,	China, Papua New Guinea, Philippines,	Indonesia Lao PDR Mongolia,
Lower-Middle-Income Countries (LMCs)	Papua New Guinea, Philippines, Thailand (6)	Thailand, (4)	Papua New Guinea, Philippines, Vietnam (6)
Upper-Middle-Income Countries (UMCs)	South Korea, (1)	South Korea, Malaysia (2)	China, Malaysia, Thailand (3)
High-Income Group High-Income Countries (HICs)	Japan, Australia, Brunei New Zealand, Hong Kong, Singapore, Taiwan (7)	Japan, Australia, Brunei New Zealand, Hong Kong, Singapore Taiwan (7)	Japan, New Zealand, Australia, Brunei, South Korea, Hong Kong, Singapore, Taiwan (8)

Notes: The classification of economies by region and income is quoted from the World Bank, World Development Report (1992, 2002, 2012a). The income range of each group is defined in Table 3.2. Island countries are not included in the table.

Table 3.2 Income range of the respective income groups (1990, 2000 and 2010)

	1990	*2000*	*2010*
Low Income	$610 or less	$755 or less	$1,005 or less
Lower Middle Income	$610 to $2,465	$756 to $2,995	$1,006 to $3,975
Upper Middle Income	$2,466 to $7,619	$2,996 to $9,265	$3,976 to $12,275
High Income	$7,620 or more	$9,266 or more	$12,276 or more

Source: World Bank (1992, 2002, 2012a) World Development Report.

Table 3.3 Shift across income groups (1990, 2000 and 2010)

East Asia and Pacific Countries	*Classification of Economies by Income Group*		
	1990	*2000*	*2010*
Cambodia	LIC	LIC	LIC
Lao PDR	LIC	LIC	LMC
Vietnam	LIC	LIC	LMC
Indonesia	LIC	LIC	LMC
North Korea	LMC	LIC	LIC
Mongolia	LMC	LIC	LMC
Philippines	LMC	LMC	LMC
Papua New Guinea	LMC	LMC	LMC
China	LIC	LMC	UMC
Thailand	LMC	LMC	UMC
Malaysia	LMC	UMC	UMC
Korea, Rep	UMC	UMC	HIC
Brunei	HIC	HIC	HIC
Hong Kong	HIC	HIC	HIC
Taiwan	HIC	HIC	HIC
Singapore	HIC	HIC	HIC
Japan	HIC	HIC	HIC
Australia	HIC	HIC	HIC
New Zealand	HIC	HIC	HIC

Source: World Bank (1992, 2002, 2012a) World Development Report; Asian Development Bank, Key Indicators of the Asia and the Pacific, various issues.

Notes
1) Myanmar is excluded from Table 3.2.
2) Out of the nineteen ADB members in the East Asia and Pacific region, only North Korea is a nonmember country. The rest of the ADB members in the region (i.e., Myanmar) and small island countries are not covered in the table due to either the unavailability of data or irrelevance for this comparative study.

Table 3.4 Four income groups and their number of countries

Income group	1990	2000	2010
LIC	5	6	2
LMC	6	4	6
UMC	1	2	3
HIC	7	7	8
Total	19	19	19

Source: Data derived from the Table 3.3.

Note: Myanmar is excluded because of the unavailability of relevant data.

Of all income groups, the biggest shifts took place within the middle-income group, particularly in the LMC group during the 1990–2010 period, which will be dealt with further in Section 3.2.4.

As for the countries in the 1990 UMC group, no country stayed with this status during the 20-year period. Countries in this group either evolved into the HIC status, or new members were able to join this group from the lower-income status. The original seven members of the HIC group in the 1990 classification were joined in 2010 by new members such as South Korea. Of all 20 countries in the sample, China has made the most remarkable jump from the LIC to UMC status between 1990 and 2010 (Table 3.3).

3.2.3   *Growth trends*

3.2.3.1   *Growth trend for the four income groups*

According to the World Bank's data (World Bank, 1992, 2002, 2012a), middle-income groups (LMC and UMC) that had gradually stepped up their average growth rate from 2.5 per cent (1980–90) developed at the highest average annual GDP growth rate (6.4 per cent) during the 2000–10 period among all income groups. By contrast, the high-income group's average growth rates gradually slowed down between 1980 and 2010 from 3.1 per cent to 1.8 per cent, the lowest rate among all groups. Rather unexpectedly, the low-income group (LIC), which had recorded the highest growth (6.1 per cent) of all four income groups in the early stage (the 1980–90 period), lowered its growth rate almost by half in the following decade, only picking up in the 2000–10 period, but not at as high a rate as before. Thus, the average level of gross national income (GNI) per capita reached some $510 in 2010, almost one-tenth of that of the upper-middle-income group (Tables 3.5a and 3.5b and Figure 3.1).

3.2.3.2   *Growth trends in the East Asian and Pacific region*

Among six low- and middle-income regions (i.e., a group of developing countries) in the world, the East Asia and the Pacific region, belonging to the LIC group in terms of per capita income in 1990 but to the LMC group in 2000 and 2010, have achieved the highest GDP growth rate since 1980 despite their low per capita GNI

Table 3.5a GDP and CO_2 emissions by world income groups

Income group	GDP ($billion)		CO_2 emissions (million tons)	
	1990	2010	1990	2010
World	22,299	63,049	22,311	33,615
Low income	916	414	n.a.	229
Middle income	2,438	19,562	9,257	16,548
Lower middle income	930	4,315	2,001	3,827
Upper middle income	1,520	15,247	7,255	12,721
High income	16,316	43,002	11,572	14,902

Sources: World Bank (1992, 2012a) World Development Report; World Bank (2012b, 2014) World Development Indicators.

Table 3.5b Changes in GDP growth rates and per capita income by world income group

	Average annual GDP growth rate (%)			GNI per capita (US$)		
	1980–1990	1990–2000	2000–2010	1990	2000	2010
World	4.0	2.6	2.8	4,200	5,150	9,097
Low income	6.1	3.4	5.5	350	420	510
Middle income	2.5	3.6	6.4	2,220	1,970	3,764
Lower middle income	2.6	3.6	6.3	1,530	1,140	1,658
Upper middle income	2.4	3.6	6.5	3,400	4,620	5,884
High income	3.1	2.4	1.8	19,590	27,510	38,658

Source: World Bank (1992, 2012a) World Development Report and World Bank (2012b, 2014) World Development Indicators.

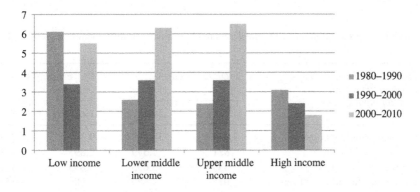

Figure.3.1 Trends in GDP growth rates since 1980 by world income group

Source: Derived from data extracted from Table 3.5b.

Note: The vertical plot shows the average annual GDP growth rate (%).

still ranking fourth in 2010 (Table 3.6). Meanwhile, two other middle-income regions, namely Europe and Central Asia and Latin America and Caribbean –both were classified as LMC in 1990 – developed into the UMC status in 2010 with the highest per capita income (over $7,000); this was achieved with a much slower growth rate of GDP compared with the East Asia or the South Asia regions throughout the three decades (1980–2010). Even with its high gross rate of GDP, South Asia's GNI per capita in 2010 was almost less than one-third of that of East Asia and the Pacific; this, in turn, was much less than half the GNI per capita of either the Latin America and Caribbean or Europe and Central Asia regions. However, all six regions were classified as middle-income status (LMC and UMC) in 2010 because South Asia and sub-Saharan Africa, which had the LIC status in 2000, successfully escaped into the LMC status. While acknowledging economic growth, the income gap between the regions still seems persistent (Tables 3.6a, 3.6b and Figure 3.2).

3.2.4   *A shift in income group status and the middle-income trap*

The term "middle-income trap" is used for a typical developing country that has become a middle-income country stagnating and failing to advance to becoming a high-income country. A middle-income trap can also take place if there is a delay in shifting economies from the low-income to middle-income status, or from the middle-income to the high-income status.

Here the study looks into the "middle-income trap" hypothesis using the sample countries in the East Asia and the Pacific region and examining the validity of the hypothesis based on the World Bank and ADB data. In the East Asia and Pacific region, only two countries (i.e., Papua New Guinea and the Philippines) remained out of the six in the same LMC classification during 1990–2010. Four LICs in 2000 (Indonesia, Lao PDR [Laos], Mongolia and Vietnam) achieved the LMC status in 2010, whereas North Korea, an LMC in 1990, was downgraded to the LIC status in 2000 (Tables 3.1 and 3.3).

Table 3.6a Gross GDP and CO_2 emissions in six low- and middle-income regions in the world

Low- and middle-income group in the world (developing regions)	GDP ($billion)		CO_2 emissions (million tons)	
	1990	2010	1990	2010
Low and Middle Income	3,334	19,997	9,399	16,778
East Asia and Pacific	821	7,579	2,895	9,571
Europe and Central Asia	489	3,055	3,893	1,417
Latin America and Caribbean	1,015	4,969	986	1,554
Middle East and N. Africa	n.a.	1,068	579	1,278
South Asia	346	2,088	782	2,253
Sub-Saharan Africa	163	1,098	464	704

Source: World Bank (1992, 2012a) World Development Report.
World Bank (2012b, 2014) World Development Indicators.

Table 3.6b Trend in GDP growth rates and GNI per capita by world developing regions

Low- and middle-income regions	Average annual GDP growth rate (%)			GNI per capita (US$)		
(Developing countries)	1980–1990	1990–2000	2000–2010	1990	2000	2010
South Asia	5.2	5.6	7.4	330	460	1,213
Sub-Saharan Africa	2.1	2.4	5.0	340	480	1,165
E. Asia and Pacific	7.8	7.2	9.4	600	1,060	3,691
Middle East & N. Africa	0.5	3.0	4.7	1,790	2,040	3,839
Latin America and Caribbean	1.6	3.3	3.8	2,180	3,680	7,802
Europe and Central Asia	2.1	−1.6	5.4	2,400	2,010	7,214
(average)	3.2	3.6	6.4	840	1,230	3,304

Source: World Bank (1992, 2002, 2012a) World Development Report.

Note: Six developing regions are arranged by 1990 GNI per capita ranking from low income to high income to the right.

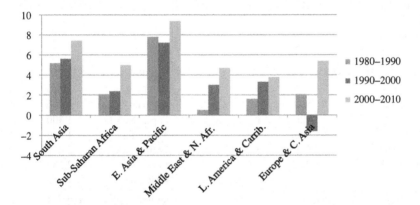

Figure 3.2 Trends in GDP growth rates in six global developing regions (1980–2010)

Source: Derived from Table 3.6b.

Note: The six regions are arranged from the low GNI per capita ranking to the right in 1990. (Vertical plot: average annual GDP growth rate [%]).

As for the number of UMC countries that increased from one (1990) to three (2010), no country stayed in this classification during the entire 1990–2010 period. South Korea, which was the only UMC in 1990, developed to be listed in the HIC category in the 2010 classification, whereas Malaysia and Thailand, which were LMCs in 1990, were both classified as UMCs in 2010. Most remarkable is what China achieved: the only country that made a big jump from the LIC status in 1990 to the UMC status in just 20 years.

Within the MIC group, the previously mentioned four countries (Papua New Guinea, Philippines, Malaysia and Thailand) have been trying to graduate to a higher-income status with little success. Although Thailand and Malaysia developed from the LMC to the UMC status, they seemed to still be unable to escape into the HIC status that South Korea succeeded in achieving in 2010. Likewise, the Philippines and Papua New Guinea have been struggling to advance to a UMC status but without a much success. Thus, they can be coined as middle-income trapped in the broader sense that they failed to escape from the "trap". However, with their relatively stable economic growth rates, two countries – Malaysia and Thailand – seem to have better chances of graduating into the high-income group; in particular, with her already high per capita income, Malaysia is in a better position (Table 3.7a).

Table 3.7a Shift of income classification by country (1990, 2010)

1990				2010		
LIC < $610				**LIC < $1,005**		
	GNI	**CO$_2$**			**GNI**	**CO$_2$**
Myanmar	n.a.	0.1	— >	Myanmar	n.a.	0.2
Vietnam	130	0.3		Cambodia	760	1.6
Cambodia	140	0.0		Aver. LIC (2)	760	0.9
Lao PDR	200	0.1				
China	370	2.2				
Indonesia	570	0.8				
Aver. LIC (6)	282	0.6				
$611 < LMC < $2,465				**$1,006 < LMC < $3,975**		
Philippines	730	0.7		Lao PDR	1,010	0.3
Papua New G.	860	0.5		Vietnam	1,100	1.7
Thailand	1,420	1.7	— >	Papua New G	1,300	0.5
Mongolia	1,430	4.6		Mongolia	1,890	4.1
Malaysia	2,320	3.1		Philippines	2,050	0.7
LMC (5)	1,352	2.1		Indonesia	2,580	1.9
				LMC (6)	1,655	1.5
$2,466 < UMC < $7,619				**$3,976 < UMC < $12,275**		
Korea, Rep	5,400	5.7	— >	Thailand	4,210	4.1
UMC(1)	5,400	5.7		China	4,260	5.8
				Malaysia	7,900	7.1
				UMC (3)	5,457	5.7
$7,620 < HIC				**$12,276 < HIC**		
Singapore	11,160	15.4		Korea, Rep	19,890	10.4
Hong Kong	11,490	4.8		New Zealand	29,050	7.8
New Zealand	12,680	7.0	— >	Hong Kong	32,900	5.3
Australia	17,000	16.8		Singapore	40,920	6.4
Japan	25,430	8.9		Japan	42,150	9.5
HIC (5)	15,552	10.58		Australia	43,740	18.6
				HIC (6)	34,775	9.7

Sources: World Bank (1992, 2002, 2012a) World Development Report and World Bank (2012b, 2014) World Development Indicators.

Note: Brunei and Taiwan, both HICs during 1990–2010, are excluded from the table.

Due to the reasons mentioned earlier, two countries – Papua New Guinea and the Philippines – seem to fit the definition of middle-income trap in the narrower sense of the term. To be precise, the two countries appeared to be trapped in the lower-middle-income status, being unable to graduate to the ranks of upper-middle-income countries, whereas Malaysia and Thailand, which are both categorized as MICs, achieved UMC status, graduating from an LMC position during the 20-year period.

3.2.5 The middle-income trap and the rate of economic growth

3.2.5.1 Lower-middle-income trap?

Although the average per capita income of six East Asian LMCs in 1990 and 2000 was certainly much lower than the world average of the LMCs (Table 3.7b), it almost caught up with the world average in 2010 due to an accelerated rate of GDP growth by these countries since 1980. However, GDP growth rates of Papua New Guinea and the Philippines were at the lowest level with less likelihood to shift to the higher-income group than the rest of the groups that joined the LMCs in 2010. The GDP average growth rates of these two countries since 1980 were consistently lower than not only those of East Asian LMCs, but also

Table 3.7b Economic growth in East Asian middle-income countries

East Asia and Pacific countries	Average annual GDP growth rate (%)			GNI per capita (US$)		
	1980–1990	*1990–2000*	*2000–2010*	*1990*	*2000*	*2010*
LMCs						
Vietnam	n.a.	7.9	7.5	130	390	1,100
Lao PDR	n.a.	6.5	7.1	200	290	1,010
Indonesia	5.5	4.2	5.3	570	570	2,580
Philippines	0.9	3.2	4.9	730	1,040	2,050
Papua New G.	1.9	4.6	3.8	860	760	1,300
Mongolia	5.6	1.0	n.a.	1,430	460	1,870
Average	3.5	4.6	5.7	653	585	1,652
World LMC	2.6	3.6	6.3	1,530	1,140	1,658
UMCs						
China	9.5	10.3	10.8	370	840	4,260
Thailand	7.6	4.2	4.5	1,420	2,010	4,210
Malaysia	5.2	7.0	5.0	2,320	3,380	7,900
Average	7.4	7.2	6.8	1,370	2,077	5,457
World LMC	2.4	3.6	6.4	3,410	4,620	5,884

Sources: World Bank (1992, 2002, 2012a) World Development Report, ADB (2012), Felipe (2012).

Note: The classification of the income group is based on the 2010 classification of the economies as listed in Table 3.1.

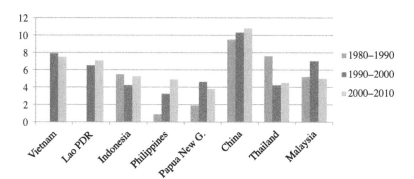

Figure 3.3 Economic growth in East Asian middle-income countries (MICs): GDP growth
rate (1980–2010)

Source: derived from Table 3.7b.

Notes
1) LMCs: Vietnam, Lao PDR, Indonesia, Philippines, Papua New Guinea. UMCs: China, Thailand,
   Malaysia.
2) LMCs and UMCs are arranged in 1990 GNI per capita ranking order from low to high income to
   the right.

of the world LMCs. Thus, Papua New Guinea and the Philippines are likely to
be left behind other member countries if this lower rate growth continues, falling into what is called the "middle-income trap".[9] If it is assumed that a certain
level of growth rate is required to avoid the middle-income trap, avoiding the
trap will be a question of how to grow fast enough to escape into the upper-
middle-income status. One ADB study suggests that a growth rate of at least
4.7 per cent average per annum is necessary to avoid a lower-middle-income
trap for LMCs (Felipe, 2012). Since both Papua New Guinea and the Philippines could not meet this requirement with their overall lower growth rates, they
are eligible for the lower-middle-income trap; only once in the 2000–10 period
did the Philippines' average annual GDP grow slightly higher than the requirement (at 4.9 per cent).

3.2.5.2   An upper middle-income trap?

Three countries (i.e., China, Malaysia, Thailand) of the UMC group in the 2010
classification of economies seem to be catching up with the global UMC per capita
income average, with higher GDP growth rates than the world UMC average.
Above all, China's rapid jump from LIC status to UMC was most notable, bringing
her per capita GNI above Thailand's. In contrast, Malaysia and Thailand, which
had suffered substantially from reduced GDP growth, failing thereby to graduate
to high-income status, may qualify for the upper-middle-income trap (Table 3.7)
in light of the lower average GDP growth rate of the Asian upper-middle-income
countries than that of their world counterparts when high-growth China is excluded

from the sample. However, the required average annual rate of GDP growth suggested by the·ADB to avoid falling into the upper-middle-income trap is 3.5 per cent per annum (Felipe, 2012). When applying this criterion, no country in the UMC group can be considered falling into the upper-middle-income trap, since all three countries in the UMC group registered higher growth rates than 3.5 per cent during the 1980–2010 period.

Only five Asian countries that have escaped the middle-income trap so far are Japan and the our "Asian tigers" (South Korea, Taiwan, Hong Kong and Singapore) out of eight high-income East Asian countries in the 2010 classification of economies (Table 3.1) (Sally, 2013). The other three countries (Macao, Australia, New Zealand) are usually excluded from the discussion of the middle-income trap because they are not regarded as having graduated from their middle-income status.

3.3 Trends in global GDP growth and CO_2 increase

According to the Environmental Kuznets Curve (EKC), environmental degradation gets worse as income per capita increases, but after a certain point (turning point), the environment will begin to improve as income further increases. This trend is portrayed as an inverted U-curve based on Grossman and Krueger's empirical study (1995).

With a view to examining the changing relationship between income growth and environmental degradation, the focus here is on rapidly developing East Asian countries that are faced increasingly with environmental predicaments.

3.3.1 *Global trends in greenhouse gas emissions and economic growth*

The relationship between economic growth and CO_2 emissions is explored in this subsection with a view to investigating the validity of the Kuznets Curve for the East Asia and Pacific region. First, the global picture will be surveyed on the basis of the world income groups (or economies) into four categories, that is, low income, lower middle income, upper middle income and high income, to find out the possible link between CO_2 emissions and economic growth at different income levels. The level of CO_2 emissions is used as a proxy for the overall level of greenhouse gas pollution because CO_2 emissions is the major component of the ecological footprint (WWF, 2006).

According to Table 3.8, the global level of CO_2 emission per capita increased at an average annual rate of 2.1 per cent over 28 years (1990–2008) as a result of comparable GDP growth rates of 2.9 per cent over the same period (World Bank, 2003, 2012b). For all four global income groups, CO_2 emissions per capita increased at a lower rate than GDP growth throughout the 1990–2008 period (Table 3.8).

CO_2 emissions (per capita metric tons) tend to increase as income rises by shifting from low-income to middle-income to high-income economies. However, the

Table 3.8 Growth of GDP and per capita CO_2 emissions for four global income groups (1990–2008, 2008, 2010)

World Income Group	CO_2 emis. growth (%)	GDP growth (%)	CO_2 emis. per capita tons	GNI per capita ($)
	1990–2008	1990–2008	2008	2010
World	2.1	2.9	4.8	9,097
Low income	3.0	4.6	0.3	510
Lower middle income	3.1	6.0	1.5	1,658
Upper middle income	3.0	3.9	5.3	5,884
High income	0.8	2.4	11.9	38,658

Source: World Bank (1992, 2002, 2012a) World Development Report; World Bank (2012b, 2014) World Development Indicators.

Notes
1) Growth rates of CO_2 and GDP are an average annual base.
2) Average annual growth rates of GDP are combined averages of two periods (1990–2001 and 2000–08).
3) The lower-middle-income group and upper-middle-income group make up the middle-income group.

growth rate of CO_2 emissions begins to reduce from the stage of lower middle income along with the declining GDP growth rate.

The high-income group produces by far the largest volume of CO_2 emissions per capita (11.9 metric tons), more than twice the upper-middle-income group, although the high-income group's annual growth rate of CO_2 (0.8 per cent) is less than one-third that of the latter. The smallest volume of CO_2 emissions per capita (0.3 tons) of all four groups was produced by the low-income group in 2008 even after two decades of accelerated GDP average annual growth rates from 3.4 per cent (1990–2001) to 5.5 per cent (2000–10) (Table 3.5b).

Among the developing countries (low- and middle-income groups), the lower-middle-income group achieved the highest annual GDP growth rate (6.0 per cent) during 1990–2008, whereas the largest emitter of CO_2 was the upper middle class in 2008. The middle-income group's larger volume of CO_2 emissions was apparently generated by its enhanced growth rate of GDP (6.4 per cent) during the 2000–10 period. Of all three groups, the high-income group had the least change of CO_2 emissions between the 1990 and 2008 period, which was, no doubt, realized by technological progress in advanced countries (Table 3.8 and Figure 3.4).

3.3.2   *Environmental Kuznets Curves at the global level*

The EKC hypothesis for the world income group is examined by looking into the relationship between CO_2 emissions and income group (Tables 3.5 and 3.4).

From Figure 3.4, derived from Table 3.8, we find that the EKC hypothesis could not be distinctively ascertained for the global relationship between income level and CO_2 emissions for both 1990 and 2008, as our findings indicated that the HICs produced the largest volume of CO_2 emissions per capita, contrary to

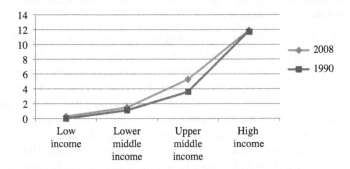

Figure 3.4 Changes in per capita CO_2 emissions by world income group (1990, 2008) (metric tons)

Source: World Bank (2012b), 2012 World Development Indicators; World Bank (2012a), World Development Report 2012.

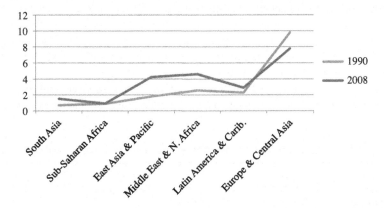

Figure.3.5 CO_2 emissions per capita: six global developing regions (1990–2008) (tons)

Source: Data from Table 3.10.

Note: Six regions listed on the horizontal plot by 1990 GNI per capita ranking order from low to high income to the right.

the standardized EKC assumption that pollution decreases as income rises after the turning point. Then if this decreasing trend of CO_2 emissions holds, CO_2 emissions would gradually be reduced as income increases, with the likelihood of enhancement of environmental protection by improved technology. In this sense, our application of the EKC hypothesis to the previously mentioned four global income groups can be partially substantiated, although with no turning point in sight. This derived global EKC shows that the world may not have yet reached the turning point. This is also borne out by another figure that portrays rising EKC trends of CO_2 emissions for six of the world's developing regions as shown in Figure 3.5.

3.3.3   Regional trend in GDP growth and CO_2 emissions: East Asia and the Pacific region

The East Asia and Pacific region, classified first as a low-income region during the 1980–90 period, then as a lower-middle-income region since 1990, had been growing at the highest growth rate of GDP throughout that period, with increases in CO_2 emissions at the highest growth rate (5.6 per cent over the years 1990 to 2008) of all six global regions (Table 3.9 and Figure 3.5), although its GNI per capita still ranked fourth in 2010 of the six regions.

With its fourth ranking per capita income, and as the third biggest CO_2 polluter of all six regions in the world toward the late 2000s, the East Asia and Pacific region is typically characterized as having a lower-middle-income status with its fastest growth rates of GDP and CO_2 emissions (Tables 3.6b. and 3.9). As Table 3.10 suggests, the 1990 EKC derived for six of the world's developing regions seems to indicate an upward trend as income rises from low-income regions (such as South Asia) to lower-middle-income regions (such as East Asia and the Middle East), whereas the 2008 EKC shows a slight downward trend as lower-middle-income regions shift to the upper-middle-income region (Latin America and Caribbean). However, the upper-middle-income Europe and Central Asia region that had the highest GNI per capita of all six regions in 1990 continued to produce the largest CO_2 emissions per capita despite its lowest annual average growth rates of CO_2 emissions and GDP during the 1980–2010 period (Table 3.9).

Thus, it follows that the growth rates of CO_2 as well as GDP tend to become higher for lower-income groups with their generally lower per capita CO_2, whereas

Table 3.9 CO_2 emissions and GDP growth rates for global low- and middle-income regions

Low- and Middle-Income Developing Regions	CO_2 emissions			Average Annual GDP Growth Rate(%)		
	aver. ann. growth(%)	% change	per capita metric tons			
	1990–2008	1990–2008	2008	1980–1990	1990–2000	2000–2010
East Asia and Pacific	5.6	185.3	4.2	7.8	7.2	9.4
Europe and Central Asia	−0.8	−19.6	7.8	2.1	−1.6	5.4
L. America and Caribbean	2.5	60.6	2.9	1.6	3.3	3.8
Middle East and N. Africa	4.2	112.5	4.6	0.5	3.0	4.7
South Asia	4.9	151.9	1.5	5.2	5.6	7.4
Sub-Saharan Africa	2.2	47.5	0.9	2.1	2.4	5.0

Source: World Bank (1992, 2002, 2012a) World Development Reports.

Note: CO_2 emission per capita growth is measured by metric tons.

Table 3.10 Per capita CO$_2$ emission and GNI for six global regions (1990–2010)

World's Six Developing Regions	CO$_2$ emis. per capita		GNI per capita	
	(metric tons)		($)	
	1990	2008	1990	2010
South Asia	0.7	1.5	330	1,213
Sub-Saharan Africa	0.9	0.9	340	1,165
East Asia and Pacific	1.8	4.2	600	3,691
Middle East and N. Africa	2.6	4.6	1,790	3,839
Latin America and Carib.	2.3	2.9	2,180	7,802
Europe and Central Asia	9.8	7.8	2,400	7,214

Source: World Bank. 2014 World Development Indicators, p.170–173; World Bank. World Development Report 2012, p.392–393.

growth rates of CO$_2$ emissions and GDP tend to be lowered accompanied by increased emissions of CO$_2$ per capita for higher-income groups.

3.3.4 What do East Asian EKCs look like?

The pattern of EKCs for a number of ADB countries in the East Asia and Pacific region is investigated here. A sample of 16 to 18 East Asian ADB member countries (Australia and New Zealand included) with relevant data was taken for this survey. This sample covers most ADB member countries in the East Asia and the Pacific, excluding South Pacific island countries. (Myanmar and North Korea are countries with full ADB membership, but they are not taken into account in this East Asia area study due to the lack of relevant data).

Based on the data in Table 3.11, two inverted U-curved EKCs (1990 and 2010) can be drawn as shown in Figures 3.6 a and 3.6b. The shape of both EKCs appears rather distorted with seemingly no turning point. The 1990 EKC (a) has two peaks, whereas the 2010 EKC (b) resembles a standardized EKC until per capita income reaches a certain level ($35,000), when the trend line starts rising even at a higher income level.

Both trend lines of the 1990 and the 2010 EKC appear, by and large, on the rising curve as income increases. In our East Asian EKCs, no single turning point can be detected as far as the data are concerned. This may suggest that East Asian countries are, for the most part, on development paths, paying generally insufficient attention to environmental protection.

The 1990 EKC with two different peaks can be accounted for by a wide range of development levels among countries with a disproportionate ratio between GNI per capita income and CO$_2$ emissions per capita in East Asian countries. Whereas the shape of the 2010 EKC resembles a standard EKC until income reaches a certain point, after this point it shows a steep upward curve. Apparently, both trend lines of the curves are rising, indicating a further increase in CO$_2$ as income

Table 3.11 CO$_2$ emissions and GNI per capita income in East Asian countries

1990			2010		
Countries	GNI ($)	CO$_2$	Countries	GNI ($)	CO$_2$
Vietnam	130	0.3	Cambodia	760	0.3
Cambodia	140	0.0	Lao PDR	1,010	0.3
Lao PDR	200	0.1	Vietnam	1,100	1.7
China	370	2.2	Papua New	1,300	0.5
Indonesia	570	0.8	Mongolia	1,890	4.1
Philippines	730	0.7	Philippines	2,050	0.7
Papua New Guin	860	0.5	Indonesia	2,580	1.9
Thailand	1,420	1.7	Thailand	4,210	4.1
Mongolia	1,430	4.6	China	4,260	5.8
Malaysia	2,320	3.1	Malaysia	7,900	7.1
South Korea	5,400	5.7	South Kore	19,890	10.4
Singapore	11,160	15.4	New Zealan	29,050	7.8
Hong Kong	11,490	4.8	Hong Kong	32,900	5.3
New Zealand	12,680	7.0	Singapore	40,920	6.4
Australia	17,000	16.8	Japan	42,150	9.5
Japan	25,430	8.9	Australia	43,740	18.6
average	5,708	4.5	average	14,732	5.4

Source: Data from World Bank, World Development Report (1992: 218–19, and 2012 a: 392–93); World Bank, World Development Indicators (2012 b: 170–172); Asian Development Bank(ADB) (2013, 2014).

Notes
1) GNI: GNI per capita ($). CO$_2$: CO$_2$ emissions per capita (metric tons).
   Average annual growth rate of GNI per capita = 5.1%, that of CO$_2$ emissions = 1.3 % for the 1990–2010 period.
2) 1990 GNP per capita from World Bank (1992) are substituted for all 1990 GNI data (except Vietnam and Cambodia). 1990 GNI for Vietnam and Cambodia are from ADB (2014:173).
3) North Korea, Taiwan, Macao, Myanmar and Brunei, included in Table 2.1, are excluded from this table due to the unavailability of data in the UN and World Bank publications.
4) Cambodia's CO$_2$ emissions per capita data of 2010 is from ADB (2013:149).

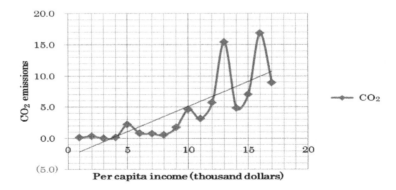

Figure 3.6a Environmental Kuznets Curves (EKCs) for East Asian countries (1990)

Source: The figure is based on Table 3.11.

Note: The vertical plot shows CO$_2$ emissions per capita (metric tons). Average GNI per capita for the sample of 16 countries = $5,708. Average CO$_2$ emissions per capita = 4.5 tons.

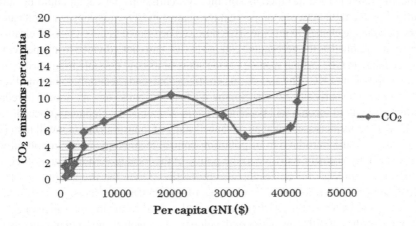

Figure 3.6b Environmental Kuznets Curves (EKCs) for East Asian countries (2010)

Source: Data derived from Table 3.11.

Note
1) The vertical plot shows CO_2 emission per capita (metric tons). 2) Average GNI per capita = $14,732. Average CO_2 emissions per capita = 5.4 tons.

increases, with intermittent setbacks and decreases before it starts picking up, seemingly at the point of shift in income level.

Reviewing for comparison the ADB's Asian EKC of 2010 derived from the enlarged sample of 42 ADB member countries,[10] we find that the trend line on the scatter plot of per capita GDP against per capita CO_2 emissions in Asia clearly resembled a standard EKC (ADB, 2012).[11] The peak of the inverted U-curve corresponds to a level of GDP per capita of $40,971 (at 2005 price levels). As far as ADB's EKC is concerned, this peak point of GDP per capita in Asian countries seems to be far from the "CO_2 turning point", since the average per capita income of the 42 ADB members was $6,107 in 2010 (Felipe, 2012).

Similarly, our East Asian EKCs depicted in our study are expected to hit the peak at some higher per capita income level if per capita income continues to increase, in light of our distorted EKCs that seem to have more than one peak, with the average GNI per capita of the sample much smaller than the one at the peak point. Thus, no single definite turning point seems to be identifiable from the trend as far as these two EKCs are concerned (Figures 3.6a and 3.6b). A rather distorted pattern of two EKCs quite distinct from the ADB's may partly be due to the limited size of the sample, including a variety of countries at different stages of development that have varied volumes of CO_2 emissions per capita.

3.3.5   Why a distorted EKC?

Between 1990 and 2010, GNI per capita and CO_2 emissions per capita increased at varying rates for respective income groups for East Asian countries. The impact of income (GNI per capita) increase on the CO_2 emissions per capita could be surmised by the ratio between the percentage change in CO_2 emissions per capita and the percentage change in income. This ratio can be termed as the CO_2–GNI elasticity that is defined as the percentage change in CO_2 emissions divided by the percentage change in GNI, which would provide some hints as to possible irregularities in the shape of the EKC. The size of this elasticity that tends generally to be small for a country at an early stage of development when CO_2 emissions are limited in relation to growth of income will become larger as economic development proceeds as CO_2 emissions increase, but at an advanced stage of industrialization it will tend to decline with the introduction of pollution-control technology. More importantly, this elasticity is easily sensitive to the policy of the local government and of technological standards for environmental protection. Often the irregularities of the EKC could be the result of the irrelevance of government measures.

Thus, the values of this elasticity are capable of indicating the relevance of government policy at different stages of development, as well as the level of efficiency in saving CO_2 emissions in the course of development as argued by Lipford and Yandle (2010: 434).[12] In other words, it implies that the smaller the amount of CO_2 emissions produced, the higher the efficiency realized by economic development, leading to a lower value of the elasticity.

Because the impact of income increase (GNI per capita) on growth of CO_2 emissions is distinctively different among the four income groups between 1990 and 2010, these could be investigated by looking at the size of the CO_2–income elasticity.

Based on Table 3.11, the average income (GNI per capita) and CO_2 emissions per capita for the four income groups of the East Asia and Pacific region are summarized in Table 3.12.

Table 3.12 Average per capita (GNI) and CO_2 emissions by income group: East Asia and Pacific region

Income group (17 countries)	1990		Income group (16 countries)	2010	
	GNI ($)	CO₂		GNI ($)	CO₂
LIC (6)	282	0.7	LIC (1)	760	0.3
LMC (5)	1,352	2.1	LMC (6)	1,655	1.5
UMC (1)	5,400	5.7	UMC (3)	5,457	5.7
HIC (5)	15,552	10.6	HIC (6)	34,775	9.7

Source: Data from Table 3.11.

Notes
1) The figures in parentheses show the number of countries. 3) The classification of income groups is based on World Bank (1992, 2012a) World Development Report.
4) CO_2 = CO_2 per capita emissions (metric tons). GNI ($) = GNI per capita.
5) Cambodia, the only LIC in 2010, produced 0.3 tons of CO_2 emissions (ADB's estimate), although the World Bank's estimate puts the figure at 1.6 tons.
6) Brunei is excluded from the table.

Major changes of CO_2 emissions per capita and GNI income per capita for each group during the 1990–2010 period are as follows:

1   LIC: CO_2 emissions became less than half, whereas average income more than doubled.
2   LMC: CO_2 emissions substantially decreased despite a minor increase in income.
3   UMC: Almost no increase in average GNI and CO_2 emissions per capita.
4   HIC: As income more than doubled, CO_2 emissions reduced by approximately 10 per cent although still producing by far the largest volume of CO_2 emissions per capita among the four groups.

Looking over the trend in CO_2 emissions and GNI by income group from Table 3.12, the average CO_2 emissions per capita increased as income groups shifted from low to high income, although it showed clearly that CO_2 emissions per capita of the LIC and LMC decreased significantly between 1990 and 2010. Another unexpected trend is that UMCs' CO_2 emissions per capita did not show any increase during the period. These trends can be regarded as rather unusual, which can partly be accounted for by the changing number of countries in the shifting of income groups during 1990 and 2010.

The relationship between CO_2 emissions and GNI income per capita by using the CO_2–GNI elasticity for each country of each income group is further investigated. The calculated results are shown in Table 3.13a and 3.13b and in Figure 3.7.

As shown by Figures 3.6a and 3.6b, the trend lines of the East Asian EKC for both 1990 and 2010 show more than one peak, even at the high-income level, that still seems to be far from the turning point. The rugged lines of the East Asian EKC seem to start at the higher income level where the income range is wide among the HIC countries, leading to distortions of the EKC. Thus, the inclusion of varieties of high-income countries seems to be contributing to render the shape of the EKC less smooth.

The overall trend of the CO_2–GNI elasticity shown in Tables 3.13a and 3.13b and in Figure 3.7 seems to coincide with the global picture except for the lower-income countries. Tables 3.13a and 3.13b and Figure 3.7 indicate relatively higher values of the CO_2–GNI elasticity figure for middle-income countries such as Thailand and Malaysia, indicating a higher growth rate of CO_2 emissions in the course of development.

The higher elasticities of Taiwan and Korea, both classified as an HIC , remind us that Korea was an upper-middle-income country until 2000 and that Taiwan barely qualified in 1990 for the HIC status, with its income level a little above the income range of the HIC.[13] Thus, the former two lower-middle-income countries are having troubles with stagnant economic growth generating a lower level of CO_2 emissions, whereas the latter two relatively newly developed HICs appear to be trying to improve efficiency of CO_2 emissions. China, which had emerged as the third UMC at the highest rate of economic growth and which is now the largest emitter of pollutants in the world, is rather unique with its low value of

Table 3.13a CO$_2$–GNI income elasticity for East Asia and Pacific countries (1990–2010)

	Elasticity
LIC (Low-income country)	
Cambodia	1.129*
LMC (Lower-middle-income country)	
Lao PDR	0.481
Vietnam	0.532
Indonesia	0.412
Philippines	0.102
Papua New Guinea	0.000
Mongolia	−0.264
Average	0.211
UMC (Upper-middle-income country)	
China	0.153
Thailand	0.805
Malaysia	0.595
Average	0.518
HIC (High-income country)	
Korea, Rep	0.467
Singapore	−0.303
Brunei	−0.033
Hong Kong	0.038
New Zealand	0.024
Australia	0.046
Japan	0.041
Average	0.040

* Cambodia's CO$_2$–GNI elasticity becomes 7.001 when the World Bank's CO$_2$ emission data (1.6) is used.

Source: Table 3.11 and ADB (2014) Key Indicators for Asia and the Pacific.
Felipe (2012).

Notes
1) CO$_2$–GNI elasticity is defined in the note of Table 3.8.
2) Brunei data are from ADB (2014: 113; Felipe, 2012).

Table 3.13b CO$_2$–GNI elasticity for four East Asian income groups (1990–2010)

East Asia and Pacific income group	*CO$_2$–GNI elasticity*
LIC (1)	1.129*
LMC (6)	0.211
UMC (3)	0.518
HIC (7)	0.040

Source: Data derived from Table 3.11.

Notes
1) CO$_2$–income elasticity =(% change of CO$_2$ emission per capita) / (% change of GNI per capita).
2) The number of countries in each income group changed during 1990–2010 as shown in Table 3.1.

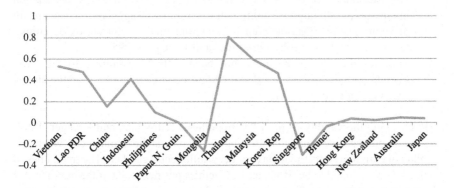

Figure 3.7 CO_2 income elasticity for East Asia and Pacific countries (1990–2010)

Source: Table 3.6a.

Note

1) The vertical plot is the CO_2–GNI elasticity. 2) Countries are listed on the horizontal plot by 1990 GNI ranking order from low to high income to the right. 3) Taiwan's data (GNI for 1990 and 2010, CO_2 for 2010) are from ADB (2014: 113, 173). 4) Taiwan's elasticity, an exceptionally high value for a high-income country, is excluded from the figure for comparative purpose because it obscures the overall trend of the EKC.

CO_2–GNI elasticity (0.153). This is largely due to the fact that China's GNI per capita increased more than ten times with a disproportionately smaller increase in CO_2 emissions per capita from 2.2 to 5.8 tons during the period (Table 3.11).[14]

Of all the countries in the sample, Singapore was the most successful country in reducing CO_2 emissions by the largest amount, as shown by the negative elasticity coefficient (−0.303).[15] Within the HIC group, Brunei was the second most efficient and successful country to combat the CO_2 problem as indicated by its CO_2–GNI elasticity (−0.033).[16]

By and large, high-income countries seem to be coping with the reduction of CO_2 emissions per capita with some success, as indicated by their lower elasticity (0.040); however, a considerable amount of environmental pollutants are still generated in high-income developed countries.

Other possible underlying causes of the distorted EKCs may be quoted as follows:

1   A small sample of countries with multitudinous structural characteristics, such as a wide range of income inequality and levels of development among the sample countries.
2   Two-thirds of the countries were low- and lower-middle-income countries in 1990, whereas a little over half of the countries were upper-middle-income and high-income countries in 2010.
3   Basically, the lower-middle-income East Asian region is rather unique in achieving the fastest growth rates of GDP and CO_2 emissions; this was achieved with a per capita income lower than the average for the world's low- and lower-middle-income regions.

4 We used only CO_2 emissions as the sources of environmental degradation in our survey, although we admit that environmental aggravation is the result of a combination of various sources, including methane, nitrous oxide, animal feces, etc., as reported by Grossman and Krueger (1995).[17]

5 Turning-point arguments have not been settled.[18] Contrary to the EKC hypothesis, our results show that the high-income group produced the largest CO_2 emissions per capita.

By checking the validity of the EKC hypothesis (Grossman and Krueger, 1995) based on our data, we found that the range of income at the turning point where the pollutant emission starts to fall has not been sufficiently clarified. The trend lines of our EKC were found to be rising, and CO_2 emissions per capita of the high-income group were not small; on the contrary, the volume of emissions was even larger than that of the middle-income group. It is thus possible to suppose that pollutant emissions may increase as income increases and that turning points are still far away.

The EKC can take various forms depending on such factors as income levels, resource endowment, technology, level of industrial development, policy frameworks, etc.[19] In particular, a wide range of gaps in income and technology among countries can be largely attributable to industrial strategy and economic policy employed that seem to be responsible for the unique shape of the East Asian EKC. A typical example is presented by three countries (North Korea, Myanmar, Cambodia) belonging to the low-income group according to the World Bank 2010 classification of economies; they were all under closed and authoritative political systems with an inward-oriented industrial strategy, whereas five high-income countries (Japan, the four Asian tigers) were able to escape the middle-income trap by shifting to an open, liberalized and outward-oriented industrialization strategy (Ota, 1999, 2000, 2002, 2003a, 2003b, 2003c, 2003d, 2003e, 2003f, 2007).[20] This shift in industrial and economic policy may provide an escape from the middle-income status to higher stages of industrial development by reducing environmental degradation with the introduced technological innovations.

3.4 Conclusion

Despite the highest growth achieved by the East Asian region, some countries could not shift to the higher-income group and stayed in the same income group for the last two decades. Out of nine middle-income countries in East Asia, four countries (i.e., Papua New Guinea and the Philippines in the lower-middle-income group and Malaysia and Thailand in the upper-middle-income group) could not graduate into the higher income group, staying in the middle-income group since 1990. However, only Papua New Guinea and the Philippines seem to be qualified for the "middle-income trap"; the two countries kept their lower-middle-income status for the entire period (1990–2010), failing to graduate to the upper-middle-income group because of their lower growth rates; in addition they enjoyed relatively low levels of CO_2 emissions. Whereas upper-middle-income Malaysia and Thailand have higher CO_2–GNI elasticities and can be broadly termed as "middle-income trapped", being unable to rise to a high income status, they had shifted earlier from the lower-middle-income to the upper-middle-income status.

China, the world largest emitter of CO_2 with a low CO_2–GNI elasticity, is currently classified as having a middle-income status, and is the only country in Asia that has jumped from the low-income to the upper-middle-income status in two decades. However, China may not be qualified for the middle-income trap in its rigorous sense despite her recent economic slowdown after two decades of 10 per cent annual growth rate. China's middle-income trap myth, if it exists, may largely be accounted for by noneconomic factors, such as air pollution and social problems, rather than by economic ones, which could be constraining sustainable development.

The results of our empirical study show that EKCs can be traceable to some extent, although their trend lines are still on the rise, seemingly away from the turning point. Our two EKC curves seem to suggest that the peak of the inverted curve may be recursive as income increases. Clearly, the East Asian EKC is still on the rising side of the curve rather than on the declining side, although further income increases may change the shape of the EKC.

The importance of an outward-oriented industrialization policy needs to be stressed in view of the five East Asian countries (Japan and the four Asian tigers) that had escaped the middle-income trap. China's case offers some lessons on how an industrial shift from self-contained economic policies to openness and reforms can be conducive to economic growth. A timely shift of the industrial strategy to more liberalized economic management may lower the EKC peaks or shorten the range of EKCs for developing countries to escape the middle-income trap with the help of introduced innovation that can cope with environmental degradation.

Notes

1 "Beijing 'airpocalypse' drives expatriates exodus". Extreme air pollution is driving expatriates out of Beijing, making it harder for companies to recruit international workers. Most environmental experts assume the problem will only worsen as the government continues to encourage the expansion of industry, coal-fired power generations and car sales across the country (Anderlini, 2013).
2 There had been more than 100 peer-reviewed EKC publications since Grossman and Krueger's path-breaking work (1995) until the publication of Yandle, Madhusudan Bhattarai and Maya Vijayaraghavan's paper (2004: 2). Nearly 400,000 pages related to 'the middle-income trap' were identified by Google (Eichengreen, Park and Shin, 2013).
3 MICs were responsible for 31 per cent of world GDP ($63 trillion in 2010), 29 per cent of world trade (2009) and 72 per cent of the world population (2010) (World Bank, 2012a: 393, 400).
4 Middle-income countries (MICs) accounted for 40 per cent of global CO_2 emissions as early as 2003 according to the UN (2007).
5 In fact, China and India were two of the top three largest polluters in the world. China is the no. 1 recipient of foreign direct investment among developing countries, not just in Asia (World Bank, 2012b).
6 The income groups are low income, US$610 or less; lower middle income, $611 to $2,465; upper middle income, $2,466 – $7,619; and high income, $7,620 or more (World Bank, 1992). Of the world's 52 middle-income countries, 38 are lower middle income and 14 are upper middle income, according to Felipe (2012) of the ADB.

7   The income-level criteria are based on the World Development Reports (World Bank, 2002; 2012a). Of the countries that were middle income in 1960, almost three-fourths remained middle income or regressed to low income by 2009. The only ones that made it to the high-income status are countries in Western Europe (Greece, Portugal, Spain, Ireland), Japan, the newly industrialized states (Israel, Mauritius, four Asian Tigers [i.e., Hong Kong, South Korea, Singapore, Taiwan]) and two island economies in Latin America (Equatorial Guinea, Puerto Rico).

8   According to Felipe (2012), there are 35 countries in the middle-income trap in the world as of 2010 of which 13 are Latin American, 11 are in the Middle East and North Africa, 6 are in sub-Saharan Africa, 3 in Asia and 2 in Europe. According to the IMF definition of middle-income status, there are six countries that stand out in East Asia: Malaysia, Thailand, Indonesia, the Philippines, Vietnam and China (Sally, 2013).

9   According to Felipe's study (Felipe, 2012), Asian LMCs that fell in the lower-middle-income trap are the Philippines and Sri Lanka, whereas Malaysia is only UMC in the upper-middle-income trap. The author used only one per capita income in 1990 PPP to define four income groups of 2010.

10 The total number of ADB member countries is 67 as of 2010 of which 48 countries are regional members; the remaining 19 countries are nonregional members. The total number of countries in the East Asia and Pacific region is 18, excluding island countries in the Pacific.

11 The data are based on ADB's survey of 374 observations drawn from 42 ADB members.

12 The term "CO_2 emission efficiency" is used by Lipford and Yandle (2010) with a similar meaning to author's CO_2–GDP elasticity in this chapter.

13 Taiwan and Korea ranked third and fourth, respectively, in the CO_2 emissions per capita country rankings among 44 ADB member countries in 2010 (ADB, 2014, p. 113). Taiwan is not a signatory to the Conference of the Parties (COP).

14 China's carbon dioxide emissions rose to 8,287 tons, which far exceeded the second ranked country (i.e., the United States) with 5,433 tons in 2010 (ADB, 2014).

15 Singapore is the only country that decreased CO_2 emissions by nearly 85 per cent; this is largely due to policy intervention in phasing down higher-polluting fuels (ADB, 2014).

16 In 2010, Brunei had the highest emissions rate at 23 tons per capita among all 44 ADB regional member countries even after the reduction of CO_2 emissions per capita by approximately 5 per cent from the 1990 level. Brunei's CO_2 emissions per capita were 24.2 tons in 1990 (ADB, 2014; World Bank, 2015).

17 Different types of pollutants were noted by Grossman and Krueger, who were the first to propound the EKC hypothesis (Grossman and Krueger, 1995). EKC turning points for various types of major pollutants are quoted by Yandle, Madhusudan Bhattarai and Maya Vijayaraghavan as follows: carbon dioxide: $37,000 to 57,000; carbon monoxide: $16,300 to 16,600; sulfur dioxide: $9,600 to 11,600 (2003 US PPP) (2004).

18 A certain range of per capita income was formerly said to be US$4000 to 8000 (1985 price PPP) (e.g., Grossman and Krueger,1995; Mabey and McNally, 1999), and the other source is per capita GDP of $37,000 to $57,000 in 2003 US dollars (Yandle, Madhusudan Bhattarai and Maya Vijayaraghavan, 2004). Grossman and Krueger first argued that economic growth tends to alleviate pollution problems once a country's per capita income reaches about $4,000 to $5,000. Mexico, with a per capita GDP of $5000, was at the critical juncture where further growth should generate increased political pressure for environmental protection (Grossman and Krueger, 1991). They found that the concentration of sulfur dioxide (SO_2) rises with per capita GDP at low levels of national income, falls with per capita GDP in the broad range between $5,000 and $14,000 (1985 US dollars) and then levels off or perhaps begins to rise again. The turning point comes at $4,119 (Grossman and Krueger, 1991). They used SO_2 as pollutants because CO_2 data were not available at that time.

19 Grossman and Krueger (1995) state that the inverted U-shape is driven by a combination of forces, such as (1) the level of output or scale of economic activity (scale effect); (2) the composition of output (structural effect); and (3) the state of technology (technical effect).

20 The successful shift from an import-substitution industrialization (ISI) strategy to an export- oriented industrialization (EOI) strategy has been one of the major important factors for East Asian high-income countries; by contrast, many of the Latin American countries stuck too long to protective import-substitution strategies, a factor reputed as being dominant in explaining their slower rate of development (Ota,1999, 2000, 2002, 2003a, 2003b, 2003c, 2003d).

References

Anderlini J. (2013) 'Airpocalypse' Drives Expats out of Beijing, *The Financial Times*, 1 April 2013. Available from: www.ft.com/intl/cms/s/0/46d11e30–99e9–11e2–83ca-00144feabdc0.html#axzz3zr5DL1CB [6 June 2013].

Asian Development Bank (ADB) (2012) *Key Indicators for Asia and the Pacific 2012, 43th Edition, Special Chapter, Green Urbanization in Asia*, Asian Development Bank, Manila.

Asian Development Bank (ADB) (2013) *Key Indicators for Asia and the Pacific 2013, 44th Edition, Special Chapter, Asia's Economic Transformation: Where to, How, and How Fast?*, Asian Development Bank, Manila.

Asian Development Bank (ADB) (2014) *Key Indicators for Asia and the Pacific 2014, 45th Edition, Special Chapter, Poverty in Asia: A Deeper Look*, Asian Development Bank, Manila.

Eichengreen B., Park D. and Shin K. (2013) Growth Slowdowns Redux: Avoiding the Middle-income Trap, *Vox*, 11 January 2013. Available from: www.voxeu.org/article/growth-slowdowns-redux-avoiding-middle-income-trap [23 October 2013].

Felipe J. (2012) *Tracking the Middle-Income Trap: What Is It, Who Is It, and Why? Part 1*, Asian Development Bank Economics Working Paper Series No.306, Asian Development Bank, Manila.

Grossman G.M. and Krueger A.B. (1991) *Environment Impacts of a North American Free Trade Agreement*, Working Paper No.3914, National Bureau of Economic Research, Cambridge, MA, pp. 1–39.

Grossman G.M. and Krueger A.B. (1995) Economic Growth and the Environment, *Quarterly Journal of Economics*, 110(2), pp. 353–377.

Izvorski I. (2011) *The Middle-income Trap, Again? The World Bank, East Asia and Pacific on the Rise: Blog*, 2 September 2011. Available from: http://blogs.worldbank.org/eastasiapacific/the-middle-income-trap-again [17 September 2013].

Lipford J.W. and Yandle B. (2010) Environmental Kuznets Curves, Carbon Emissions and Public Choice, *Environment and Development Economics*, 15(4), pp. 417–438.

Mabey N. and McNally R. (1999) *WWF-UK: Foreign Direct Investment and the Environment*, WWF-UK Report, November 1999. Available from: www.oecd.org/investment/mne/2089912.pdf [21 November 2013].

Ota T. (1999) Ajia no Keizaihatten-Kenishugitaisei-Minshuka (Economic Development – Authoritarian Regime – Democratization in Asia), 22, *Keiei Kenkyusho Ronshu* (Management Research Institute Papers), Department of Management, Toyo University, Tokyo, pp. 111–130.

Ota T. (2000) Kensho: Ajia no seijitaisei no henka to keizaiseicho (Empirical study: Transformation of political regime and economic growth in Asia), 23, *Keiei Kenkyusho Ronshu*

(Management Research Institute Papers), Department of Management, Toyo University, Tokyo, pp. 109–144.

Ota T. (2002) Ajia Keizai Hatten niokeru Sangyo Seisaku no Tenkai (Industrial policy and Economic Development in Asia), 56, *Keiei Ronshu* (Management Review), Department of Management, Toyo University, Tokyo, pp. 95–106.

Ota T. (2003a) Ajia no Seiji Seido to Keizai Hatten (Development of Political Regime and Economic Growth – Part I), 58, *Keiei Ronshu* (Management Review), Department of Management, Toyo University, Tokyo, pp. 145–158.

Ota T. (2003b) Ajia no Seiji Seido to Keizai Hatten (Development of Political Regime and Economic Growth – Part II), 59, *Keiei Ronshu* (Management Review), Department of Management, Toyo University, Tokyo, pp. 93–100.

Ota T. (2003c) Ikou Keizai ni Okeru Sangyo Seisaku: Chugoku Keizai Hatten ni Okeru Keizai Tokku no Yakuwari (Industrial Policy in Transitional Economy: the Role of China's Special Economic Zones in Economic Development), 60, *Keiei Ronshu* (Management Review), Department of Management, Toyo University, Tokyo, pp. 129–144.

Ota T. (2003d) *Ajia no Seiji-seido to Sangyou Seisaku no Yakuwari* (Asian Development Path – The Role of Industrial Policy Under Changing Political Systems), Bunshindo Publishing Co, Tokyo.

Ota T. (2003e) *Economic Growth and Transformation of Political Regime in Asia*, 18, Les Cahiers De L'Association Tiers-Monde, XVIIIeme Journees sur Developpement, Theme: Liberalisation, Transferts De Connaissances et Developpement, Paris, pp. 173–188.

Ota T. (2003f) *The Role of Special Economic Zones in China's Economic Development as Compared with Asian Export Processing Zones 1979–1995*, Asia in Extenso, University of Poitiers, Poitiers.

Ota T. (2007) Special Economic Zones in China's Economic Development as Compared with Asian Export Processing Zones, in *Special Economic Zones – Global and Indian Experiences*, (ed) Prabha Shastri R., The Icfai University Press, Hyderabad, pp. 71–105.

Sally R. (2013) *Asia and the Middle-income Trap*, Institute of Economic Affairs, 18 October 2013. Available from: www.iea.org.uk/blog/asia-and-the-middle-income-trap [1 February 2014].

U.N. (2007) Development Cooperation with Middle-income Countries, *Special Conference on Development Cooperation with Middle-Income Countries*, 1–2 March 2007, Madrid. Available from: www.un.org/esa/ffd/events/2007mic/micE.pdf [4 November 2013].

World Bank (1992) *World Development Report 1992: Development and the Environment*, Oxford University Press, New York.

World Bank (2002) *World Development Report 2002: Building Institutions for Markets*, Oxford University Press, New York.

World Bank (2003) *World Development Report 2003: Sustainable Development in a Dynamic World – Transforming Institutions, Growth, and Quality of Life*, Oxford University Press, New York.

World Bank (2012a) *World Development Report 2012: Gender Equality and Development*, Oxford University Press, New York.

World Bank (2012b) *World Development Indicators*, World Bank. Available from: http://data.worldbank.org/data-catalog/world-development-indicators [30 November 2012].

World Bank (2014) *World Development Indicators*, World Bank. Available from: http://data.worldbank.org/data-catalog/world-development-indicators [8 September 2014].

World Bank (2015) *World Development Indicators*, World Bank. Available from: http://data.worldbank.org/data-catalog/world-development-indicators [11 October 2015].

WWF (2006) *Living Planet Report 2006*, Gland, Switzerland/London/Oakland, CA: Worldwide Fund/Global Footprint Network/Zoological Society of London.

Yandle B., Madhusudan Bhattarai M. and Maya Vijayaraghavan M. (2004) Environmental Kuznets Curves: A Review of Findings, Methods, and Policy Implications, *Research Study*, 2, pp. 1–16.

4 Economic and social importance of the growing natural fiber market

China's role in the international cotton market

Carolina Gavagnin and M. Bruna Zolin

4.1 Introduction

The 2008 global crisis has severely affected the textile filament industry, including natural fibers, and particularly cotton. Cotton is the world's most important natural fiber. It supplies an important part of the textile industry that employs more labor globally than any other industry. The textile industry has played a decisive role in the processes of development of some Asian countries (e.g., China, India, Hong Kong and Bangladesh) by providing substantial employment and significant contributions to export earnings. In developed countries, one of the main reasons for its great importance is in terms of its employment rate, which has been greatly reduced by the 2008 economic crisis and by competition from lower-cost countries in the developing world, creating concerns about the entire textile manufacturing systems and associated labor markets in developed countries.

Research on the cotton market tends to focus on the distortions that industrialized countries cause in the international market due to the high level of subsidies given to this crop (Baffes, 2003, 2007; Gillson *et al.*, 2004; Anderson and Martin, 2008; Shahin, 2008). Generally, the guilty parties are identified as the United States and the EU. Although the pre eminent role is played by China in this area (as the world's main consumer, producer and importer), the effects produced by this country on the international cotton market tend to be underestimated. In absolute terms, the Chinese government subsidizes the sector offering the highest level of support worldwide since 2009–10 (ICTSD, 2013), even if, in relative terms (per unit of product), the EU is the largest subsidizer.

Although cotton is naturally a perennial plant (its life cycle is about 10 years), in extensive plantations it is grown as an annual crop. It is thus subject to annual change if and when other crops prove to be more profitable. Cotton is an extremely widespread vegetable textile fiber – the most widespread in the world. According to UNCTAD (2014) in 2007–08, out of the 65 countries where cotton is grown, 52 are developing countries, 21 are classified as least-developed countries and 22 (33 per cent of the total) are located in the Asian continent.

Cotton is one of the oldest crops in the world, and international trade in cotton can be traced back at least a thousand years (Findlay and O'Rourke, 2003). Since the Industrial Revolution it has experienced widespread growth. It is an important natural resource for millions of consumers, a major source of export revenues in some developing countries and a source of income and means of survival for a multitude of small and poor farmers, generally located in rural areas. In developed countries – such as the United States and the European Union countries – cotton is cultivated on large industrial farms with the support of government subsidies. Thanks to the aid received from Western countries, agricultural land turned into massive cotton plantations in non developed countries provides cheap raw materials for export or to mass-produce products.

Currently the majority of the world's cotton is grown in developing countries where labor costs are low. According to UNCTAD (2014), labor costs in the textile industry represent approximately one-sixth of total production costs, and rising labor costs have eroded the comparative advantage held by developed countries in terms of technology and better infrastructures in favor of low-cost economies. Approximately 100 million farmers in developing countries, working small plots of 2 to 15 acres, provide the world with two-thirds of its cotton (Takacs, 2012). In a large number of developing countries agriculture fulfils a major economic role, which is confirmed by its large contribution to the gross domestic product (GDP) and its high employment rate.

Since China's accession to the World Trade Organization, the country has achieved enormous progress, which has been enhanced by the central government's cotton policies (Yong, 2011b). In 2011, the Chinese government began to store cotton in order to support the domestic price paid to farmers. By 2012, China had amassed an inventory equivalent to 85 per cent of the total national annual production. "With more than 10 million tons of inventory, Beijing in theory could do without imports for 5–6 years," says Kevin Latner, executive director of Cotton Council International (CCI), a body promoting American cotton. The hypothesis, however, is not accurate.

> China has repeatedly made it clear its goal is price stability. And its action so far has served rather to rebalance the market: when international prices fall, they buy more cotton which by the way is a great deal, because then they can sell it on the local market at higher prices.
>
> (Bellomo, 2013)

The world's cotton market is facing a lot of problems, aggravated by the continuing economic crisis. More specifically, the main issues can be summarized as follows:

- Environmental deterioration: One major component of environmental degradation is the depletion of fresh water. Cotton is, indeed, a water-intensive crop. In addition, pesticides and other chemicals are widely used in order to reduce yield losses and facilitate crop harvests. Pesticides can harm humans, animals and beneficial organisms and reduce biodiversity. Heavy use of chemicals on poor-quality soil contributes to a loss of fertility and downstream pollution. According to CottonConnect (2014), around 50 per cent of pesticides used in developing countries are for cotton cultivation. Utilization of genetically modified organisms is widespread in cotton production; nevertheless, the debate on the benefits and costs arising from this crop is quite controversial and deals mainly with environmental consequences. Over the past decade, increasing awareness of environmental concerns has led the market for organic cotton to grow. Organic cotton is currently produced in 18 countries: the main producer is India, followed by Turkey, China, Tanzania and the United States (Textile Exchange, 2013).

- Economic relevance: 90 per cent of cotton farmers are concentrated in developing countries. The dominant farm structure (around 2 hectares) is the small farm, endowed with limited resources, but generating income to support family food needs (CottonConnect, 2014). Some of the poorer developing countries depend on cotton for their livelihood: cotton is a major component of their export revenues – which are indispensable for investing in infrastructure and basic services such as education and health care – and is the only source of income for local farmers. But as long as they do not apply innovative techniques and utilize specialist workers, they will lack competitiveness and will not be able to match rich countries' export prices, where the cotton trade is distorted by government subsidies to the sector.
- Social concerns: Child labor and slavery are the main social concerns, particularly in Uzbekistan, which is the world's third largest cotton exporter. Its booming cotton industry, which largely supplies the European market, is underpinned by a system of state-sponsored forced labor, particularly of children (Siegle, 2013).[1] Forced labor is a big concern in cotton plantations in Pakistan, India and Brazil (BCI, 2006).

Starting from these premises, this research seeks to assess the role of China in the world cotton market, analyzing which factors and to what extent they have affected Chinese cotton production, consumption and international trade over the first 12 years of the twenty-first century.

First, after a brief presentation of the adopted methodology to be used, an overall picture of the world cotton market is provided. Then a deepening review of the Chinese cotton market and the repercussions of China's behavior worldwide are dealt with. The impact that some macroeconomic variables have on the phenomenon of Chinese behavior is described by means of a correlation matrix. The findings and conclusions of the research are presented at the end of the chapter.

4.2   Materials and methods

A brief presentation of the world cotton market (production, consumption and trade) is obtained by using the following statistical sources: the Food and Agriculture Organization (FAO), the World Bank, the United States Department of Agriculture (USDA), Indexmundi, the International Cotton Advisory Committee (ICAC), Cotton Outlook (Cotlook) and PCI Fibres.

The FAOSTAT database provides up-to-date data relating to production and trade of agricultural crops by country, specifically harvested area, yield, imports and exports. The World Development Indicators (WDI) is the primary World Bank data catalogue presenting the most current and accurate global development data available at global and national levels. USDA's Foreign Agricultural Service contains current and historical official data on supply, use and trade of agricultural commodities for the United States and key producing and consuming countries, including China. All Indexmundi data about agricultural commodities are sourced from the USDA. ICAC, whose purpose is to assist governments in fostering a healthy world cotton economy (Valderrama, 2005), provides statistics on world cotton production, consumption and trade. In doing so, it strives to identify emerging changes in the structure of the world cotton market. Cotlook and PCI Fibres are the official source of cotton and manmade fiber prices, respectively. The period taken into account is 2000–12.

As far as the Chinese market is concerned, the study considers its relationship with the major variables affecting production, consumption and international trade.

The wide range of varieties of cotton grown worldwide reflects differences in cotton prices. Hence the need for standardization in a global cotton price indicator. Nowadays there are basically two points of reference for cotton prices: the Cotlook A Index and the New York Futures Exchange (NYFE). The former reflects cotton prices in the everyday physical cotton market, whereas the latter is a purely speculative market. The A Index, compiled by Cotlook Ltd., a private company in Liverpool, is indeed the most often quoted indicator of average international prices. It is calculated by averaging the offer values of the cheapest five quotations for delivery to East Asia for middling-quality cotton of 1⅛inches.[2] In this chapter the Cotlook A Index is referred to as the cotton price indicator.

Since 2002 the Chinese Cotton Index (CC Index) reflects cotton prices in China. It is an indicator of the Type 328 cotton price level, calculated as the daily average of offer prices received by 200 Chinese mills.

In order to analyze Chinese cotton production, consumption and trade, the study selected some influencing variables – namely, cotton prices, cotton substitute prices, harvested area, productivity and government investment for cotton production.

In order to measure a proxy of these variables, the study used the following indicators, respectively: the CC Index, the PCI synthetic fibers index, the cotton harvested area, the quantity of cotton produced per hectare and government expenditure in the primary sector.

Cotton consumption, in addition to cotton prices and cotton substitute prices, is supposed to be affected by the average standard of living (GDP per capita) and population trends.

The variables influencing the international cotton trade are assumed to be the price of cotton, the price of cotton substitutes and the exchange rate yuan/US dollar. The study aims to measure the linear association between production (consumption, imports and exports) and each of the previously listed variables through the Pearson correlation index (r).

4.3   The world cotton market: stylized facts

India has been well known for its textile goods since ancient times. During the second half of the seventeenth century, cotton goods in Europe were imported from India. The Industrial Revolution, however, changed the international competitive advantages, and India lost its leader position. Britain subsequently became the world's most important textile producer, even exporting to India. Rising wages and raw cotton prices in Britain were compensated for by competitive advantages in productivity. With globalization, the developed countries (particularly in Europe and for the clothing industry) delocalized, and European companies have gradually divested production, and some countries (especially in Asia) have taken advantage of this situation. At the beginning of the twenty-first century, Europe appears to be returning to Asia what the Industrial Revolution had taken away. As a general trend, however, since the 1970s cotton's share of world textile fiber consumption has started to decline and give way to chemical fibers, although cotton still remains the most important natural fiber.

Currently, cotton textile manufacturing is the most important industry within the textile sector, even if the volume is lower compared with the 1960s because of competition with synthetic fibers. Cotton, an important natural fiber, is produced mainly in the United States, India, China, Egypt, Pakistan and Eastern Europe (Table 4.1). India has the largest area cultivated for cotton production, but China is the largest producer and consumer of cotton in the world. Developing countries account for 81 per cent of global cotton production (ICTSD, 2013).

The textile industry and, consequently, the cotton industry, had and continues to have an important role in the EU. Among the member states, Italy is the leading manufacturer of textile products, followed by Germany, the United Kingdom and France. Turkey is included among the world's leading cotton consumers (Table 4.1). Because of the end of protectionism due to the expiration of the

Table 4.1 The cotton market: main producing and consuming countries (estimates 2013)

Country	Production (1,000 480-lb bales)	Share of world production (%)	Consumption (1,000 480-lb bales)	Share of world consumption (%)
China	34,000	28.95	36,000	33.12
India	28,000	23.84	22,750	20.93
United States	13,500	11.50	3,505	3.22
Pakistan	9,500	8.09	11,725	10.79
Brazil	7,000	5.96	4,050	3.73
Turkey	2,250	1.92	6,100	5.61
European Union	1,599	1.36	973	0.90
Rest of World	21,575	18.37	23,600	21.71
World	117,424	100.00	108,703	100.00

Source: Indexmundi and USDA.

Multi-Fiber Arrangement (1994), the European Union has been open to greater global competition, particularly from China, India and other Asian countries, fuelling concrete fears and concerns within its borders. According to Scheffer (2012), the European textile and clothing industry is highly export oriented; however, it is at a disadvantage in terms of supply to lower- and middle-income countries. The dimensions of the EU industry declined substantially between 2000 and 2010. The turnover of the industry decreased by 25 per cent (slightly more in textiles), whereas employment decreased by 50 per cent. In terms of demand, the clothing and home textiles market in Europe is slowly growing in volume but is stable in value. Even if the luxury segment has performed well, the gap in growth compared with developing countries is not sufficient to cover losses through competition.

The growth of world cotton production in recent years, according to ICAC (2013), was due to the growth in productivity rather than to an increase in land allocated to production. Much of this increase is attributable to China (Table 4.3).

In the world cotton market, there is a pronounced concentration in production and consumption: the leading cotton-producing economies also account for a large share of cotton consumption (ICAC, 2012a). The main actors in the world cotton market are China, India, the United States, Pakistan, Brazil and Turkey (Table 4.1). China and India account for 53 per cent of world production and 54 per cent of total consumption.

In dynamic terms, starting from 2010, world production exceeds consumption without attenuating the increase in world prices. In 2012 an improvement in consumption and a reduction in the quantity produced corresponded to a significant reduction in prices due to stock accumulation on the Chinese market (Figure 4.1).

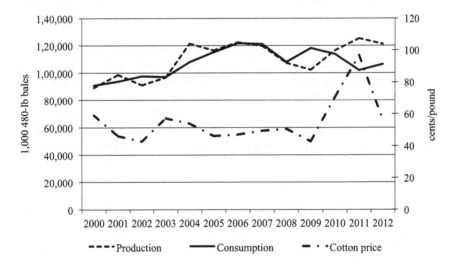

Figure 4.1 The world cotton market: production, consumption and cotton price (2000–2012)

Source: Authors' elaboration based on USDA and Cotlook data.

Note: Cotton price calculated as yearly average price (A index).

4.4   Supply and demand determinants

Many factors have affected and are affecting the world cotton market, both on the supply side and the demand side.

More specifically, the main determinants of cotton supply are the price of cotton, the profitability of alternative products, the costs of production, the size of buffer stocks, changes in technology, environmental constraints and public policies (Theriault, Serra and Sterns, 2013).

Cotton demand, in addition to price changes in cotton and cotton substitutes, is influenced by consumer tastes and preferences, demographic factors, income and the general level of prices (Baffes, Ataman Aksoy and Beghin, 2005).

As expected, in relation to the global trend in cotton production, consumption and trade in the period between 2000 and 2012 appear to be influenced by cotton price[3] movements (Figure 4.1): peaks in the cotton price are followed by an increase in cotton production and a contraction in cotton demand, as happened in 2011; whereas, when the cotton price decreases, as in 2009, global consumption leaps up and production goes down.

Since the 1960s, the use of synthetic fibers has increased dramatically, causing the natural fiber industry to lose much of its market share. Since late 1990s, cotton and natural fibers in general have been gradually surpassed by manmade fibers (MMF) – among which nylon, polyester and acrylic are the most common. This global shift in preferences has been mainly influenced by MMF's lower cost (Carmichael, 2015).

In 2012 world demand for fibers – natural and manmade – exceeded 80 million tons, and taking into account the demand for cotton and manmade fibers in the same year, the share of cotton demand equalled 31.6 per cent of total demand (Table 4.2). Global demand for manmade fibers is projected to further increase (Morris and Wagneur, 2012).

In relation to international trade, since 2000 the volume of traded cotton has been constantly increasing until reaching its peak in 2005 (Figure 4.2), when all textile trade was integrated into World Trade Organization rules and textile quotas were eliminated with the Multi-Fiber Agreement (ESCAP, 2008). The economic crisis that hit the world commodities markets in 2008, leading to unprecedented high prices, resulted in a contraction of the cotton trade. Since 2011 a decrease in the general price levels of commodities has sustained international trade recovery.

Table 4.2 World fiber consumption: share of cotton and manmade fibers (2007, 2010, 2012)

World fiber consumption (Million tons)			*Share of cotton consumption (%)*			*Share of MMF consumption (%)*		
2007	*2010*	*2012*	*2007*	*2010*	*2012*	*2007*	*2010*	*2012*
67,736	69,728	83,500	36.3	32.9	31.6	55.5	60.1	60.9

Source: FAO and ICAC.

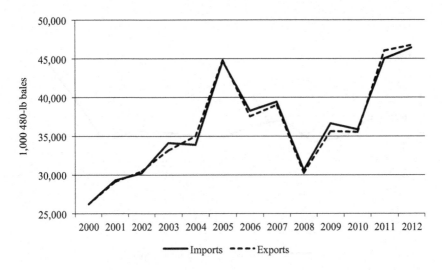

Figure 4.2 The world cotton market: imports and exports (2000–2012)
Source: Authors' elaboration based on USDA data.

Cotton prices, as with other basic commodities, are subject to large fluctuations (FAO *et al.*, 2011). Extreme price volatility leads to high uncertainty in economies, and the stronger the country's dependency on commodities and the more open the economy is, the greater the uncertainty.

Price volatility is influenced by the substitution effect caused by competition with synthetic fibers, exchange rate fluctuations, demand, the application of new technologies and cultivation techniques, subsidies granted to cotton producers – particularly in developed countries – and unpredictable weather events (Marwaha, 2011).

World cotton trade and production are highly affected by government policy intervention. Subsidies to the cotton sector include direct support to production, border protection (such as tariffs and quotas), crop insurance subsidies and minimum support price mechanisms. According to ICAC (2013), in 2012 about 49 per cent of world cotton production received direct government assistance. The impact of direct and indirect subsidies on cotton prices is not easily measurable, and prices are an extremely important variable for some developing countries – namely countries located in Western and Central Africa – who heavily rely on cotton export revenues. Support to the cotton industry in developed countries is a major cause of contention for many developing countries: in 2004 the World Trade Organization was led to deal with "the cotton problem" as a separate issue (Baffes, 2011: 8).

World subsidies seem to have a negative influence on cotton prices (Figure 4.3). If ICAC data are considered, it is found that when direct assistance to the cotton industry diminishes, the A index leaps up, such as in 2004 and 2011; vice versa, in 2002 and 2005, the amount of subsidy provided to the world cotton industry increased and cotton prices decreased (ICAC, 2013).

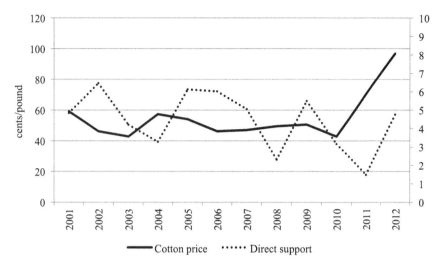

Figure 4.3 World direct assistance to cotton and cotton price (2000–2012)
Source: Authors' elaboration based on ICAC data.

4.5   The Chinese market

China is at the center of the global cotton market, as the world's largest cotton-producing, consuming and importing country (Table 4.3). China imports cotton from the United States, India, Australia and Uzbekistan in particular (Meyer, Mac-Donald and Kiawu, 2013).

Although China maintains its primacy in the market, especially due to its massive cotton imports, production and consumption have recently shown a decreasing pattern. Figure 4.4 depicts the trend of the Chinese cotton market in the period 2000–12.

After a constant increase in production and consumption, in 2008 the cotton market in China suffered a slight contraction, partly related to the overall economic crisis that hit world commodities.

However, the China Cotton Association (2014) ascribes the decrease in cotton production to lower acreage; increasing costs of labor, fertilizer and seed; low technological adaptation; preferential government support to grain crops; and volatile prices.

As far as technological adaptation is concerned, in the early 1990s China became the first country to commercialize genetically modified (GM) plants, starting with the virus-resistant tobacco, applied on a large scale. At that time, in other parts of the world scholars were discussing whether or not genetically modified organisms (GMOs) pose a risk to health (Jia and Peng, 2002). Among modified organisms, Bt cotton – an engineered variety made by US biotech giant Monsanto – is the most grown transgenic crop in China. Bt cotton makes up 95 per cent of China's

Table 4.3 Chinese cotton production, consumption and imports (2000, 2004, 2008, 2012)

	2000		2004		2008		2012	
	China 1,000 480-lb bales	*World share %*	*China 1,000 480-lb bales*	*World share %*	*China 1,000 480-lb bales*	*World share %*	*China 1,000 480-lb bales*	*World share %*
Production	20,300	22.78	30,300	24.95	36,700	34.00	35,000	28.43
Consumption	22,725	25.04	37,250	34.54	42,750	39.38	36,000	33.55
Imports	230	0.88	6,385	18.85	6,996	22.86	20,327	44.09

Source: USDA.

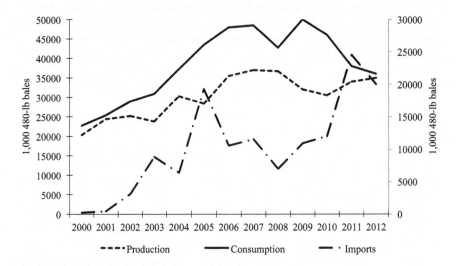

Figure 4.4 The Chinese cotton market: production, consumption and imports (2000–2012)
Source: Authors' elaboration based on USDA data.
Note: Imports are represented on the secondary vertical axis.

vast cotton plantations. Chinese researchers express very different and discordant opinions on the merits of Bt cotton. According to Lu *et al.* (2010) and Huang *et al.* (2010), the introduction of Bt cotton has led and is leading to strong environmental benefits (with favorable economic benefits by the reduction in production costs) in addition to the cultivated soil and benefits to neighboring farmers' soils. According to these authors, since its introduction in 1997, pesticide use has halved, and their study showed this led to a doubling of natural insect predators such as ladybirds, lacewings and spiders. In addition, the authors highlighted that such crops can promote biocontrol services in agricultural areas. However, according to *The Guardian* (Sample, 2010) millions of hectares of farmland in northern China have been struck by infestations of bugs following the widespread adoption of Bt cotton. Outbreaks of infestations of myriads of bugs, which can devastate around 200 varieties of fruit, vegetable and corn crops, have risen dramatically in the past decade, as cotton farmers have shifted from traditional cotton crops to GM varieties, scientists said.

Because global economic growth is expected to remain slow and uncertain, the price of cotton fiber is higher and more volatile than that of manmade fiber.

Consumption has also decreased in the Chinese market. Nevertheless, the China Textile Industry Association claims that growing per capita incomes and rising standards of living will be the main driver of cotton consumption recovery (Meador and Xinping, 2013).

China's accession to the World Trade Organization in December 2001 reduced the Chinese government's former strict control of trade. Cotton imports tripled in 2005 after the removal of textile and clothing global trade quotas (Yong, 2011a). High cotton imports are a consequence of low cotton production relative to high consumption – over the years the amount of cotton consumed by Chinese mills far exceeded the amount of Chinese harvested cotton, thus leaving mills dependent on imported cotton.

China is not only the largest producer of cotton, but is also the largest manmade fiber–producing country in the world. China's manmade fiber industry follows a constantly increasing pattern, with its production scale averaging at about 24 million metric tons in 2012 (ICAC, 2012b). In addition to price differences with respect to cotton and natural fibers in general, other major factors that have contributed to growth in the manmade fiber market in China are rising prosperity, population growth and the growing demand from Chinese industry for advanced products (Morrison, 2012).

The Chinese government supports cotton production by controlling imports and by applying border protection measures based on quotas and duties[4] with an effective tariff of 40 per cent on cotton imported without a quota. In addition, China maintains a strategic reserve of cotton – managed by the China National Cotton Reserve Corporation (CNCRC) agency – serving as a national buffer stock. The government releases cotton to the market from the reserve when there is shortage and replenishes it when there is abundance, thus supporting prices. Thus, China's behavior greatly influences the market price,[5] both at domestic and international levels. The efforts of China (given the rules on international trade) to ensure high prices to domestic producers required a significant accumulation of stocks – purchased on the international market – especially in 2011. Government policies, which are soon expected to result in China holding almost half of the world's cotton stocks, represent a major reason for China's commanding influence in the cotton market (Cotton Incorporated, 2013). Any CNCRC decision involving cotton stocks potentially has an impact on the global price direction. The United States, the world's leading cotton exporter, sees half of its cotton production imported by China and would not get along without it (Bellomo, 2013).

Direct assistance in China totalled $3.1 billion in 2011–12 and reached an estimated $5.8 billion in 2012–3 (ICAC, 2013).

4.6   Results

In such a context and in order to identify the variables that have the greatest impact on production, consumption and trade of Chinese cotton, a correlation matrix was drawn up. The study uses the Pearson product-moment correlation coefficient, defined as the covariance of the two considered variables, divided by the product of their standard deviations. The period taken into account is 2000–12.[6]

The identified determinants are three indices, respectively the CC Index, the A index and, considering the substitution effect, the PCI index. Among the variables related to supply, the availability of land and productivity were considered. Taking into account the high level of government support to the cotton sector, government investment is included among the independent variables with regard to production. For the consumption function, the price of cotton adds to the GDP per capita. The price of oil has not been examined because previous studies have concluded that only very weak links exist between the price of oil and the price of textile fibers (ICAC, 2010). As for trade, the relationship with price indices and the exchange rate has been investigated.

We have obtained the following values for *r* (scatter plots in the appendix), as depicted in Table 4.4.

As far as cotton production is concerned, the results show it to be positively correlated with cotton prices, land dedicated to cotton harvesting, productivity and government investment and negatively correlated to synthetic fiber prices.

In particular, there is a strong positive linear association between production, land area allocation and productivity, but, as expected, high negative correlation

Table 4.4 Correlation between Chinese cotton production, consumption, imports, exports and their determinants (2000–2012)

	Chinese cotton production	Chinese cotton consumption	Chinese cotton imports	Chinese cotton exports
Cotton price – CC Index	0.42	0.26		
Cotton price – A index			0.70	0.37
MMF price – PCI Index	−0.71	0.70	0.67	−0.60
Land	0.84			
Productivity	0.82			
Government investment	0.34			
GDP per capita		0.56		
Total population		0.70		
Exchange rate yuan/$			−0.64	0.47

Source: FAO, the World Bank and USDA.

Note: Government expenditure in agriculture, forestry and fisheries, according to the central government budget, data available for 2002–2010 period.

with synthetic fiber prices. This can be explained by the recent ever-increasing recourse to advanced technology and to the substitution effect between cotton and synthetic fibers.

Cotton consumption in China is positively correlated to synthetic fiber prices, GDP per capita and population size. A positive correlation between consumption and cotton prices was found. The same happens for cotton imports. This value does not reflect what was expected and can be probably ascribed to the limited number of observations per each variable in the analysis – namely 13 – and, as for imports, to the boost following China's accession to the WTO, the 2005 trade quotas removal and the distortions caused by massive government support. A deeper analysis considering a larger historical timeframe series of observations would clarify whether the result is robust or biased.

As for imports and exports, the results show that there is a strong correlation with synthetic fiber prices and the exchange rate. Contrary to what is expected, between 2000 and 2012 when the yuan depreciated, imports decreased and exports increased. Despite China's accession to the World Trade Organization in 2001, the Chinese government's control – although less strict – is still exercised through specific trade policies.

4.7 Is the primacy of China going to last? Concluding remarks

The importance of cotton stems from its connection to both the agricultural sector and the textile industry. This raw material is cultivated in many developing countries, providing income and employment. But world cotton trade and production are highly affected by government policy interventions, especially if these are implemented in developed countries.

The cotton market is governed by a few countries – indeed, production and consumption are profoundly concentrated in just a few regions globally. An exception is represented by China. China is the leading actor in the cotton market at the global level, being the world's largest producer, consumer and importer of cotton. Indeed, Chinese cotton public policy, based namely, on a cotton reserve system and on import quotas, has a strong influence on the world cotton market. The massive concentration of global cotton buffer supplies in China provides the country with the power to balance the market: when the international cotton price decreases, China stockpiles cotton and buys abroad and then sells it to the domestic market at a higher price, and vice versa.

But what are the main factors influencing the Chinese cotton market? How do they correlate to cotton production, consumption and international trade in China? By identifying the main macroeconomic variables for each aspect of the market and studying their behavior over the last 13 years, the direction and the size of their correlation were analyzed.

The calculations have revealed that cotton production in China is influenced by the size of the harvested area dedicated to cotton cultivation and land productivity, whereas cotton consumption is strongly correlated with the increase in population and living standards (GDP). Cotton imports and exports are correlated to exchange rate movements. Considering government policies supporting trade would be helpful to deepen the analysis of the relationship.

A negative correlation between cotton prices and cotton production and imports was found. This might be ascribed to the limited number of observations per each aggregate variable of the analysis. Additional research is needed: a larger historical timeframe series of observations should be considered – especially considering the recent global economic crisis – in order to confirm the robustness of the results or, alternatively, to determine their bias.

The main result emerging from the analysis is the strong impact of prices on the cotton market – the price of cotton, but most of all, the price of cotton substitutes. Competition with cheaper and technologically advanced manmade fibers is indeed one of the biggest challenges that the cotton sector is facing. For farmers, prices are the driving force: unstable crop prices, together with bad weather and high fertilizer or seed costs, are capable of wiping out their profits and pushing them to plant other crops.

Having said that, is the primacy of China in the cotton market going to last? China, and consequently the world cotton market, is facing a number of challenges due to the influence of economic, social and environmental issues. The small size of farms prevents the achievement of economies of scale; in the absence of government support, their survival may be put at risk. Moreover, there are too many different cultivated varieties of cotton, often of poor quality, especially in China. Considering that land is a limited factor and any increase in the surface area for harvesting cotton reduces the area allocated to other staple crops, food production concerns arise. The main cotton consumer countries are developing countries where per capita income is increasing and population is growing. The demand for cotton seems destined to grow, although at a slower pace because of the shift in preferences towards manmade fibers. In terms of production costs, the increase in labor costs should reduce the comparative advantage based on the production costs in China and shift demand to countries with abundant and cheaper labor (Bangladesh and Vietnam, for example).

Among the environmental concerns needing to be considered are the high water requirements of the crop, the abundant use of chemical inputs, the conflicting results of the effects on the soil and on human health of GM cotton, the treatment of waste materials (plastic residues) and the limitation of the most important factor of production (land).

Concerning social issues, the extreme dependence on income derived from the cultivation of cotton – in particular its importance to rural and poor people in developing countries – has to be mentioned. Equally, large amounts of the world's cotton are still produced in slavery-like conditions, and child labor in the cotton industry is also a current issue.

Considering all these elements, it is very likely that in the future there could be a shift, if not in cotton production, in cotton consumption and, consequently, in the textile industry to countries with economies with lower labor costs and fewer environmental restrictions and where future projections forecast increasing income per capita and population growth rates.

Notes

1 Schools are closed down for the duration of the cotton harvest, and children, some as young as 10 years old, are sent to the fields to pick cotton by hand for little or no pay. Students who fail to meet their targets or refuse to work are reportedly punished with detentions and beatings or can even face expulsion from school. Human rights groups estimate that up to 200,000 children are involved each year.
2 Since 2004 the geographical basis of the quotations is for delivery to the Far East, in view of the cotton trade flows since China's accession to the WTO. The terms quoted are Cost and Freight (CFR). Since August 2015 the base quality changed to middling 1⅛ inches. Changes in location and staple length reflect shifts in cotton trading patterns.
3 From this point forward the study will refer to the Cotlook A Index as the cotton price, unless otherwise specified.
4 Under its accession agreement to the WTO, China is obliged to establish a calendar-year tariff-rate quota.
5 From 1954 to 1988 China applied a system of centralized procurement and sale of cotton. Procurement (price paid to the cotton farmers) and selling prices (price at which the public authority sold the cotton to the textile enterprises) were decided by the central government. In 1999, in view of its accession to the WTO, the Chinese government decided to open the cotton market, and cotton procurement and selling prices were decided according to market supply and demand.
6 Due to data availability constraints.

References

Anderson K. and Martin W. (2008) Why Developing Countries Need Agricultural Policy Reform to Succeed under Doha, in *Developing Countries and the WTO: Policy Approaches*, (eds) Sampson G.P. and Chambers W.B., New York: United Nations University Press, pp. 19–40.

Baffes J. (2003) *Cotton and Developing Countries: A Case Study in Policy Incoherence*, World Bank Trade Note, 10(10), International Trade Department, Washington, DC, The World Bank Group.

Baffes J. (2007) *Distortions to Cotton Sector Incentives in West and Central Africa*, The World Bank. Available from http://siteresources.worldbank.org/INTTRADERESEARCH/Resources/544824–1146153362267/Benin_0708.pdf [Accessed: 15 November 2015].

Baffes J. (2011) *Cotton Subsidies, the WTO, and the 'Cotton Problem'*, Policy Research Working Paper No 5663, The World Bank Development Economics, Development Prospects Group & Poverty Reduction and Economic Management Network.

Baffes J., Ataman Aksoy M. and Beghin J.C. (2005) *Cotton: Market Setting, Trade Policies, and Issues*, Policy Research Working Paper No. 3218, The World Bank, Washington.

BCI (2006) *Scoping Research on Labour and Social Issues in Global Cotton Cultivation*, Final Report, The Better Cotton Initiative (BCI) Steering Committee. Available from: http://storage.globalcitizen.net/data/topic/knowledge/uploads/20111012131831705.pdf [Accessed: 20 October 2015].

Bellomo S. (2013) Con scorte record la Cina controlla il mercato del cotone, *Il Sole 24 Ore*, 22 May 2013. Available from: www.ilsole24ore.com/art/finanza-e-mercati/2013–05–22/scorte-record-cina-controlla-064542.shtml?uuid=AbY6L1xH [Accessed: 7 October 2015].

Carmichael A. (2015) Man-Made Fibers Continue To Grow, *Textile World*, 3 February 2015. Available from: www.textileworld.com/Issues/2015/_2014/Fiber_World/Man-Made_Fibers_Continue_To_Grow [Accessed: 28 September 2015].

China Cotton Association (2014) *China Cotton Report*, 2(5). Available from: www.english.
china-cotton.org/ [Accessed: 7 October 2015].

CottonConnect (2014) *Cotton Connect Impact*. Available from: www.cottonconnect.org/
[Accessed: 10 October 2015].

Cotton Incorporated (2013) *Chinese Cotton Policy: Decisions and Effects*. Available from:
www.cottoninc.com/corporate/Market-Data/SupplyChainInsights/Chinese-Cotton-
Policy/ [Accessed: 5 August 2015].

ESCAP (2008) *Unveiling Protectionism: Regional Responses to Remaining Barriers in the
Textiles and Clothing Trade*, United Nations Economic and Social Commission for Asia
and the Pacific (ESCAP), New York.

FAO, Ifad, UNCTAD, WFP (2011) *Price Volatility in Food and Agricultural Markets:
Policy Responses*, Food and Agricultural Organization.

Findlay R. and O'Rourke K.H. (2003) Commodity Market Integration, 1500–2000, in *Globalization in Historical Perspective*, (eds) Bordo M.D., Taylor A.M. and Williamson
J.G., Chicago: University of Chicago Press, pp. 13–64.

Gillson I., Poulton C., Balcombe K. and Page S. (2004) *Understanding the Impact of Cotton Subsidies on Developing Countries*, Overseas Development Institute, London.

Huang J., Mi J., Lin H., Wang Z., Chen R., Hu R., Rozelle S. and Pray C. (2010) A Decade
of Bt Cotton in Chinese Fields: Assessing the Direct Effects and Indirect Externalities of
Bt Cotton Adoption in China, *Science China, Life Sciences*, 53(8), pp. 981–991.

ICAC (2010) *Cotton: Review of the World Situation*, International Cotton Advisory Committee (ICAC), 63(3), www.icac.org/cotton_info/publications/reviews/2010/english/
erev1_10.pdf.

ICAC (2012a) *Cotton: Review of the World Situation*, International Cotton Advisory Committee (ICAC), 65(5), www.icac.org/cotton_info/publications/reviews/2010/english/
erev1_10.pdf.

ICAC (2012b) Manmade Fibres: Current Situation and Developments Aimed at Sustainability, *International Cotton Advisory Committee (ICAC) 71st Plenary Meeting*, Inter-
laken, Switzerland.

ICAC (2013) *Production and Trade Policies Affecting the Cotton Industry*, September
2013, International Cotton Advisory Committee (ICAC), Washington, DC.

ICTSD (2013) *Cotton: Trends in Global Production, Trade and Policy*, Information Note,
International Centre for Trade and Sustainable Development (ICTSD), Geneva.

Jia S.R. and Peng Y.F. (2002) GMO Biosafety Research in China, *Environmental Biosafety
Research*, 1(1), pp. 5–8.

Lu Y., Wu K., Jiang Y., Xia B., Li P., Feng H., Wyckhuys K.A. and Guo Y. (2010) Myriad
Bug Outbreaks in Multiple Crops Correlated with Wide-Scale Adoption of Bt Cotton in
China, *Science China Life Sciences*, 328(5982), pp. 1151–1154.

Marwaha S. (2011) Impacting Factors on Global Cotton Price, *The Indian Textile Journal*,
July 2011, pp. 72–79.

Meador M. and Xinping W. (2013) *Peoples Republic of China: Cotton and Products
Annual 2013*, Gain Report No. 13017, Beijing: United States Department of Agriculture
(USDA) Foreign Agricultural Service.

Meyer L., MacDonald S. and Kiawu J. (2013) *Cotton and Wool Outlook*, CWS-13e, Washington, DC: United States Department of Agriculture (USDA).

Morris D. and Wagneur C. (2012) *India, The Market for Natural and Man-made Fibres,
Textiles and Textile Manufactures to 2012*, Comité International de la Rayonne et des
Fibres Synthétiques (CIRFS), Brussels.

Morrison W.M. (2012) *China's Economic Conditions*, Congressional Research Service (CRS) Report for Congress, Library of Congress, Washington, DC.

Sample I. (2010) Scientists Call for GM Review after Surge in Pests around Cotton Farms in China, *The Guardian*, 13 May 2010. Available from: www.theguardian.com/environment/2010/may/13/gm-crops-pests-cotton-china [Accessed: 30 October 2015].

Scheffer M.R. (2012) *In-Depth Assessment of the Situation of the T&C Sector in the EU and Prospects*, Final Report prepared for European Commission Enterprise and Industry DG, Saxion Universities, Enschede, The Netherlands.

Shahin M. (2008) The Cotton Initiative, in *Developing Countries and the WTO: Policy Approaches*, (eds) Sampson G.P. and Chambers W.B., New York: United Nations University Press, pp. 41–61.

Siegle L. (2013) Why Does Cotton Production Still Cause Slave Labour?, *The Guardian*, 27 October 2013. Available from: www.theguardian.com/environment/2013/oct/27/cotton-production-slave-labour-uzbekistan [Accessed: 3 September 2015].

Takacs H. (2012) Sustainable Cotton Production in India: A Case Study in Strategic Corporate Social Responsibility, *International Journal of Business and Social Research (IJBSR)*, 2(3), pp. 1–10.

Textile Exchange (2013) *Farm & Fibre Report 2011–2012.* Available from: http://farmhub.textileexchange.org/upload/library/Farm%20and%20fiber%20report/Farm_Fiber%20Report%202011–12-Small.pdf [Accessed: 11 November 2015].

Theriault V., Serra R. and Sterns J.A. (2013) Prices, Institutions, and Determinants of Supply in the Malian Cotton Sector, *Agricultural Economics*, 44(2), pp. 161–174.

UNCTAD (2014) *Agricultural Products: Cotton*, United Nations Conference on Trade and Development. Available from: www.unctad.info/en/Infocomm/Agricultural_Products/Cotton/Description/ [Accessed: 11 November 2015].

Valderrama C.A. (2005) *A Profile of the International Cotton Advisory Committee*, International Cotton Advisory Committee. Available from: www.new-rules.org/storage/documents/ffd/valderrama.pdf [Accessed: 27 August 2015].

Yong W. (2011a) *How WTO Accession Has Changed China and the Road Forward*, Centre for International Governance Innovation (CIGI), 19 May 2011. Available from: www.cigionline.org/publications/2011/5/how-wto-accession-has-changed-china-and-road-forward [Accessed: August 2015].

Yong W. (2011b) *China's Development since WTO Accession*, East Asia Forum: Economics, Politics and Public Policy in East Asia and the Pacific, 6 October 2011. Available from: www.eastasiaforum.org/2011/10/06/chinas-development-since-wto-accension/ [Accessed: 13 August 2015].

Appendix

Scatter plots

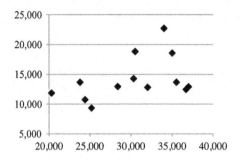

Figure 4.A1 Correlation between production and the CC Index, 1,000 480-lb bales and yuan/ton (2000–2012)

Source: Authors' elaboration based on USDA and Cotton Outlook's data.

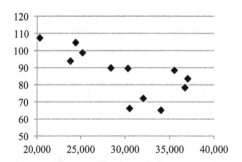

Figure 4.A2 Correlation between production and the PCI Index, 1,000 480-lb bales and cents/pound (2000–2011)

Source: Authors' elaboration based on PCI Fibres and USDA's data.

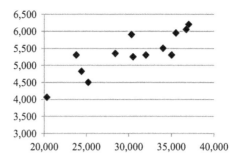

Figure 4.A3 Correlation between production and land, 1,000 480-lb bales and 1,000 HA (2000–2012)

Source: Authors' elaboration based on USDA's data.

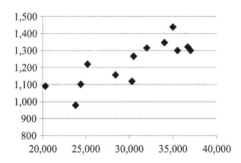

Figure 4.A4 Correlation between production and productivity, 1,000 480-lb bales and kg/ HA (2000–2012)

Source: Authors' elaboration based on USDA's data.

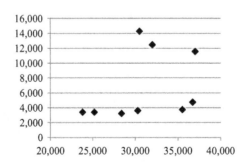

Figure 4.A5 Correlation between production and government investment, 1,000 480-lb bales and US$ (2002–2010)

Source: Authors' elaboration based on FAO and USDA's data.

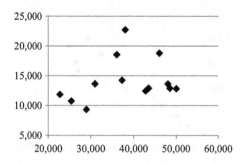

Figure 4.A6 Correlation between consumption and the CC Index, 1,000 480-lb bales and yuan/ton (2000–2012)

Source: Authors' elaboration based on USDA and Cotton Outlook's data.

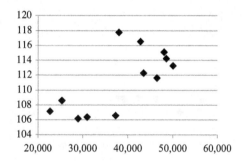

Figure 4.A7 Correlation between consumption and the PCI Fibre Index, 1,000 480-lb bales and cents/pound (2000–2011)

Source: Authors' elaboration based on PCI Fibres and USDA's data.

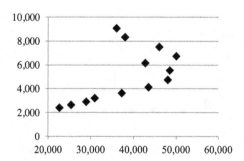

Figure 4.A8 Correlation between consumption and GDP per capita, 1,000 480-lb bales and US$ (2000–2012)

Source: Authors' elaboration based on World Bank and USDA's data.

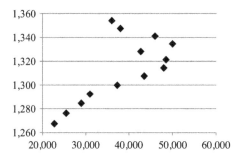

Figure 4.A9 Correlation between consumption and total population, 1,000 480-lb bales and thousands (2000–2012)

Source: Authors' elaboration based on FAO and USDA's data.

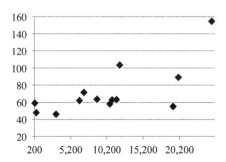

Figure 4.A10 Correlation between imports and the A index, 1,000 480-lb bales and cents/ pound (2000–2012)

Source: Authors' elaboration based on USDA and Cotton Outlook's data.

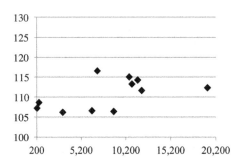

Figure 4.A11 Correlation between imports and the PCI Index, 1,000 480-lb bales and cents/ pound (2000–2011)

Source: Authors' elaboration based on PCI Fibres and USDA's data.

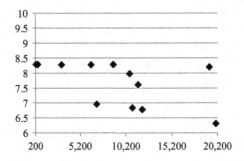

Figure 4.A12 Correlation between imports and the exchange rate, 1,000 480-lb bales and yuan/$ (2000–2012)

Source: Authors' elaboration based on World Bank and USDA's data.

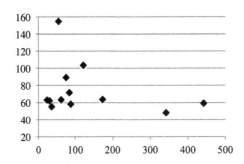

Figure 4.A13 Correlation between exports and the A Index, 1,000 480-lb bales and cents/pound (2000–2012)

Source: Authors' elaboration based on USDA and Cotton Outlook's data.

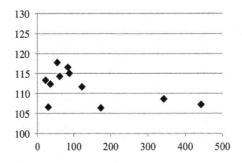

Figure 4.A14 Correlation between exports and the PCI Index, 1,000 480-lb bales and cents/pound (2000–2011)

Source: Authors' elaboration based on PCI Fibres and USDA's data.

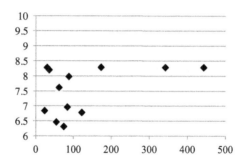

Figure 4.A15 Correlation between exports and the exchange rate, 1,000 480-lb bales and yuan/$ (2000–2012)

Source: Authors' elaboration based on World Bank and USDA's data.

Part II

Corporate strategy and social responsibility

5 The influence of national characteristics on corporate social, environmental and governance performance

Eduardo Ortas, Igor Alvarez, Ainhoa Garayar and Jacques Jaussaud

5.1 Introduction

Following growing social and environmental concerns, both in the public consciousness and at the company level in the last decades of the twentieth century (Campbell, 2003), an increase in the number of voluntary initiatives and codes of business conduct in the field of corporate social responsibility (CSR) and sustainable development have been identified since the 1990s (Rasche, 2009). Various instruments have been proposed by different national and international organizations, including nongovernmental foundations and organizations (OECD, 2001; UNRISD, 2002; EC, 2003, 2004; Waddock, 2004, 2008). The United Nations Global Compact (UNGC), which was first outlined at the 1999 World Economic Forum in Davos by Secretary-General Kofi Annan, is the largest CSR initiative in the world (Ruggie, 2004; Rasche, Waddock and McIntosh, 2012; Kell, 2013). It was launched in July 2000, and as of 2015 has more than 12,700 participants. According to the United Nations Global Compact Office (UNGCO, 2013), Spain, France and Japan are the countries with the highest number of participating firms.

According to a number of researchers (Bennie, Bernhagen and Mitchell, 2007; Cetindamar and Husoy, 2007; Byrd, 2009; Janney, Dess and Forlani, 2009; Runhaar and Lafferty, 2009) the main reasons for companies to adopt the UNGC initiative are the following: (1) the companies' commitment to act in an ethical way, in terms of sustainable development or corporate citizenship; (2) improvement of companies' image and access to foreign markets; and (3) as a response to the pressure of stakeholders, including customers. Only a few studies, however, have analyzed whether the adoption of the UNGC – as a driver of CSR performance – has truly stimulated the companies' environmental, social and corporate governance performance (Ayuso and Roca, 2010; Garayar and Calvo, 2012; Arevalo *et al.*, 2013). Furthermore, the moderating effect of the commitment to UNGC in the relationship between companies' social performance (CSP), companies' environmental performance (CEP), corporate governance performance (CGP) and corporate financial performance (CFP) seems to be unexplored.

This chapter contributes to the literature on corporate social and environmental responsibility by analyzing from a neoinstitutional perspective the differences in CSP, CEP and CGP between the three countries with the most companies committed to the UNGC (i.e., Spain, France and Japan). The research will contribute to a better understanding of the premises established by Adams, Hill and Roberts (1998), who argue that differences across countries are complex, thus requiring further investigation on country-specific effects. Furthermore, this research also focuses on analyzing whether the country-specific differences moderate the relationship between CSP, CEP and CGP and CFP of companies from the previously mentioned countries. The empirical investigation is based on a sample of 125 French, Spanish and Japanese companies committed to the UNGC and is carried out through regression analysis.

The results show that (1) the Spanish and French companies achieve similar levels of social and corporate governance performance and higher levels than those achieved by the Japanese firms; (2) on the other hand, Japanese firms seem to be more committed to environmental issues than their Spanish and French counterparts; and (3) finally, the country-specific characteristics seem to significantly influence the relationship between corporate social, environmental, corporate governance and financial performance.

The rest of the chapter is organized as follows. The second section introduces the theoretical approach, reviews the previous research on the topic and develops the working hypotheses. The third section is devoted to the study's empirical methodology. The results achieved are shown in Section 5.4. Finally, Section 5.5 contains further discussion and lists the conclusions of the research.

5.2 Theoretical background and hypotheses

5.2.1 Theoretical background

Neoinstitutional theory is often used to explain why firms in different countries adopt different CSR priorities. Socially accepted rules and beliefs embedded in the cultural characteristics of a nation influence the actions of its members and organizations (DiMaggio and Powell, 1991a, 1991b; Selznick, 1996), such as in the case of CSR practices (Boiral, 2003, 2007; Frederick, 2006; Hiss, 2009).

Neoinstitutional theory (Meyer and Rowan, 1991; DiMaggio and Powell, 1991b) addresses the question of how and why the environment affects organizational structure and practices. DiMaggio and Powell's emphasis centers on understanding the reasons for institutional resemblance among companies. What factors have an influence when it comes to promoting similarities between firms? DiMaggio and Powell (1991b) differentiate between two types of isomorphism: competitive and institutional isomorphism. Competitive isomorphism relates to efficiency (technical or economic explanations): when there is a cheaper, better or more efficient way of doing things, competitive forces encourage firms to adopt such a new approach. Institutional isomorphism is a more complex process which develops according to three kinds of mechanisms: coercive, normative and mimetic ones.

Coercive isomorphism is the result of formal pressures (e.g., laws) and informal pressures (e.g., agreements and codes of conduct) exerted on firms or by the cultural beliefs of the surrounding society. As far as CSR is considered, coercive isomorphism may include regulations related to the issuing of social and environmental information (Larrinaga-González, 2007).

Normative isomorphism results from the professionalization of those people who make decisions in firms. The professionalization of firms' management – via business schools offering specialization courses, for instance – leads managers to have a similar way of perceiving, interpreting, understanding and solving the problems their firms are facing. In other words, they end up developing similar cognitive mind-sets from which they develop similar patterns of behavior and provide similar solutions. There is, for instance, controversy as to whether practices in social responsibility achieve good economic results. However, according to Larrinaga-González (2007), firms often participate in a CSR initiative, like the UNGC, not in search of better financial results, but as a response to certain values shared by other firms, in order to gain legitimacy.

As far as mimetic isomorphism is concerned, uncertainty perception may explain why firms tend to mimic their competitors. In the case under review, firms may be motivated to adopt a social responsibility initiative as a way to strengthen their social legitimacy because their competitors are doing so (Larrinaga-González, 2007). According to Bansal (2005) mimetic pressures explain the motivation of a group of Canadian companies in environmentally sensitive sectors to promote sustainable development. Aerts, Cormier and Magnan (2006), on their side, find that coercive and mimetic institutional pressures have a significant effect on plans to begin issuing information of an environmental nature.

This neoinstitutional theoretical framework is particularly useful because our objective is to explore the companies' CSP, CEP and CGP in their contexts (Baxter and Chua, 2003; Bebbington, Higgins and Frame, 2009; Ball and Craig, 2010). This theoretical framework appears to be relevant as each of the three kinds of mechanisms (coercive, normative and mimetic) may be at work to promote CSR and sustainable development strategies and practices (Bansal, 2005).

5.2.2 *Literature review and hypotheses development*

Companies' commitment to CSR is strongly influenced by national and transnational organizations and agencies. A number of scholars have investigated the reasons for such a large acceptance of the UNGC initiative (Vormedal, 2005; Bennie, Bernhagen and Mitchell, 2007; Cetindamar and Husoy, 2007; Byrd, 2009; Janney, Dess and Forlani, 2009; Runhaar and Lafferty, 2009; Ayuso and Mutis, 2010; Ayuso and Roca, 2010; Perez-Batres, Miller and Pisani, 2010, 2011; Garayar and Calvo, 2012; Arevalo *et al.*, 2013). Practitioners and the UNGCO itself have also published a number of studies in order to identify such motives (UNGCO, 2007, 2009, 2010, 2012, 2013; Accenture and UNGC, 2010). The main reasons are to improve reputation and increase employee satisfaction (Runhaar and Lafferty, 2009), as well as improving the firms' image (Cetindamar and Husoy, 2007; Runhaar and Lafferty, 2009; Ayuso and Roca, 2010), learning better practices, achieving competitive advantages and facilitating strategic changes when implementing the principles (Waddock, Mirvis and Ryu, 2008; Ayuso and Roca, 2010; Arevalo *et al.*, 2013).

However, CSR practices and CSR initiatives may differ from country to country, at least to some extent, as a consequence of different national social, political and economic conditions (Maignan and Ralston, 2002; Aaronson, 2003; Welford, 2004, 2005; Chapple and Moon, 2005; Kimber and Lipton, 2005). According to Brammer *et al.* (2006), when internationalizing, firms face pressures from a growing number of different stakeholders because of social, cultural, legal, regulatory, and economic characteristics in each country (Hofstede, 1980; Schwartz, 1994).

Welford (2004) studied the differences for companies from the United Kingdom, Norway, Hong Kong and Singapore. In Singapore, which is a very open economy, firms focus on external aspects of CSR, whereas in Norway they emphasize social policies; in Hong Kong, an economy that was traditionally linked with the United Kingdom, the focus is on internal aspects of CSR. According to Welford (2005), CSR is linked with a country's economic development: the more developed the country is, the more CSR practices are implemented.

Baughn *et al.* (2007) compare two themes of CSR, environmental and social issues, in 14 Asian countries with companies from Western Europe, Australia, New Zealand, the United States, Canada, the Middle East and Africa. They find strong relationships between CSR and a country's economic, political and social contexts. This reflects, according to them, the importance of a country's development of such institutional capacity to promote and support CSR practices. Huge differences are identified among Asian firms themselves: Japan, Taiwan and Singapore, for example, demonstrate levels of social and environmental CSR on a par with or above that seen in other developed countries, whereas Pakistan and Bangladesh show levels of CSR that fall below the average found in Eastern and Central Europe, as well as in Latin America and Africa.

Aaronson (2003) analyzes the differences between firms from the United Kingdom and the United States. Although the two nations enjoy similar political and entrepreneurial cultures, they have taken significantly different approaches to CSR policies. The British authorities have made both domestic and global CSR a priority and have stressed that British businesses must act ethically everywhere. Therefore, British companies' disclosure was at that time more comprehensive than that of US firms.

According to Smith, Adhikari and Tondkar (2005) and Kolk and Perego (2010) companies from countries with a stronger stakeholder orientation (civil law) issue more and higher-quality corporate environmental reports than companies from countries emphasizing shareholder orientation (common law). The former are more sensitive to stakeholders' needs (Ball, Kothari and Robin, 2000; Simnett, Vanstrealen and Chua, 2009) and their legal system is more oriented towards the protection of different stakeholders. Thus, according to Frías-Aceituno, Rodriguez-Ariza and García-Sánchez (2012), companies located in civil-law countries are likely to disclose more on social and environmental issues than companies located in

Anglo-Saxon countries, because the common-law legal system is oriented to protecting shareholders first (Prado-Lorenzo, García-Sánchez and Blazquez-Zaballos, 2013). Bushman, Pietroski and Smith (2004), on the contrary, investigate voluntary governance disclosures on the basis of a sample of 1,000 companies from 46 countries; they conclude that governance transparency is higher in common-law countries with a high judicial efficiency.

France, Japan and Spain, the three countries under investigation in this chapter because they have the highest number of firms committed to the UNGC initiative, offer contrasting institutional characteristics (Aoki, 1988), with contrasting legal and judicial traditions (Amann *et al.*, 2007). A Christian cultural background versus a Confucian cultural background may lead to a different emphasis on social versus environmental priorities, for instance. Another example is that a still strong tradition in Japan, compared with France and Spain, not to mention the United States, is to avoid resorting to litigation in order to solve conflicts, which are settled through informal and undisclosed arrangements. Such a tradition may matter as far as governance transparency is concerned, for instance.

Ortas *et al.* (2015), on the basis of the same data drawn from the UNGC, using a descriptive methodology (HJ biplot method), find that Spanish and French firms achieve similarly high levels of social and corporate governance performance, whereas Japanese firms are more committed to environmental issues. They find such results in line with the institutional and cultural backgrounds of European Latin countries on the one hand, that is, France and Spain, and a Confucian country on the other side, namely Japan.

On the basis of the whole of the literature that has been presented briefly, in a neoinstitutional perspective the H1 hypothesis is formulated as follows:

H1: Companies from different countries with different institutional backgrounds will have different priorities in terms of social, environmental and corporate governance performance.

Furthermore, CSR activities by firms may be valued differently by shareholders in countries with different cultural and institutional backgrounds (Amann *et al.*, 2007). Cultural differences between Japan and Western countries have been widely addressed (Nakane, 1970; Hofstede, 1980, for instance). Institutional differences that may matter here include specific interfirmal relationships, namely *keiretsu* group relationships in Japan (Aoki, 1988; Miyashita and Russel, 1994), the weight of direct finance (Aoki, 1988) and the share of foreign shareholders in respective stock exchanges (Amann *et al.*, 2007). As a consequence, the economic benefits, including from a financial perspective, derived from CSR activities may differ from country to country. In return, financial performance may affect CSR efforts differently from country to country, as financial objectives and respective CSR objectives (social, environmental and corporate governance) may differ according to the country. As a consequence, hypothesis H2 is formulated as follows:

H2: The relationship between CSR performance and financial performance of a firm is affected according to its country's institutional background.

5.3 Sample delimitation and methodology

5.3.1 Corporate financial, social, environmental and governance performance measures

This research focuses on companies from the three countries with the most firms committed to the UNGC initiative: Spain, France and Japan. The data used in this work are twofold: (1) data related to firms' CSP, CEP and CGP; and (2) market data related to companies' financial performance (FP). Data has been collected from the ASSET4 database of Datastream (Thomson Reuters, Inc.), which provides objective and systematic environmental, social and governance (ESG) data using more than 280 key performance indicators on more than 4,000 global companies, including Morgan Stanley Capital International (MSCI) World, MSCI Europe, STOXX 600, National Association of Securities Dealers Automated Quotation (NASDAQ) 100, Australian Securities Exchange (ASX) 300 and MSCI Emerging Markets companies. This dataset, such as that provided by the Kinder, Lydenberg and Domini (KLD) database, is recognized as providing the most complete ratings of ESG performance and social responsibility.

The database search provided a total of 203 companies that were monitored from 2005 to 2012, thus totaling 1,624 firm-years grouped in ten primary economic sectors in the Global Industry Classification Standard (GICS) system. However, for 78 firms there was no full match between firms' FP and companies' CSP, CEP and CGP for the entire period under investigation. The study thus ended with a final sample of 125 firms and 1,000 firm-years (see Appendix 2 for complete details about each company).

The firms' FP has been measured through two market-based measures drawn from the Datastream database: (1) companies' total annual market return (CMR) and (2) companies' financial risk (CFR). CMR is defined as the equity return earned by stockholders on a yearly basis, and CFR (i.e., the volatility of the companies' stock prices) is defined by the standard deviation of the companies' returns. It is worth mentioning that the measurement of CFP through market-based and accounting-based measures both have their advantages and limitations. On the one hand, accounting-based measures focus on firms' historical assessment of accounting profitability, capturing indicators such as return on assets (ROA), asset growth, operating revenue, etc., which can be biased due to the differences in accounting procedures and managerial manipulation. On the other hand, market-based measures are less susceptible to accounting rules and managerial manipulation because they refer to investors' evaluations and expectations of firms' performance. However, stock prices may be affected by external phenomena not related to firms' intrinsic financial performance. Nevertheless, this forward-looking measure is used to define firms' CMR and CFR.

Companies' performance on social (CSP), environmental (CEP) and corporate governance (CGP) has been measured by the scores of each company on the social, environmental and corporate governance composite indexes, such as provided by the ASSET4 database. These composite indexes comprise variables that capture a wide range of stakeholders' performance issues, assessed by independent external social audits (Orlitzky, Schmidt and Rynes, 2003) that apply social and environmental screens, thus reflecting companies' social, environmental and corporate governance strengths and weaknesses. Selected composite indexes in this research are defined as follows (further information about the measurement of the composite indexes is in Appendix 1):

- CSP measures a company's capacity to generate trust and loyalty with its workforce, customers and society, a key factor in determining its ability to generate long-term value. This composite index results from a weighted score of the companies' strengths and weaknesses on indicators related to (1) product responsibility; (2) community; (3) human rights; (4) diversity and opportunity; (5) employment quality; (6) health and safety; and (7) training and development.
- CEP measures a company's impact on living and nonliving natural systems, including the air, land and water, as well as complete ecosystems. It reflects to which extent a company uses best management practices to avoid environmental risks and capitalize on environmental opportunities. This composite index results from a weighted score of the companies' strengths and weaknesses on indicators related to (1) emissions reduction; (2) product innovation; and (3) resource consumption reduction.
- CGP measures systems and processes of a company which ensure that its board members and executives act in the best interests of its shareholders. This composite index results from a weighted score of the companies' strengths and weaknesses on indicators related to (1) board functions; (2) board structure; (3) compensation policy; (4) vision and strategy; and (5) shareholder rights.

These composite indexes take values from 0 to 100. The higher the companies' score on each composite index, the higher the companies' performance on social, environmental or corporate governance.

The following outlines briefly the methodology used in order to test the H1 and H2 hypotheses.

5.3.2 *Methodology*

This section introduces two different econometric models aiming to empirically detect if (1) the companies' country context influences their level of CSP, CEP and CGP; and (2) the companies' country context moderates the relationship between the companies' CSP, CEP and CGP and their financial performance (measured by the firms' CMR and CFR). In both cases, the research focuses on dependency models because they are able to predict the impact of some explanatory variables, considered simultaneously, on the behavior of a given dependent variable.

The first model contains three equations and aims to verify if the different companies' country contexts influence the companies' performance in the following three dimensions: (1) social, (2) environmental and (3) corporate governance. The proposed model is provided by the following set of equations:

$$CSP_{i,t} = \beta_1 CSP_{i,t-1} + \beta_2 CSP_{i,t-2} + \beta_3 CSP_{i,t-3} + ... + \beta_n CSP_{i,t-n} \qquad (5.1)$$
$$+ \phi_i Country + \varepsilon_t$$

$$CEP_{i,t} = \beta_1 CEP_{i,t-1} + \beta_2 CEP_{i,t-2} + \beta_3 CEP_{i,t-3} + ... + \beta_n CEP_{i,t-n} \qquad (5.2)$$
$$+ \phi_i Country + \varepsilon_t$$

$$CGP_{i,t} = \beta_1 CGP_{i,t-1} + \beta_2 CGP_{i,t-2} + \beta_3 CGP_{i,t-3} + ... + \beta_n CGP_{i,t-n} \qquad (5.3)$$
$$+ \phi_i Country + \varepsilon_t$$

where $CSP_{i,t}$ refers to the level of corporate social performance of company i in the period t (5.1), $CEP_{i,t}$ refers to the level of corporate environmental performance of company i in the period t (5.2), $CGP_{i,t}$ refers to the level of corporate governance performance of company i in the period t (5.3), *Country* is a binary variable that takes the value 1 if a company i belongs to Spain or France and 0 if a company i belongs to Japan, and ε_t refers to the equations' disturbance terms. The reason why we consider French and Spanish firms on the one hand (*Country* equals 1 in their cases) and Japanese firms on the other hand (*Country* equals 0 for them) is because of the results of Ortas *et al.* (2015) mentioned in the literature review section: Spanish and French firms achieve similarly high levels of social and corporate governance performance, whereas Japanese firms are more committed to environmental issues. The significance of the ϕ_i parameters will indicate if the companies' level of CSP, CEP and CGP is influenced by the geographical context in which the companies operate.

The second dependency model is proposed in order to detect if the companies' country context moderates the relationship between the firms' CSP, CEP and CGP and their FP. The proposed model is provided by the following set of equations:

$$CSP_{i,t} = \sum_{s=1}^{n} \beta_i CMR_{i,t-s} + \sum_{s=1}^{n} \beta_i CFR_{i,t-s} + \phi_i Country + \varepsilon_t \qquad (5.4)$$

$$CEP_{i,t} = \sum_{s=1}^{n} \beta_i CMR_{i,t-s} + \sum_{s=1}^{n} \beta_i CFR_{i,t-s} + \phi_i Country + \varepsilon_t \qquad (5.5)$$

$$CGP_{i,t} = \sum_{s=1}^{n} \beta_i CMR_{i,t-s} + \sum_{s=1}^{n} \beta_i CFR_{i,t-s} + \phi_i Country + \varepsilon_t \qquad (5.6)$$

where $CSP_{i,t}$ refers to the level of corporate social performance of company i in the period t (5.4), $CEP_{i,t}$ refers to the level of corporate environmental performance of company i in the period t (5.5), $CGP_{i,t}$ refers to the level of corporate governance performance of company i in the period t (5.6), $CMR_{i,t}$ is the total annual market return of company i in the period t, $CFR_{i,t}$ is the financial risk of company i in the period t, *Country* is a binary variable that takes the value 1 if a company i belongs to Spain or France and 0 if a company i belongs to Japan, and, finally, ε_t refers to the equations' disturbances.

As can be appreciated, both models use past values of different independent variables to explain the value of different dependent variables. The problem of what the optimal lag-length selection is for each equation is solved by implementing the Akaike's information criterion (AIC) and Schwarz's information criterion (SIC). It is worth mentioning that the implementation of the SIC criterion allows us to detect the appearance of eventual better levels of goodness of fit in the equations with more parameters, thus providing more robust results.

5.4 Results

5.4.1 Descriptive analysis

Table 5.1 summarizes the descriptive statistics for the companies' level of CSP, CEP, CGP, CMR and CFR for the full sample from 2005 to 2012. As can be appreciated, the companies in the sample enjoy higher scores on social and environmental performance than on corporate governance performance. Specifically, the

Table 5.1 Descriptive statistics of the companies' corporate social performance (CSP), environmental performance (CEP), governance performance (CGP), corporate market return (CMR) and corporate financial risk (CFR) (2005–2012)

		Mean	*Median*	*Maximum*	*Minimum*	*Std. Dev.*	*Skewness*	*Kurtosis*	*Obs.*
2005–2012	**CSP**	66.8837	79.5500	98.7000	3.4400	30.3631	−0.8511	2.2822	1000
	CEP	72.9865	87.2650	96.9600	9.3000	27.1683	−1.1876	2.9200	1000
	CGP	32.8726	20.2250	95.2900	1.4900	28.9782	0.7145	20.8045	1000
	CMR	0.0416	0.0159	2.5989	−0.8554	0.3671	1.1350	6.9237	1000
	CFR	0.0213	0.0194	0.0567	0.0077	0.0078	1.1131	4.3539	1000
2012	**CSP**	83.9933	89.8400	97.4200	13.3200	16.3833	−2.4353	9.3717	125
	CEP	87.5286	91.7600	94.2100	27.1200	11.0049	−3.2454	15.0924	125
	CGP	41.4242	36.4000	94.7800	1.6000	28.7322	0.3585	1.7091	125
	CMR	0.0439	0.0335	0.7449	−0.6806	0.2565	0.2247	3.6609	125
	CFR	0.0192	0.0179	0.0567	0.0093	0.0068	1.9055	9.4218	125
2011	**CSP**	83.8410	89.6900	97.4800	5.4700	18.0155	−2.4468	9.3145	125
	CEP	85.8173	90.5400	94.3900	21.2500	13.5226	−2.8459	11.2065	125
	CGP	43.3803	35.4400	93.1000	1.8600	28.9327	0.3841	1.7115	125
	CMR	−0.1421	−0.1282	0.2564	−0.7154	0.2024	−0.2904	2.7751	125
	CFR	0.0225	0.0215	0.0563	0.0115	0.0062	1.7878	9.5963	125

(*Continued*)

Table 5.1 (Continued)

		Mean	Median	Maximum	Minimum	Std. Dev.	Skewness	Kurtosis	Obs.
2010	**CSP**	66.7836	80.8900	97.6700	4.1400	31.0419	−0.8413	2.1997	125
	CEP	74.0642	89.0100	94.8400	9.3000	26.5233	−1.2479	3.1510	125
	CGP	35.7529	20.9200	95.2600	2.1700	30.9088	0.6184	1.8529	125
	CMR	0.1402	0.1314	0.9579	−0.5080	0.2761	0.3444	3.4704	125
	CFR	0.0186	0.0181	0.0312	0.0117	0.0044	0.8702	3.3210	125
2009	**CSP**	66.8583	78.9700	97.8000	3.9600	30.3996	−0.7970	2.2029	125
	CEP	74.5549	88.1800	94.3600	10.0100	25.6157	−1.2964	3.2848	125
	CGP	34.4303	20.3700	92.0300	1.4900	30.2338	0.5947	1.8674	125
	CMR	0.2148	0.1707	1.8376	−0.4375	0.3983	1.0959	4.8693	125
	CFR	0.0261	0.0257	0.0534	0.0136	0.0068	0.6685	3.9599	125
2008	**CSP**	66.0768	76.2900	97.6800	3.5300	29.5139	−0.8876	2.4766	125
	CEP	72.0757	86.7800	94.0100	9.6900	27.5759	−1.1978	2.9320	125
	CGP	29.5052	16.1800	95.2900	1.5600	27.9657	0.8432	2.2979	125
	CMR	−0.3464	−0.3806	0.3812	−0.8554	0.2257	0.4796	3.1727	125
	CFR	0.0334	0.0332	0.0534	0.0189	0.0068	0.2194	2.7041	125
2007	**CSP**	58.7950	69.6300	97.8900	3.4400	32.0759	−0.4841	1.7532	125
	CEP	67.0459	82.2500	94.8400	9.8900	29.9324	−0.8599	2.1451	125
	CGP	27.6527	14.1700	93.1000	1.5800	27.8063	0.9592	2.5486	125
	CMR	−0.0883	−0.1163	0.5369	−0.5459	0.2197	0.4817	3.1242	125
	CFR	0.0184	0.0179	0.0302	0.0086	0.0043	0.3114	2.7219	125
2006	**CSP**	56.0922	62.6600	98.5400	5.2600	31.8778	−0.3056	1.6445	125
	CEP	62.0513	73.5100	96.6600	12.4500	30.7604	−0.4252	1.6269	125
	CGP	25.4541	13.4900	94.1200	2.1200	25.8506	1.1437	2.9868	125
	CMR	0.0804	0.0497	1.2427	−0.5418	0.2839	1.1635	5.5462	125
	CFR	0.0178	0.0173	0.0306	0.0095	0.0044	0.5606	2.8628	125
2005	**CSP**	52.6296	55.0200	98.7000	6.3800	32.5078	−0.0314	1.4705	125
	CEP	60.7539	70.7300	96.9600	12.9700	31.4611	−0.3025	1.4593	125
	CGP	25.3808	13.0500	90.6700	2.2900	25.7464	1.0586	2.7312	125
	CMR	0.4305	0.3380	2.5989	−0.3532	0.4092	1.9012	9.2920	125
	CFR	0.0148	0.0144	0.0235	0.0077	0.0037	0.4153	2.5441	125

Note: For every period of the sample considered.

considered firms achieve better levels of CEP (72.98) than in the other two dimensions (CSP = 66.88 and CGP = 32.87).

The maximum and minimum values of the CSP, CEP and CGP composite indexes reveal a wide diversity in the values of the firms' performance in those three dimensions. For example, the most successful company in terms of CSP achieves a score of 98.7, whereas the least successful reaches a value of 3.44. It is

Table 5.2 Correlations between firms' financial, environmental, social and governance performance

	CSP	CEP	CGP	CMR	CFR
CSP	1				
CEP	0.7373	1			
CGP	0.5965	0.3660	1		
CMR	0.0820	0.0832	0.0382	1	
CFR	0.1007	0.0862	0.1562	0.3132	1

This table shows the cross-correlations between the companies' corporate social performance (CSP), environmental performance (CEP), governance performance (CGP), corporate market return (CMR) and corporate financial risk (CFR).

worth mentioning that the same pattern is observed when examining the companies' levels of CEP and CGP. These issues suggest the existence of different stakeholder orientations among the companies in the sample. In general, a positive trend is observed in the companies' levels of CSP, CEP and CGP along the entire time period analyzed, thus suggesting a growing commitment of the companies to the social, environmental and corporate governance business dimensions.

Market-based data indicate a slightly different trend in CMR and CFR. The positive trend in CMR identified in 2005 and 2006 seems to be truncated by the emergence of the global financial crisis that led to the main developed countries entering into a period of economic recession. This effect is revealed by an average negative market return displayed by the companies in 2007 and 2008. This structural economic setting seems also to have affected stock volatility since 2007, such as indicated by the values of CFR.

Table 5.2 shows the cross-correlations between the variables under investigation (i.e., CSP, CEP, CGP, CMR and CFR) for the full time period. As can be observed, CSP is strongly and positively correlated with firms' CEP and positively correlated with companies' CGP, whereas CGP is positively correlated with firms' CEP but with less intensity. Furthermore, although the market-based measures of companies' FP are positively correlated with the firms' CSP, CEP and CGP, correlation coefficients are of minor magnitude. Finally, CMR is slightly correlated with financial risk (CFR), an issue that is consistent with the notion that a more volatile stock should be compensated with a higher return.

5.4.2 Regression analysis

This section focuses on analyzing whether the companies' country context influences their level of CSP, CEP and CGP and if it plays a moderating role in the relationship between the companies' CSP, CEP, CGP and CFP. Accordingly, the estimates of model 1 (i.e., equations (5.1) to (5.3)) and model 2 (i.e., equations (5.4) to (5.6)) are shown in Tables 5.4 and 5.5, respectively. The optimal laglength selection for each model is shown in Table 5.3. According to the AIC and

Table 5.3 Optimal lag-length selection for the explanatory models

Eq. (5.1) Impact on CSP			Eq. (5.2) Impact on CEP		
Lag (year)	AIC	SIC	Lag (year)	AIC	SIC
1 (2011)	10.1623	10.2993	**1 (2011)**	9.6914	9.8113
2 (2010)	10.1676	10.3014	**2 (2010)**	9.7001	9.8203
3 (2009)	**10.1800**	**10.3189**	**3 (2009)**	**9.7141**	**9.8245**
4 (2008)	10.1750	10.3145	**4 (2008)**	9.7003	9.8199
5 (2007)	10.1743	10.3136	**5 (2007)**	9.7001	9.8191
6 (2006)	10.1701	10.3104	**6 (2006)**	9.6945	9.8165
7 (2005)	10.1677	10.3061	**7 (2005)**	9.6923	9.8133

Eq. (5.3) Impact on CGP			Eq. (5.4) Impact on the CSP-CFP relation		
Lag (year)	AIC	SIC	Lag (year)	AIC	SIC
1 (2011)	9.2669	9.3348	**1 (2011)**	9.1323	9.2911
2 (2010)	9.2691	9.3356	**2 (2010)**	9.1421	9.3003
3 (2009)	**9.2752**	**9.3423**	**3 (2009)**	**9.1455**	**9.3069**
4 (2008)	9.2730	9.3397	**4 (2008)**	9.1432	9.3055
5 (2007)	9.2701	9.3375	**5 (2007)**	9.1430	9.3052
6 (2006)	9.2694	9.3365	**6 (2006)**	9.1366	9.2919
7 (2005)	9.2692	9.3361	**7 (2005)**	9.1303	9.2903

Eq. (5.5) Impact on the CEP-CFP relation			Eq. (5.6) Impact on the CGP-CFP relation		
Lag (year)	AIC	SIC	Lag (year)	AIC	SIC
1 (2011)	8.6523	8.9912	**1 (2011)**	8.9521	8.9903
2 (2010)	8.6598	8.9945	**2 (2010)**	8.9533	8.9934
3 (2009)	**8.6621**	**8.9993**	**3 (2009)**	**8.9699**	**9.1001**
4 (2008)	8.6612	8.9978	**4 (2008)**	8.9602	9.0522
5 (2007)	8.6601	8.9965	**5 (2007)**	8.9592	9.0301
6 (2006)	8.6576	8.9889	**6 (2006)**	8.9500	8.9948
7 (2005)	8.6411	8.9802	**7 (2005)**	8.9423	8.9871

The table shows the values reached by the AIC and the SIC for each lag of the econometric models (i.e., equations (5.1) to (5.6)). The best lag-length selection is shown in bold.

SIC, the optimal lag-length for the three equations of the first model is three lags: that is, companies' CSP, CEP and CGP of the last period (i.e., 2012) are measured by their values in the previous three years (i.e., 2011, 2010 and 2009). On the other hand, according to the AIC and SIC, the moderating role of the companies' geographical context between the firms' CSP, CEP, CGP and CFP is implemented by using three lags.

Table 5.4 Influence of the companies' country context on environmental, social and governance performance

Equation (1) Impact on CSP	$\beta_1(CSP_{2011})$	$\beta_2(CSP_{2010})$	$\beta_3(CSP_{2009})$	$\phi_i(Country)$
	0.1499	0.3430	0.8533**	13.0925
	(0.3562)	(0.4702)	(0.4158)	(8.0294)
Equation (2) Impact on CEP	$\beta_1(CEP_{2011})$	$\beta_2(CEP_{2010})$	$\beta_3(CEP_{2009})$	$\phi_i(Country)$
	0.9760***	1.1032***	−0.0104	−10.5084***
	(0.0462)	(0.3569)	(0.3145)	(2.7666)
Equation (3) Impact on CGP	$\beta_1(CGP_{2011})$	$\beta_2(CGP_{2010})$	$\beta_3(CGP_{2009})$	$\phi_i(Country)$
	0.1479	0.4952*	−0.1619	38.8156***
	(0.2606)	(0.2507)	(0.2250)	(7.3866)

This table shows the estimates of equations (5.1) to (5.3), aiming to show the impact of the companies' geographical context on firms' CSP, CEP and CGP. The values in parentheses refer to the standard errors.

*** Significant at the 1% level, ** significant at the 5% level, * significant at the 10% level.

The estimates contained in Table 5.4 indicate that the firms' CSP is partially explained by their social performance achieved in the past periods, as the coefficient for 2009 is significant at the 5 percent level. It is interesting to note that the nonsignificance of the ϕ_i parameter for equation (5.1) reveals that the country context of the different companies does not have an influence on their CSP levels, an issue that confirms the previous results obtained by the implementation of the HJ-biplot by Ortas *et al.* (2015) on the same set of data. Furthermore, Table 5.6 also reveals that the CEP and CGP achieved by the companies depend on their values in different periods. We notice the following two behaviors: (1) the firms' CEP levels in 2012 are positively influenced by their performance achieved in 2010 and, to a lesser extent, in 2011; and (2) the firms' CGP levels in 2012 are only influenced by their performance in 2010.

With regard to the objectives of this research, it is important to examine the sign and significance of the ϕ_i parameters. Looking at the estimates, it can be concluded that the companies' country context determines the firms' CEP and CGP levels. However, its impact on companies' CEP and CGP is of a different nature. On the one hand, the negative sign of the first parameter indicates that the Spanish and French firms score lower on environmental issues than the Japanese firms. On the other hand, the positive sign of the last ϕ_i parameter reveals that Spanish and French firms score better on corporate governance issues than Japanese ones. Such results are in line with the ones by Ortas *et al.* (2015), who use the same dataset but a different methodology. It is important to note that the influence of the significant ϕ_i parameters on firms' CEP and CGP is of a different magnitude. The higher value of the ϕ_i parameter in equation (5.3) than that obtained in equation (5.2) clearly indicates that the influence of being Spanish or French on the firms' CGP is of a higher magnitude than the effect of being Japanese on the companies' CEP.

Table 5.5 Moderating effect of companies' geographical context on firms' relation between environmental, social, governance and financial performance

$\beta_1(CMR_{2011})$	$\beta_2(CMR_{2010})$	$\beta_3(CMR_{2009})$	$\beta_4(CFR_{2011})$	$\beta_5(CFR_{2010})$	$\beta_6(CFR_{2009})$	$\phi_i(Country)$
Equation (5.4) Impact on the CSP–CFP relation						
40.9730***	16.4615**	−12.2386**	−1166.9943**	−1461.7333*	−918.1202	24.9697***
(11.9772)	(8.1358)	(5.7978)	(508.0232)	(795.6950)	(554.1835)	(5.1076)
Equation (5.5) Impact on the CEP-CFP relation						
34.8435***	14.8774**	−9.7495*	−1216.5061***	−1819.9254***	−841.4461*	12.6449***
(10.4138)	(7.0739)	(5.0410)	(441.7118)	(691.8343)	(481.8469)	(4.4409)
Equation (5.6) Impact on the CGP–CFP relation						
−0.4176	−2.4148	−2.5479	−195.3677	−1418.0132**	−135.2340	44.7292***
(10.0686)	(6.8394)	(4.8739)	(427.0700)	(668.9015)	(465.8747)	(4.2937)

This table provides the estimates of equations (5.4) to (5.6), aiming to show the moderating role of the companies' geographical context to the relation between firms' CSP, CEP, CGP and CFP. The values in parentheses refer to the standard errors.
*** Significant at the 1% level, ** significant at the 5% level, * significant at the 10% level.

In short, this leads us to regard hypothesis H1, according to which "Companies from different countries with different institutional backgrounds will have different priorities in terms of social, environmental and corporate governance performances", as validated. France and Spain are rather different than Japan from a cultural and institutional point of view and compared to Japan are rather close to each other; as a consequence, French and Spanish firms are close in terms of CSR, whereas Japanese firms present a different profile.

The estimates of Table 5.5 reveal a different impact of CFP on CSP, CEP and CGP. The companies' annual market return has a strong and positive effect on firms' performance on social and environmental issues. This result is in line with the idea that a more profitable firm has higher slack resources and is more able to invest in social and environmental-related issues. The only exception is the impact of firms' CMR in 2009 on companies' CSP and CEP. This may be explained by the negative effects suffered by the companies because of the impact of the global financial crisis on their market returns. Table 5.5 also reveals that firms' CMR seems not to have an effect on their levels of CGP. In general, firms' financial risk has a negative influence – at different lags – on companies' CSP, CEP and CGP levels. This result is in line with the idea that investors identify low-CSP, low-CEP and low-CGP firms to be riskier investments.

More interesting to the objectives of this research is the fact that the companies' country context plays a crucial role in the relationship between the firms' CSP, CEP, CGP and CFP. Specifically, the positive sign of the ϕ_i parameters reveals that the financial factors have a higher influence on firms' CSP, CEP and CGP for the French and Spanish firms than for the Japanese ones. Finally, we find a higher impact of the country context on the relationship between financial factors and the companies' CGP and CSP than on the relationship between financial factors and the environmental dimension.

Thus, hypothesis H2, according to which "The relationship between CSR performance and financial performance of a firm is affected according to its country's institutional background", may be regarded as validated too.

5.5 Concluding remarks

In a neoinstitutional approach (DiMaggio and Powell, 1991a, 1991b; Meyer and Rowan, 1991), firms from different countries often adopt different management styles, implement different organizational choices and even weigh differently main business objectives, such as profitability, growth and CSR objectives. Based on such an approach, it was expected that firms from France, Japan and Spain, the three countries with the most firms committed to the UNGC initiative, would rank differently in terms of social, environmental and corporate governance issues as priorities in their CSR policies, and thus would perform differently in these three different fields. This led to our H1 hypothesis, according to which "Companies from different countries with different institutional backgrounds, will have different priorities in terms of social, environmental and corporate governance performances". Furthermore, in line with Amann *et al.* (2007), it was expected that the link between CSR performance and financial performance would be moderated by the institutional environment of firms, namely of the country they come from. This led to hypothesis H2, according to which "The relationship between CSR performance and financial performance of a firm is affected according to its country's institutional background".

In order to test H1 and H2, a sample of 125 firms was carefully drawn from the three countries, with relevant data on their CSP, CEP, and CGP on one side, and on their CFP on the other side (CMR and CFR). With the help of a regression analysis, both hypotheses are validated.

More specifically, Spanish and French firms achieve similarly higher levels of social and corporate governance performance than Japanese firms, but the latter are more committed to environmental issues than are the former. Furthermore, financial performance has a greater influence on the three dimensions of CSR performance (social, environmental and corporate governance) for French and Spanish firms than for Japanese ones.

One may thus wonder why CSR is more environment oriented in Japanese firms than in French and Spanish firms. This may result from various national characteristics, such as the high population concentration in Japan in huge urban areas, which led to them being highly sensitive to environmental issues from the 1970s onwards. One may also consider the influence of Confucian and Buddhist conceptions of the relationship between mankind and nature, which contrasts to some extent with the Christian one (Ortas *et al.*, 2015). One may also wonder why CSR is less governance oriented and even socially oriented in Japanese companies than in French and Spanish companies. In broad terms, a stronger inclination in the case of Japan to informal and undisclosed arrangements may partly explain this outcome, among other institutional reasons.

Appendix 1
Topics comprised in the CSP, CEP and CGP composite indexes

CSP composite index subdivisions:

- *Product responsibility:* This category measures a company's management commitment and effectiveness towards creating value-added products and services upholding the customer's security. It reflects a company's capacity to maintain its license to operate by producing quality goods and services integrating the customer's health and safety through accurate product information and labeling.
- *Community:* This category measures a company's management commitment and effectiveness towards maintaining the company's reputation within the general community (local, national and global). It reflects a company's capacity to maintain its license to operate by being a good citizen (donations of cash, goods or staff time, etc.), protecting public health (avoidance of industrial accidents, etc.) and respecting business ethics (avoiding bribery and corruption, etc.).
- *Human rights:* This category measures a company's management commitment and effectiveness towards respecting the fundamental human rights conventions. It reflects a company's capacity to maintain its license to operate by guaranteeing the freedom of association and excluding child, forced or compulsory labor.
- *Diversity and opportunity:* This category measures a company's management commitment and effectiveness towards maintaining diversity and equal opportunities in its workforce. It reflects a company's capacity to increase its workforce loyalty and productivity by promoting an effective life–work balance, a family-friendly environment and equal opportunities regardless of gender, age, ethnicity, religious or sexual orientation.
- *Employment quality:* This category measures a company's management commitment and effectiveness towards providing high-quality employment benefits and job conditions. It reflects a company's capacity to increase its workforce loyalty and productivity by distributing rewarding and fair employment benefits, and by focusing on long-term employment growth and stability by promoting from within, avoiding layoffs and maintaining relations with trade unions.

- *Health and safety:* This category measures a company's management commitment and effectiveness towards providing a healthy and safe workplace. It reflects a company's capacity to increase its workforce loyalty and productivity by integrating into its day-to-day operations a concern for the physical and mental health, well-being and stress levels of all employees.
- *Training and development:* This category measures a company's management commitment and effectiveness towards providing training and development (education) for its workforce. It reflects a company's capacity to increase its intellectual capital, workforce loyalty and productivity by developing the workforce's skills, competences, employability and careers in an entrepreneurial environment.

CEP composite index subdivisions:

- *Emissions reduction:* This category measures a company's management commitment and effectiveness towards reducing hazardous environmental emissions in its production and operational processes. It reflects a company's capacity to reduce air emissions (greenhouse gases, F-gases, ozone-depleting substances, NOx and SOx, etc.), waste, hazardous waste, water discharges and spills and their impact on biodiversity and to partner with environmental organizations to reduce the environmental impact of the company in the local or broader community.
- *Product innovation:* This category measures a company's management commitment and effectiveness towards supporting the research and development of eco-efficient products or services. It reflects a company's capacity to reduce the environmental costs and burdens for its customers, thereby creating new market opportunities through new environmental technologies and processes or also eco-designed, dematerialized products with extended durability.
- *Resource reduction:* This category measures a company's management commitment and effectiveness towards achieving an efficient use of natural resources in the production process. It reflects a company's capacity to reduce the use of materials, energy or water and to find more eco-efficient solutions by improving the supply chain management.

CGP composite index subdivisions:

- *Board functions:* This category measures a company's management commitment and effectiveness towards following best-practice corporate governance principles related to board activities and functions. It reflects a company's capacity to have an effective board by setting up the essential board committees with allocated tasks and responsibilities.
- *Board structure:* This category measures a company's management commitment and effectiveness towards following best-practice corporate governance principles related to a well-balanced membership of the board. It reflects a

company's capacity to ensure a critical exchange of ideas and an independent decision-making process through an experienced, diverse and independent board.

- *Compensation policy:* This category measures a company's management commitment and effectiveness towards following best-practice corporate governance principles related to competitive and proportionate management compensation. It reflects a company's capacity to attract and retain executives and board members with the necessary skills by linking their compensation to individual or company-wide financial or extra-financial targets.
- *Vision and strategy:* This category measures a company's management commitment and effectiveness towards the creation of an overarching vision and strategy integrating financial and extra-financial aspects. It reflects a company's capacity to convincingly show and communicate that it integrates the economic, social and environmental dimensions into its day-to-day decision-making processes.
- *Shareholder rights:* This category measures a company's management commitment and effectiveness towards following best-practice corporate governance principles related to its shareholder policy and equal treatment of shareholders. It reflects a company's capacity to be attractive to minority shareholders by ensuring them equal rights and privileges and by limiting the use of anti-takeover devices.

Appendix 2

List of the companies in the sample

ID French companies

1 Air France-KLM
2 Alcatel-Lucent
3 Alstom
4 Bollore
5 Bouygues
6 Carrefour
7 Casino Guichard
8 CNP assurances
9 Credit Agricole
18 Renault
19 Saint Gobain
20 Sanofi
21 Schneider electric
22 SCOR se
23 SEB
24 Societe Generale
25 Sodexo
26 Technip

Japanese companies

34 Aeon
35 Ajinomoto
36 All Nippon airways
37 Asahi group holdings
38 Asahi Kasei
39 Astellas Pharma
40 Benesse holdings
41 Canon marketing, Japan
42 Casio computer
51 DIC
52 Dowa holding
53 Ebara
54 Fuji electric
55 Fujikura
56 Fujitsu
57 Fukuoka financial group
58 Hirose electric
59 Hitachi chemical
68 Komatsu
69 Kyocera
70 Minebea
71 Mitsubishi electric
72 Mitsubishi heavy inds.
73 Mitsubishi ufj finl. Group
74 Mitsubishi
75 Mitsui chemicals
76 Mitsui osk lines
85 Resona holdings
86 Ricoh
87 Ryohin keikaku
88 Seiko Epson
89 Sekisui chemical
90 Shimizu
91 Shin-etsu chemical
92 Shinko elec. inds.
93 Shiseido
102 Tokio marine holdings
103 Tokyo electron
104 Toppan printing
105 Toshiba
106 Toto
107 Yamaha
108 Yokogawa electric

Spanish companies

109 Abengoa
118 Ferrovial
119 FCC
120 Gamesa
121 Gas natural
122 Indra sistemas
123 NH hoteles
124 Red electrica corpn.
125 Repsol YPF

10 Danone
11 Dassault Systemes
12 Klepierre
13 L'oreal
14 Lafarge
15 Lagardere groupe
16 Natixis
17 Peugeot

27 Tele-performance
28 Thales
29 Total
30 Valeo
31 Veolia environnement
32 Vinci
33 Vivendi

43 Chiyoda
44 Citizen holding
45 Cosmo oil
46 Dai Nippon printing
47 Daiichi sankyo
48 Daikin industries
49 Daiwa securities group
50 Dentsu

60 Hitachi high-techs.
61 Hitachi
62 Inpex
63 Itochu
64 JSR
65 KAO
66 Kikkoman
67 Kirin holdings

77 Mitsui
78 Mizuho finl. Group
79 Nissan motor
80 Obayashi
81 Olympus
82 Omron
83 Osaka gas
84 Renesas electronics

94 Sojitz
95 Sumitomo Mitsui Financial Group
96 Sumitomo Mitsui Trust Holding
97 Sumitomo Mitsui Trust Holding
98 Sysmex
99 Takeda pharmaceutical
100 Teijin
101 Terumo

110 Abertis infraestructuras
111 Acciona
112 ACS
113 Banco popular español
114 Bankinter 'r'
115 BBVA
116 Ebro foods
117 Endesa

References

Aaronson S.A. (2003) Corporate Responsibility in the Global Village: The British Role Model and the American Laggard, *Business & Society Review*, 108(3), pp. 309–338.

Accenture and UNGC (2010) *A New Era of Sustainability*, United Nations Global Compact-Accenture CEO Study 2010, New York: Accenture Institute for High Performance.

Adams C.A., Hill W. and Roberts C.B. (1998) Corporate Social Reporting Practices in Western Europe: Legitimating Corporate Behavior?, *The British Accounting Review*, 30(1), pp. 1–21.

Aerts W., Cormier D. and Magnan M. (2006) Intra-industry Imitation in Corporate Environmental Reporting: An International Perspective, *Journal of Accounting and Public Policy*, 25(3), pp. 299–331.

Amann B., Caby J., Jaussaud J. and Piniero J. (2007) Shareholder Activism for Corporate Social Responsibility: Law, and Practices in the United States, Japan, France and Spain, in *The New Corporate Accountability, Corporate Social Responsibility and the Law*, (eds) McBarnet D., Voiculescu A. and Campbell T., Cambridge University Press, Cambridge, pp. 336–364.

Aoki M. (1988) *Information, Incentives and Bargaining in the Japanese Economy*, Cambridge University Press, Cambridge.

Arevalo J.A., Aravind D., Ayuso S. and Roca M. (2013) The Global Compact: An Analysis of the Motivations of Adoption in the Spanish Context, *Business Ethics: A European Review*, 22(1), pp. 1–14.

Ayuso S. and Mutis J. (2010) El Pacto Mundial de las Naciones Unidas – ¿una herramienta para asegurar la responsabilidad global de las empresas?, *Globalización, competitividad y Gobernanza, Universia*, 4(2), pp. 28–38.

Ayuso S. and Roca M. (2010) *Las empresas españolas y el Pacto Mundial*, Documento de Trabajo Cátedra MANGO RSC, 8.

Ball A. and Craig R. (2010) Using Neo-institutionalism to Advance Social and Environmental Accounting, *Critical Perspectives on Accounting*, 21(4), pp. 283–293.

Ball R., Kothari S.P. and Robin A. (2000) The Effect of International Institutional Factors on Properties of Accounting Earnings, *Journal of Accounting and Economics*, 29(1), pp. 1–51.

Bansal P. (2005) Evolving Sustainably: A Longitudinal Study of Corporate Sustainable Development, *Strategic Management Journal*, 26(3), pp. 197–218.

Baughn, C.C., Bodie, N.L. and McIntosh, J.C. (2007) Corporate Social and Environmental Responsibility in Asian Countries and Other Geographical Regions, *Corporate Social Responsibility and Environment Management*, 14, pp. 189–205.

Baxter J. and Chua W.F. (2003) Alternative Management Accounting Research – Whence and Whither, *Accounting, Organizations and Society*, 28(2–3), pp. 97–126.

Bebbington J., Higgins C. and Frame B. (2009) Initiating Sustainable Development Reporting: Evidence from New Zealand, *Accounting, Auditing & Accountability Journal*, 22(4), pp. 588–625.

Bennie L., Bernhagen P. and Mitchell N.J. (2007) The Logic of Transnational Action: The Good Corporation and the Global Compact, *Political Studies*, 55(4), pp. 733–753.

Boiral O. (2003) ISO 9000: Outside the Iron Cage, *Organization Science*, 14(6), pp. 720–737.

Boiral O. (2007) Corporate Greening through ISO 14001: A Rational Myth?, *Organization Science*, 18(1), pp. 127–146.

Brammer S.J., Brooks C. and Pavelin S. (2006) Corporate Social Performance and Stock Returns: Evidence from Disaggregate Measures, *Financial Management*, 35(3), pp. 97–116.

Bushman R.M., Pietroski J. and Smith A. (2004) What Determines Corporate Transparency?, *Journal of Accounting Research*, 42(2), pp. 207–252.

Byrd L.S. (2009) Collaborative Corporate Social Responsibility: A Case Study Examination of the International Public Relations Agency Involvement in the United Nations Global Compact, *Corporate Communications: An International Journal*, 14(3), pp. 303–319.

Campbell D. (2003) Intra- and Intersectoral Effects in Environmental Disclosures: Evidence for Legitimacy Theory?, *Business Strategy Environnement*, 12, pp. 357–371.

Cetindamar D. and Husoy K. (2007) Corporate Social Responsibility Practices and Environmentally Responsible Behaviour: The Case of the United Nations Global Compact, *Journal of Business Ethics*, 76(2), pp. 163–176.

Chapple W. and Moon J. (2005) Corporate Social Responsibility (CSR) in Asia: A Seven-country Study of CSR Web Site Reporting, *Business & Society*, 44(4), pp. 415–441.

DiMaggio P.J. and Powell W.W. (1991a) Introduction, in (eds.) Dimaggio P.J. And Powell W.W., *The New Institutionalism in Organizational Analysis*, The University of Chicago Press, Chicago and London, pp. 1–38.

DiMaggio P.J. and Powell W.W. (1991b) The Iron Cage Revisited: Institutional Isomorphism and Collective Rationality in Organizational Fields, in (eds.) Dimaggio P.J. And Powell W.W *The New Institutionalism in Organizational Analysis*, The University of Chicago Press, Chicago and London, pp. 63–82.

European Commission (2003) *Mapping Instruments for Corporate Social Responsibility*, Luxembourg: Employment & Social Affairs.

European Commission (2004) *ABC of the Main Instruments of Corporate Social Responsibility*, Luxembourg: Employment & Social Affairs.

Frederick W.C. (2006) *Corporation Be Good! The Story of Corporate Social Responsibility*, Dog Ear Publishing, Indianapolis.

Frías-Aceituno J.V., Rodriguez-Ariza L. and García-Sánchez I.M. (2012) The Role of the Board in the Dissemination of Integrated Corporate Social Reporting, *Corporate Social Responsibility and Environmental Management*, 20(4), pp. 219–233.

Garayar A. and Calvo J.A. (2012) Joining the UN Global Compact: An Institutional Approach, *Revista de Contabilidad*, 15(2), pp. 311–355.

Hiss S. (2009) From Implicit to Explicit Corporate Social Responsibility: Institutional Change as a Fight for Myths, *Business Ethics Quarterly*, 19(3), pp. 433–451.

Hofstede G. (1980) *Culture's Consequences*, Sage Publications, Beverly Hills.

Janney J.J., Dess G. and Forlani V. (2009) Glass Houses? Market Reactions to Firms Joining the UN Global Compact, *Journal of Business Ethics*, 90(3), pp. 407–423.

Kell G. (2013) 12 Years Later: Reflections on the Growth of the UN Global Compact, *Business & Society*, 52(1), pp. 31–52.

Kimber D. and Lipton P. (2005) Corporate Governance and Business Ethics in the Asia–Pacific Region, *Business & Society*, 44(2), pp. 178–210.

Kolk A. and Perego P. (2010) Determinants of the Adoption of Sustainability Assurance Statements: An International Investigation, *Business Strategy and the Environment*, 19, pp. 182–198.

Larrinaga-González C. (2007) Sustainability Reporting: Insights from Neoinstitutional Theory, in *Sustainability Accounting and Accountability*, (eds) Unerman J., O'Dwyer B. and Bebbington J., Routledge, London, pp. 150–167.

Maignan I. and Ralston D.A. (2002) Corporate Social Responsibility in Europe and the US: Insights from Businesses' Self-presentations, *Journal of International: Business Studies*, 33, pp. 497–514.

Meyer J.W. and Rowan B. (1991) Institutionalized Organizations: Formal Structure as Myth and Ceremony, in (eds.) Dimaggio P.J. And Powell W.W., *The New Institutionalism in Organizational Analysis*, The University of Chicago Press, Chicago/London, pp. 41–62.

Miyashita K. and Russel D. (1994) *Keiretsu, Inside the Hidden Japanese Conglomerates*, New York: McGraw Hill.

Nakane C. (1970) *Japanese Society*, Tuttle Classics, Tokyo.

OECD (2001) *Codes of Corporate Conduct: Expanded Review of their Contents*, OECD Working Papers on International Investment 2001/6, Directorate for Financial, Fiscal and Enterprise Affairs.

Orlitzky M., Schmidt F. and Rynes S. (2003) Corporate Social and Financial Performance: A Meta-analysis, *Organization Studies*, 24(3), pp. 403–441.

Ortas E., Alvarez I., Jaussaud J. and Garayar A. (2015) The Impact of Institutional and Social Context on Corporate Environmental, Social and Governance Performance of Companies Committed to Voluntary Corporate Social Responsibility Initiatives, *Journal of Cleaner Production*, 108(A), pp. 673–684.

Perez-Batres L.A., Miller M.M. and Pisani, M.J. (2010) Sustainability and the Meaning of Global Reporting for Latin American Corporations, *Journal of Business Ethics*, 51(2), pp. 193–209.

Perez-Batres L.A., Miller V.V. and Pisani M.J. (2011) Institutionalizing Sustainability: An Empirical Study of Corporate Registration and Commitment to the United Nations Global Compact Guidelines, *Journal of Cleaner Production*, 19(8), pp. 843–851.

Prado-Lorenzo J.M., García-Sánchez I.M. and Blazquez-Zaballos A. (2013) El impacto del sistema cultural en la transparencia corporativa, *Revista Europea de Dirección y Economía de la Empresa*, 22(3), pp. 143–154.

Rasche A. (2009) Toward a Model to Compare and Analyze Accountability Standards–The Case of the UN Global Compact, *Corporate Social Responsibility and Environmental Management*, 16(4), pp. 192–205.

Rasche A., Waddock S. and McIntosh M. (2012) The United Nations Global Compact: Retrospect and Prospect, *Business & Society*, 52(1), pp. 6–30.

Ruggie J.G. (2004) The Global Compact: An Extraordinary Journey, in *Raising the Bar: Creating Value with the UN Global Compact*, (eds) Fussler C., Cramer A. and van der Vegt S., Greenleaf Publishing, Sheffield, UK, pp. 15–17.

Runhaar H. and Lafferty H. (2009) Governing Corporate Social Responsibility: An Assessment of the Contribution of the UN Global Compact to CSR Strategies in the Telecommunications Industry, *Journal of Business Ethics*, 84, pp. 479–495.

Schwartz H. (1994) Are There Universal Aspects in the Structure and Contents of Human Values?, *Journal of Social Issues*, 50(4), pp. 19–45.

Selznick P. (1996) Institutionalism "Old" and "New", *Administrative Science Quarterly*, 41(2), pp. 270–277.

Simnett R., Vanstrealen A. and Chua W.F. (2009) Assurance on Sustainability Reports: An International Comparison, *The Accounting Review*, 84(3), pp. 937–967.

Smith J., Adhikari A. and Tondkar R. (2005) Exploring Differences in Social Disclosures Internationally: A Stakeholder Perspective, *Journal of Accounting and Public Policy*, 24(2), pp. 123–151.

UNGCO (2007) *United Nations Global Compact Annual Review 2007*, United Nations Global Compact Office, New York.

UNGCO (2009) *United Nations Global Compact Annual Review 2009*, United Nations Global Compact Office, New York.

UNGCO (2010) *United Nations Global Compact Annual Review 2010*, United Nations Global Compact Office, New York.

UNGCO (2012) *United Nations Global Compact Annual Review 2012*, United Nations Global Compact Office, New York.

UNGCO (2013) *United Nations Global Compact Annual Review 2013*, United Nations Global Compact Office, New York.

UNRISD (2002) *Promoting Socially Responsible Business in Developing Countries: The Potential and Limits of Voluntary Initiatives*, United Nations Research Institute for Social Development, New York.

Vormedal I. (2005) *Governance through Learning: The UN Global Compact and Corporate Responsibility*, Report n° 7/05, Program for Research and Documentation for a Sustainable Society-ProSus-, Oslo: University of Oslo.

Waddock S. (2004) Creating Corporate Accountability: Foundational Principles to Make Corporate Citizenship Real, *Journal of Business Ethics*, 50(4), pp. 313–327.

Waddock S. (2008) Building a New Institutional Infrastructure for Corporate Responsibility, *The Academy of Management Perspectives*, 22(3), pp. 87–108.

Waddock S., Mirvis P.H. and Ryu K. (2008) *Learning, Practice, Results: In Good Company*, United Nations Global Compact Office, Boston College and Accountability.

Welford R. (2004) Corporate Social Responsibility in Europe and Asia: Critical Elements and Best Practice, *Journal of Corporate Citizenship*, 13, pp. 31–47.

Welford R. (2005) Corporate Social Responsibility in Europe, North America and Asia, *Journal of Corporate Citizenship*, 17, pp. 33–52.

6 Does corporate social responsibility enhance the international transfer of environmental management?

Tatsuo Kimbara and Kazuma Murakami

6.1 Introduction

Since the 1990s, the development of the triple bottom line (Elkington, 1998), the Global Compact and ISO26000 indicate that firms must achieve social responsibility in their economic, social, and environmental dimensions. In particular, environmental protection requirements have become important for the sustainability of the Earth.

For sustainable development, Agenda 21 is a UN guide for individuals, businesses, and governments in making choices for less environmentally destructive developments. Multinational enterprises (MNEs) in developed countries operating globally can, in particular, contribute to environmental preservation. They can play a critical role in the reduction of negative environmental impacts through the transfer of advanced environmentally friendly practices and technologies. Various MNE practices and technologies could improve the environmental preservation capacity and performance of the host economy when eco-friendly technologies and practices are transferred to the host country. This kind of contribution toward sustainable development is required as a component of corporate social responsibility (CSR).

This chapter analyzes the relationship between CSR and the transfer of environmental management in the firms' overseas operations. It examines what practices and technologies firms transfer under what conditions and the driving forces of such transfers in relation to CSR. The literature review in the second section briefly considers the concept of CSR in the existing studies to clarify the concept in relation to environmental issues. The third section explains the data and the variables used in this chapter, and the fourth section indicates the analytical model used. The fifth section discusses the results of the analysis, and the sixth section summarizes the conclusions and the implications of the study.

6.2 Literature review

CSR is defined as a concept whereby companies integrate social and environmental concerns in their business operations and interactions with their stakeholders on a voluntary basis, going therefore beyond their legal obligations (European

Commission, 2001). In contrast, the World Business Council for Sustainable Development (WBCSD, 1999: 3) defines CSR as "the commitment by business to contribute to economic development while improving the quality of life of the workforce as well as of the community and society at large". CSR is the relationship between firms and society. It imposes obligations resulting from the social contract between business and society (Lantos, 2001). The essential function of CSR is to understand societal needs and recognize societal expectations (De Schutter, 2008). The nature of CSR changes when the role of the firms changes with the passage of time.

Historically, the origins of CSR are found in socially responsible investment (SRI) in the early twentieth century (Lantos, 2001). SRI was begun so as to avoid investments with firms in the alcohol, gambling, and tobacco industries from the perspective of Christian ethics. In the 1960s and 1970s, SRI expanded to exclude the armaments industry because of disagreement with the Vietnam War. In those decades, environmental pollution and lack of consumer protection were criticisms fired at big business. In 1976, the OECD published the MNE code of conduct, "OECD MNEs Guideline", and a revised version was published in June 2000. From the late 1980s to the 1990s, sustainability became a global concern. The protection of the environment was understood as an important CSR requirement.

Administratively, the US government established the Equal Employment Opportunity Commission in 1965, the Environmental Protection Agency in 1970, and the Consumer Product Safety Commission in 1972. Through these measures of institutional legitimacy, employees, consumers, and the community are recognized as important stakeholders. In 1999, the Secretary General of the UN proposed a code of conduct, the UN Global Compact, in relation to human rights, labor, the environment, and anticorruption. These moves resulted in the publication of ISO26000 in 2011. ISO26000, which defines the social responsibility of all kinds of organizations, lists seven core issues: governance of organizations, human rights, labor practices, the environment, fair business practices, consumer issues, and community involvement and development. Thus, ISO26000 emphasizes social policies as a common responsibility for all organizations.

Following the Global Reporting Initiative (GRI), the UN Global Compact, and ISO26000 guidelines, MNEs came to recognize the necessity of adopting systematic supply chain management because the guidelines include child labor and human rights protection in developing countries. CSR practices in supply chain management are required to implement effective preservation of the environment and establish fair practices with respect to labor and employment conditions. In addition to this, SCOPE 3, which was published in 2011, asked firms to calculate and disclose their greenhouse gas (GHG) emissions data in the supply chain as a whole. Furthermore, another requirement is that the natural resources to be used in the supply chain are not disputed resources. Thus, it became necessary for firms to prove the integrity of their entire supply chain.

Friedman (1970) presented one extreme view of CSR. He argued that when firms pursue their own profit, the economy as a whole gains maximum benefit. He believed that the CSR of firms is to increase profits. Consequently, Friedman criticized CSR advocates because CSR is used as a tool by corporate management to strengthen its own position.

Similar criticism was made of the Porter hypothesis in the 1990s, which indicated the compatibility of economic development and the protection of the environment (Walley and Whitehead, 1994). Research interest in the relationship between the economy and the environment has shifted to studying the relationship between CSR and financial performance (Zhelyazkov, 2012). The question then becomes what the functions or components of CSR are. Even though CSR has become increasingly important, the concept is controversial (Wan-Jan, 2006). Elkington (1998) proposed a new concept with sociological, environmental, and economic dimensions, which he termed the triple bottom line. CSR increasingly attracts theoretical and practical interests. Similarly, Carroll (1991) points out the economic, legal, ethical, and altruistic dimensions of CSR. He depicts CSR as a pyramid based on these four dimensions. Lantos (2001, 2002) then classified CSR into ethical CSR, altruistic CSR, and strategic CSR, which takes into consideration the communication activity required to achieve business goals. Schwartz and Carroll (2003) modified Carroll's pyramid by classifying CSR into three fields: economic, legal, and ethical.

Economic theory has argued over CSR from two contrasting approaches. One approach, which supports shareholder sovereignty, argues for the maximization of shareholder value (Friedman, 1970). The other approach supports stakeholder sovereignty, which implies that firms depend on various stakeholders and need to satisfy the requirements of each stakeholder (Hall and Soskice, 2001).

Similarly, in the field of corporate law, there are two dominant approaches to explain CSR. The shareholder approach stresses ownership rights. This approach asserts shareholders' benefit and is negative except for economic CSR. In contrast, the contractual approach regards corporate CSR as a social contract with stakeholders. The contractual approach views a firm as having a bundle of contractual obligations with various stakeholders. This approach emphasizes that all stakeholders commit to firms in a myriad of ways. The employee is involved in the firm in terms of intellectual capital, the customer in his reliance on the firm, and the community in its support of the education and the tax system. CSR, therefore, needs to consider the requirements of all stakeholders.

Porter, who contributed significantly to the development of competitive strategy theory, emphasized the strategic view of CSR (Porter, 2003). Porter and Krammer (2006) classified CSR into two types. In the first type, CSR is the responsibility of business to respond to the introduction of regulations. This understanding of CSR is that of passive compliance in following regulations such as those requirements for pollution control. Social criticism intensified against the antisocial activities on the part of big businesses and led to the code of conduct for MNEs (Hawk, 1977; OECD, 2000). Firms are inclined to respond passively to comply with the regulations introduced.

The second type is strategic CSR. Porter and Krammer (2006) argue that the responsibility of firms is to create activities providing value for both society and the firms. This view emphasizes that when firms intensify their CSR involvement and enjoy high market evaluation, they improve their competitive advantage and their market performance (Lantos, 2001; Porter and Krammer, 2006).

So, it is emphasized that firms should invest in CSR as a part of a corporate strategy to obtain a competitive advantage in the market. This is because the success of firms depends on the existence of adequate infrastructure, appropriate and high-quality education for future employees, collaboration with local suppliers, the high quality of institutions, and the protection of the law. Investment in CSR means a differentiation strategy, which generates new demand and puts a premium price on the products or services provided (McWilliams and Siegel, 2001).

The European Commission (EC, 2001) stresses that a firm's CSR practice leads to high societal evaluation and that it positively affects economic performance. It summarizes four reasons for the positive impact of CSR. First, CSR commitment improves labor conditions, enhances employee organizational loyalty, and motivates increased employee productivity. It can also attract capable human resources. Second, responsible behavior to reduce resource consumption and pollution requires efficient resource utilization. Third, when firms have close relationships with various external stakeholders, firms strengthen stable relationships with them. Fourth, when investors and consumers agree with the increased commitment of firms in CSR activities, it will be reflected by investment in the capital market and consumer purchasing in the product or service market.

The concept of CSR and its theoretical model have changed with the passage of time. CSR is a required societal function that firms have. Each society has its own ethical norms, culture, and religious beliefs. Thus, CSR is fundamentally affected by the social conditions in which firms exist. Even though the CSR concept is disseminating in society and firms, the concept itself remains equivocal. The components of CSR are contingent upon the specific conditions in each society. However, as globalization of the economy and society proceeds, the concept of CSR becomes more standardized, particularly under the influence of the GRI guidelines, the UN Global Compact, and ISO26000. Thus, the content of CSR reports by firms increasingly converges. Therefore, corporate management needs to appropriately respond to the claims on CSR. One of the main dimensions of CSR is environmental issues. Next, the study analyzes environmental practices as a part of CSR and their transfer to different organizations.

It is believed that this research is the first to analyze the relationship between CSR assessment and the international transfer of environmental management. Even though there are existing studies about the international transfer of individual environmental practices such as innovation (Beise and Rennings, 2005; Popp, 2006, 2011; Rennings *et al.*, 2006; Phene and Almeida, 2008), environmental management practices (Florida and Kenney, 1991; Szulanski, 1996), or knowledge (Gupta and Govindarajan, 2000; Pérez-Nordtvedt *et al.*, 2008; Ockwell *et al.*, 2010), no research on the relationship between CSR and the international transfer of environmental practices can be found. It is significant to ascertain the effect that CSR has on the international transfer of practices and how to transfer and diffuse practices to the host country through foreign direct investment. This study, therefore, analyzes the international transfer of environmental management in relation to CSR.

6.3 Data and variables

6.3.1 Data

Data used in this paper are from two sources. First, CSR data are obtained from the CSR assessments by Toyo Keizai Shinpo Sha (2011) "CSR Company Directory 2010". This database has the largest CSR ratings data available in Japan in terms of the number of firms and headings assessed. CSR assessment is similar to environmental rating in the sense that both include environmental assessment. Environmental rating, however, is different from CSR assessment since the former rating does not include social contribution, employment, human resource management, and corporate governance, which the latter assessment does.

The CSR assessment published in 2010 is done for 1,104 firms in September 2009. The assessment has four fields: corporate governance, environmental protection, employment and human development management, and social contribution. The evaluation in each field is a grade of AAA, AA, A, B, or C.

First, corporate governance has 21 headings, which include the unit responsible for CSR, the CSR director, the CSR policy, the ethical code of conduct, and manuals. The aggregate assessment is based on the evaluation of the 21 headings. Second, environmental protection has 21 headings, which include the existence of a responsible organizational unit for the environment, environmental policy, environmental accounting, ISO14001 rating in domestic and overseas operations, the green procurement system, and the midterm plan for CO_2 emissions reduction. Third, employment and human resource management has 24 headings, which include the ratio of women employees to total employees, ratio of females who occupy a position on the board of directors, length of maternity leave, the employment ratio of individuals with a disability, and the frequency ratio of labor accidents. Finally, social contribution has 19 headings, which include the presence of an organizational unit responsible for customer care, a product safety and customer relations unit, the degree of collaboration with nonprofit organizations (NPOs) and nongovernmental organizations (NGOs), ISO19001 certification, and volunteer activity in society.

Thus, CSR assessment for each field provides a score of AAA, AA, A, B, or C. The study uses these five grades converted into a 5-point scale: 5, 4, 3, 2, and 1, respectively. Because there are four fields, the maximum CSR score for a firm is 20 points.

The second data source is the questionnaire survey that was conducted in January and February 2011.[1] From the survey, data were collected on the international transfer of environmental management. The study used Vietnamese researchers in the translation of the questionnaire from Japanese into Vietnamese, and discussions were undertaken on the method for data collection. Vietnamese research assistants were hired to conduct face-to-face interviews with company managers using the structured questionnaire. The number of effective responses obtained was 96. They are linked with the CSR database to obtain 30 sample firms. The study uses this limited sample for the analysis.

6.3.2 *Variables*

The main variables in this study are external factors, the parent firm, strategy of the foreign subsidiary, and the environmental practice and system used in the subsidiary (Tables 6.1 and 6.2). This framework includes significant dimensions in the analysis of strategic management and organization theory.

The external factors have three indicators: GOV means the host government environmental regulation is strict; COM means the community has strong demands on the environment; and CUS means the customer requirements in the market are strong. Next, the indicators of the parent firm are the CSR assessment and owner-ship ratio of Japanese parent firms (JOWN). Of the 30 sample firms, 29 parent

Table 6.1 Descriptive statistics

Variable			Mean	SD
External factor	GOV	Government environmental regulations and mandates are strict	3.800	(0.847)
	COM	Community's demand in Vietnam for environmental performance is strong	3.000	(1.203)
	CUS	Customer's demand in Vietnam market for environmental performance is strong	3.867	(0.937)
Organization of parent firm	CSR	Parent company's CSR assessment score	16.067	(2.959)
	JOWN	The ownership ratio of Japanese parent firms	94.433	(13.640)
Environmental strategy	LDS	Leadership on environmental issues by top management is strong	4.143	(0.591)
	GOAL	Your company has specific goals for reducing environmental burdens	4.167	(0.699)
Management system	ISO	Your company has obtained ISO14001 certification	2.690	(0.604)
	REP	Your company's emission data are reflected to parent company's environmental report	2.933	(0.365)
	GREN	The green procurement level of your company is equal to those of companies in Japan	3.148	(0.949)

Note: The items are measured in a Likert-type 5-point scale, except for ISO and REP, which are measured at 3 points.

Note: The CSR score for one firm is from 4 to 20 points.

Table 6.2 Correlation among variables

		1	2	3	4	5	6	7	8	9
1	GOV	1.00								
2	COM	0.71**	1.00							
3	CUS	0.10	0.21	1.00						
4	CSR	0.14	0.09	−0.11	1.00					
5	JOWN	−0.42*	−0.14	0.28	−0.24	1.00				
6	LDS	0.28	0.11	−0.02	0.28	−0.44*	1.00			
7	GOAL	0.52**	0.20	0.04	0.19	−0.34	0.46*	1.00		
8	MANA	0.30	0.23	−0.03	0.13	−0.24	0.21	0.59**	1.00	
9	GREN	−0.05	0.24	0.20	0.47*	0.28	0.25	0.02	−0.20	1.00

Note: ISO and REP are combined and summed up as MANA.

Note: **$p < 0.01$, * $p < 0.05$.

firms (96.7 percent) have obtained ISO14001 certification. Hence, the rate of adoption of ISO14001 in the parent firms is very high.

The indicators of strategic factors of the subsidiary are measured in terms of leadership (LDS) and goal of environmental management (GOAL). The organizational practices are measured using three indicators: ISO14001 (ISO), environmental report (REP), and green procurement (GREN). The items are measured in a Likert-type 5-point scale, except ISO and REP, which are measured in 3 points. ISO and REP are combined as MANA, and the scores are added up. JOWN is measured by the ownership ratio of Japanese parent firms.

6.3.3 Hypothesis and methodology

The CSR assessment adopted evaluates 85 headings on their degree of CSR activities and provides an aggregate evaluation for each firm. This assessment is based on the evaluation of various issues about the environment and social aspects as mentioned earlier. Looking at CSR pressure and the issue of competitive advantage, a firm needs to transfer physical resources and organizational capabilities to the entire organization to efficiently and effectively implement operations. However, various practices in the subsidiaries are not necessarily the same as in the parent companies.

It is assumed that high-scoring CSR firms tend to be proactively involved in environmental management because such firms take positive action in relation to the environmental and social aspects of business. With the perception of this background, firms adapt to regulations such as the Restrictions of Hazardous Chemicals (RoHS) in electrical and electronic equipment and the Registration, Evaluation, Authorization, and Restriction of Chemicals (REACH). This leads to the following hypothesis:

Hypothesis: High-scoring CSR firms tend to transfer their environmental management to overseas operations.

This hypothesis is tested in this study. In the model, CSR is an explanatory variable, and the transfer of environmental management is an explained variable. An explained variable uses two indicators: environmental management (MANA) and green procurement (GREN). In addition, the control variables are government regulation (GOV), customer requirement (CUS), and community requirement (COM) as external factors; GOAL and LDS as strategic factors; and the ownership ratio of Japanese parent firms.

The study uses 2009 CSR data, which were published in 2010, and dependent variables as in 2010. Whether the study uses t period or t-1 period for CSR data is not critical because the transfer is not completed at a specific point in time. Rather, CSR assessment reflects the overall measures and accumulated results of past efforts and is the result of past practices and organizational capabilities. Therefore, the study uses data about transfer from the survey in 2010, compared to CSR data in 2009.

The model, which examines the effect of CSR assessment on the transfer of environmental management, adopted factors such as government regulation, strategy of subsidiary, and CSR assessment of parent firms, depending on preceding studies on the transfer of knowledge and capabilities (Cohen and Levinthal, 1990; Gupta and Govindarajan, 2000; Porter and Krammer, 2006).

In relation to the determinants of international transfer of management, the importance of absorptive capacity is often emphasized. However, the study's model does not directly include absorptive capacity. The focus of the study is foreign subsidiaries under the control of MNEs, not the transfer of knowledge and skill from one society to another. Absorptive capacity is an equivocal concept used in knowledge transfer or learning in the dimensions of individuals, organizations, and society (Lane *et al.*, 2006). Currently, the common indicators of absorptive capacity are not available. The target of the analysis is the overseas operation of MNEs, which is an internalized operation. The study aims to examine the practices of MNEs and the system or procedure, indirectly reflecting the absorptive capacity.

The analytical model is shown next. Model 1 uses MANA, and Model 2 uses GREN as the explained variables. There is a high correlation between GOAL and LDS of strategic factor ($r = 0.458$, $p < 0.05$). Accordingly, patterns are estimated using two indicators separately. The dummy variables mean that when the number of employees is less than 300, it is 0. When the number is greater than 300, it is 1.

Model 1: MANA $= \beta_{m1}$GOV $+ \beta_{m2}$COM $+ \beta_{m3}$CUS $+ \beta_{m4}$CSR
$+ \beta_{m5}$JOWN$+\beta_{m6}$LDS(GOAL) $+ \beta_{m7}$D_scale   (6.1)

Model 2: GREN $= \beta_{g1}$GOV$+\beta_{g2}$COM $+ \beta_{g3}$CUS $+ \beta_{g4}$CSR
$+ \beta_{g5}$JOWN $+ \beta_{g6}$LDS(GOAL) $+ \beta_{g7}$D_scale   (6.2)

6.4 Results

Based on the models, the data was analyzed using ordinary least squares (OLS). The results are shown in Table 6.3. The results show the following important points.

Table 6.3 Results of analysis

	Model 1 (MANA)				Model 2 (GREN)			
	Co-efficient	t value	Co-efficient	t value	Co-efficient	t value	Co-efficient	t value
GOV	0.229	0.699	−0.276	−0.991	−0.408	−1.650	−0.441	−1.474
COM	−0.055	−0.190	0.219	0.944	0.533	2.278*	0.542	2.129*
CUS	−0.154	−0.749	−0.159	−1.002	0.100	0.606	0.133	0.766
CSR	−0.059	−0.289	−0.113	−0.742	0.510	3.200**	0.557	3.328**
JOWN	−0.091	−0.379	−0.071	−0.400	0.434	2.361*	0.326	1.768
LDS	0.020	0.084			0.309	1.853		
GOAL			0.623	3.360**			0.070	0.347
D_scale	0.510	2.515*	0.454	2.899**	−0.038	−0.232	−0.035	−0.196
Constant	5.402	2.714*	4.406	3.239**	−4.145	−1.897	−2.003	−1.009
Adj R²		0.097		0.433		0.446		0.352
F value		1.400		4.060**		3.872**		3.018*
DW		1.898		2.365		2.304		2.275

Note: **$p < 0.01$, * $p < 0.05$.

First, CSR assessment has a significant positive relationship with the transfer of green procurement. When leadership (LDS) is used as a strategic variable, green procurement shows a significant positive relationship to ownership of parent firms (JOWN) and community (COM), as well as to CSR assessment (CSR). That is, CSR, the ownership ratio by parent firms and community demand, affect green procurement together. Firms with high CSR assessment are likely to implement the transfer of environmental practices. On this point, the study's hypothesis is supported.

Second, the regulation of the host government is not significant to green procurement (GREN) and environmental management (MANA). In fact, it is evident that MNEs are required to submit environmental reports such as air, water, and chemicals to the supervisory office of the host government. Regulation by the host government does not seem to be a driving force of the transfer. This depends on whether the regulation by the host government works as minimum criteria or as a strict goal to be achieved.

The actual influence of the host country is not straightforward because community (COM) has a positive relationship to the transfer. It is supposed that direct regulation by the host government has a relatively weak influence on green procurement practice, but the local community has an explicitly positive effect. The inhabitants of the region where firms locate often have direct complaints against environmental problems, but the subsidiary in an industrial zone may have fewer complaints by residents because of locational reasons.

Third, ISO14001 and the environmental report into environmental management system (MANA) are integrated. The environmental goal (GOAL) has a significant positive relationship to the environmental management system (MANA). This result indicates that the environmental management system is strongly related to the degree to which the management goal of the subsidiary is embedded in the management philosophy. When MANA and GREN are compared, green procurement must be implemented because it is a mandatory governmental requirement and should be implemented as CSR.

Fourth, the size of firms plays a decisive role in establishing environmental management systems. It is generally understood that large firms receive more external pressures to act in socially responsible ways. Furthermore, large firms are more likely to develop environmental management systems than smaller firms because they have more resources to adapt to such pressures. So, the larger the firm size, the stronger the relationship between the environmental management system and CSR. The results in Table 6.3 indicate that firm size is positively related to MANA.

However, CSR does not show a significant relationship to MANA. At the subsidiary level, the study finds that CSR is not significantly related to MANA. There may be two reasons for this. First, the environmental management system may not be well established in the overseas subsidiary, compared with the parent firm, because of the subsidiary's development stage or because of the firm size. Second, this difference suggests the existence of a gap in capabilities between parent firms and subsidiaries. The subsidiaries in Vietnam in the study's sample were, on average, established in 2001. So, the accumulated level of experience and capabilities in environmental management practices seem to be lower in the subsidiaries than in the parent firms. Most probably, the environmental management systems of the subsidiaries are under the process of formation. Because of these reasons, different relationships can be found between parent firms and subsidiary firms with regard to CSR and MANA.

Fifth, CSR assessment means external assessment. Firm behavior is not solely determined by external factors. The driving force of the international transfer of environmental management should include internal factors of the firm. Therefore, an environmental management system led by corporate policy and green procurement are inevitable for the implementation of such practices. As is found in the study of technology transfer and knowledge transfer, external factors and strategy are both regarded as the main determinants (Gupta and Govindarajan, 2000; Jeppesen and Hansen, 2004). This holds true for the international transfer of environmental practices.

6.5 Conclusion

In this chapter, the study analyzed the relationship between CSR assessment and the international transfer of environmental management by Japanese firms. In preceding studies, some analyses were done on the relationship between CSR and economic performance. However, these studies did not analyze the transfer of environmental practices to overseas operations. This research examined this issue based on a survey of Japanese-related firms in Vietnam. The results of the analysis reveal that CSR assessment of parent firms promotes the transfer of environmental practices to overseas operations.

To conclude, it is understood that the environmental policy and strategy of the parent firms are the driving force of the international transfer of environmental management. Therefore, for sustainability in the global sense, the environmental strategy and management systems in MNEs are important and effective in the transfer to developing countries. Social consciousness for sustainability promotes good firm behavior.

However, there are limitations in the study. The study was implemented in only one country, and the number of firms in the sample was limited. It is necessary to verify the study's findings in another area or country with a larger sample. In spite of these limitations, the research provides useful findings and contributes to the development of new research issues. To manage GHG emissions, more proactive corporate strategies are necessary. For that purpose, the acceptance by firms of a strong social philosophy helps improve the practices of the firms globally. For MNEs, it is important to promote the transfer of environmental management practices and, at the same time, to implement CSR.

Note

1 Four hundred manufacturing firms are listed from the directories of Japanese-affiliated companies in Vietnam by Toyo Keizai Shinpo Sha and JETRO (Japan External Trade Organization). They were asked to join the survey by telephone and email.

References

Beise M. and Rennings K. (2005) Lead Markets and Regulation: A Framework for Analyzing the International Diffusion of Environmental Innovations, *Ecological Economics*, 52, pp. 5–17.

Carroll A.B. (1991) The Pyramid of Corporate Social Responsibility: Toward the Moral Management of Organizational Stakeholders, *Business Horizons*, 34(4), pp. 39–48.

Cohen W.M. and Levinthal D.A. (1990) Absorptive Capacity: A New Perspective on Learning and Innovation, *Administrative Science Quarterly*, 35(1), pp. 128–152.

De Schutter O. (2008) Corporate Social Responsibility: European Style, *European Law Journal*, 14(2), pp. 203–236.

Elkington J. (1998) *Cannibals with Forks: The Triple Bottom Line of 21st Century Business*, Capstone Publishing Ltd, Oxford.

European Commission (2001) *Green Paper: Promoting a European Framework for Corporate Social Responsibility*, COM (2001) 366 final, 18 July 2001, Brussels.

Florida R. and Kenney M. (1991) Transplanted Organizations: The Transfer of Japanese Industrial Organization to the U.S., *American Sociological Review*, 56(3), pp. 381–398.

Friedman M. (1970) Social Responsibility of Business Is to Increase Its Profit, *The New York Times Magazine*, 13 September 1970, pp. 211–214.

Gupta A.K. and Govindarajan V. (2000) Knowledge Flows within Multinational Corporations, *Strategic Management Journal*, 21(4), pp. 473–496.

Hall P.A. and Soskice D. (2001) *Varieties of Capitalism: International Foundation of Comparative Advantage*, Oxford University Press, Oxford.

Hawk B.E. (1977) The OECD Guidelines for Multinational Enterprises: Competition, *Fordham Law Review*, 46(2), pp. 241–276.

Jeppesen S. and Hansen M.W. (2004) Environmental Upgrading of Third World Enterprises through Linkages to Transnational Corporations: Theoretical Perspectives and Preliminary Evidence, *Business Strategy and the Environment*, 13(4), pp. 261–274.

Lane P.J., Koka B. and Pathak S. (2006) The Reification of Absorptive Capacity: A Critical Review and Rejuvenation of the Construct, *The Academy of Management Review*, 31(4), pp. 833–863.

Lantos G.P. (2001) The Boundaries of Strategic Corporate Social Responsibility, *Journal of Consumer Marketing*, 18(7), pp. 595–630.

Lantos G.P. (2002) The Ethicality of Altruistic Corporate Social Responsibility, *Journal of Consumer Marketing*, 19(3), pp. 205–232.

McWilliams A. and Siegel D. (2001) Corporate Social Responsibility: A Theory of the Firm Perspective, *The Academy of Management Review*, 26(1), pp. 117–127.

Ockwell D., Watson J., Mallett A., Haum R., Mackerron R.G. and Verbeken V. (2010) *Enhancing Developing Country Access to Eco-innovation: The Case of Technology Transfer and Climate Change in a Post-2012 Policy Framework*, Working Paper No.12, OECD Publishing, Paris.

OECD (2000) *OECD Guidelines for Multinational Enterprises*, Organisation for Economic Cooperation and Development (OECD), Paris.

Pérez-Nordtvedt L., Kedia B.L., Datta D.K. and Rasheed A.A. (2008) Effectiveness and Efficiency of Cross-border Knowledge Transfer: An Empirical Examination, *Journal of Management Studies*, 45(4), pp. 714–744.

Phene A. and Almeida P. (2008) Innovation in Multinational Subsidiaries: The Role of Knowledge Assimilation and Subsidiary Capabilities, *Journal of International Business Studies*, 39(5), pp. 901–919.

Popp D. (2006) International Innovation and Diffusion of Air Pollution Control Technologies: The Effects of NOx and SO_2 Regulation in the US, Japan, and Germany, *Journal of Environmental Economics and Management*, 51(1), pp. 46–71.

Popp D. (2011) International Technology Transfer, Climate Change, and the Clean Development Mechanism, *Review of Environmental Economics and Policy*, 5(1), pp. 131–152.

Porter M.E. (2003) CSR: A Religion with Too Many Priests?, European Business Forum, Autumn, 15, 1 October 2003.

Porter M.E. and Krammer M.R. (2006) Strategy and Society: The Link between Competitive Advantage and Corporate Social Responsibility, Harvard Business Review, 4(12), pp. 78–92.

Rennings K., Ziegler K., Ankele K. and Hoffman E. (2006) The Influence of Different Characteristics of the EU Environmental Management Auditing Scheme on Technical Environmental Innovations and Economic Performance, *Ecological Economics*, 57(1), pp. 45–59.

Schwartz M. and Carroll A.B. (2003) Corporate Social Responsibility: A Three Domain Approach, *Business Ethics Quarterly*, 3(4), pp. 503–530.

Szulanski G. (1996) Exploring Internal Stickiness: Impediments to the Transfer of Best Practice within the Firm, *Strategic Management Journal*, Special Issue, 17, pp. 27–43.

Toyo Keizai Shinpo Sha (2011) CSR Company Directory 2010, Toyo Keizai Shinpo Sha, Tokyo.

Walley N. and Whitehead B. (1994) It's Not Easy Being Green, *Harvard Business Review*, 72(3), pp. 46–52.

Wan-Jan W.S. (2006) Defining Corporate Social Responsibility, *Journal of Public Affairs*, 6(3–4), pp. 176–184.

WBCSD (1999) *Meeting Changing Expectations: Corporate Social Responsibility*, World Business Council for Sustainable Development (WBCSD), Geneva.

Zhelyazkov G. (2012) Challenges and Impact of CSR on Business Performance in Bulgaria, *Trakia Journal of Sciences*, 10(4), pp. 36–41.

7 The status of financial accounting standards for SMEs in Japan and the Philippines

Sadako Inoue

7.1 Introduction

Today, more than 120 countries or organizations have adopted the International Financial Reporting Standards (IFRS), issued by the International Accounting Standards Boards (IASB). In addition, the IASB published the International Financial Reporting Standards for Small and Medium-sized Entities (IFRS for SMEs) in July 2009, taking into account the special needs of SMEs and emerging economies, etc. (IASB, 2009a). However, the enforcement of the IFRS for SMEs has been left entirely to the discretion of each country, and so, more than 80 countries, led by developing countries, have adopted the IFRS for SMEs or announced plans to do so, but others, including many developed countries, have set individual standards for their SMEs (IASB, 2013). In Asia, the Philippines were one of the first countries to have adopted the IFRS for SMEs in 2010, and Japan has set individual standards for SMEs. Also, with respect to adoption of the IFRS, which are generally used by large or publicly accountable entities, the Philippines adopted the IFRS compulsorily in 2005, but Japan has adopted it optionally so far. There are differences between these two countries in terms of their approaches to the adoption of not only the IFRS for SMEs, but also the IFRS.

The purpose of this study is to examine how the financial accounting standards for SMEs are constituted in these two countries with different characteristics from the perspective of the concepts of a standards model and the approaches to standards setting. This research perspective is not new. The concepts of a standards model were discussed in terms of the 'Big GAAP versus Little GAAP' until the 1990s. Moreover, the arguments involving standards setting are similar to recent discussions on whether the standards should be set within the framework of the generally accepted accounting principles (GAAP) or not.

The theoretical construct of this study is mainly based on arguments developed at the International Accounting Standards Board (IASB, 2004) and the Accounting Standards Board of Canada (AcSB, 2007). The resulting two discussion papers deal with whether or not accounting standards for SMEs should be developed and related matters, namely, focusing on the concepts of a standards model and approaches to standards setting. First, the concepts of a standards model signify the extent to which standards should be applied in a standalone document and the extent to which the single-standard and the dual-standard concepts are present in the concepts. The single-standard concept fundamentally suggests that similar transactions or circumstances should be treated the same, regardless of a company's size, and therefore the standards for SMEs should not be set separately. The dual-standard concept suggests that the standards for SMEs should be constituted aside from the standards for large or publicly accountable entities and should be a self-contained standalone set of financial accounting and reporting standards. Then, the approaches to standards setting, consisting of the top-down approach and the bottom-up approach, are used to develop the standards for SMEs. The former requires that the standards for SMEs be a simplified version of the standards for large or publicly accountable entities; the latter requires that they should be enacted in accordance with tax acts, company laws, etc., which SMEs must comply with. These concepts and approaches are connected to each other and could be useful in making a matrix that analyzes the positioning of the standards for SMEs in Japan and the Philippines.

This research draws from secondary data and an interview, which was held in August 2013 (Inoue, 2014), to describe the development of accounting standards for SMEs in Japan and the Philippines. Through a comparison of the status of accounting standards for SMEs in the two countries with different views on the adoption of the IFRS, the study will be able to clarify the characteristics and homologous points of the two countries. The information will be useful for other countries that are struggling to decide what accounting standards should be adopted for SMEs and will help them in arriving at more informed and rational decisions under different circumstances.

7.2   Analysis categories for the status of SMEs' accounting standards

IASB (2004)

In order to develop accounting standards suitable for SMEs, IASB (2004) was published as a discussion paper in June 2004. It first discusses whether the IASB should develop special financial reporting standards for SMEs (IASB, 2004). There are two views concerning the principal alternatives. One is that the IASB should not develop them because the IFRS is considered suitable for all entities including SMEs. The objective of financial statements as set out in the *Framework for the Preparation and Presentation of Financial Statements* issued by the International Accounting Standards Committee (IASC, 1989), Paragraph 12, states the following:

> The objective of a financial statement is to provide information about the financial position, performance and changes in the financial position of an entity which could be useful to a wide range of users in making economic decisions.

The standards for the general-purpose financial statements of entities required to follow the IFRS, along with public accountability, would meet the needs of all users of financial statements. Therefore, the adoption of a single set of accounting standards appropriate for all entities, regardless of size, might be suggested. This view is called 'the single-standard concept' in this study.

The other view is that the board should establish special standards for SMEs (i.e., the IFRS for SMEs) and indicate the types of entities for which it believes these standards are suitable. This, however, does not mean SMEs would be prohibited from using the IFRS. The IASB notes that the users of financial statements of SMEs might not be interested in some information contained in general-purpose financial statements as much as users of financial statements of entities with public accountability. On the other hand, the users of financial statements of SMEs may need some information that is not presented in the financial statements of large or publicly accountable entities. Such differences suggest that a separate set of financial reporting standards suitable for SMEs may be appropriate and may be justified on the basis of cost–benefit considerations. The extent of the differences between the IFRS and standards for SMEs will be decided on the basis of user needs and cost–benefit analyses. This view is called 'the dual-standard concept' in this study.

AcSB (2007)

The AcSB stated that 'one size does not necessarily fit all' and decided to pursue separate strategies for public enterprises, private enterprise (i.e., SMEs[1]), and not-for-profit organizations in its Strategic Plan, issued in 2006. With respect to SMEs, the board examined the needs of the users of SMEs' financial statements in order to determine what financial reporting approach would be best. AcSB (2007) is the discussion paper that analyzes issues the AcSB is considering in its strategic review of financial reporting by SMEs. According to the paper, there are three possible types of approaches to developing accounting standards for SMEs (AcSB, 2007, paragraph 58):

1   A top-down approach based on standards for publicly accountable entities (i.e., the IFRS).
2   A standalone approach based on the IASB's proposed IFRS for SMEs.
3   An independently developed set of Canadian standards, based on various sources, including, but not necessarily restricted to, the IFRS and Canadian accounting standards.

First, the top-down approach would start with public entities' GAAP (i.e., the IFRS) and have embedded within it certain different treatments available only to SMEs. This approach is similar to the differential reporting model that is a part of the current Canadian GAAP. In AcSB (2007), the term 'differential' applies to requirements specifically for SMEs that modify the general standards in certain narrowly circumscribed respects. Thus, an important characteristic of this approach is modifying GAAP in order to suit SMEs' circumstances on the assumption of the single-standard concept. Next, the standalone approach means that all of the relevant accounting requirements are contained in a single document. Therefore, it suggests that material that is irrelevant or seldom applicable would be excluded, and references to other documents should be avoided, or, at least, minimized. In addition, an important objective of this approach is a substantial reduction in the volume and complexity of the accounting requirement. This can be achieved by condensing and simplifying the standards that are applicable to publicly accountable entities.

In comparison with the first approach, the standalone approach is different from the point of attaching great importance to developing accounting standards only for SMEs. This is based on the dual-standard concept. However, both have similar characteristics in terms of the perspective on the approaches to standards setting because they focus on adjusting general accounting standards within GAAP. Such an approach that sets them within GAAP is called 'the top-down approach' in this study.

The third approach is developing a set of Canadian standards independently, which would, to a large degree, be a fresh start. When these standards are developed, a vast amount of intellectual capital would be invested. They would be developed in the context of Canadian circumstances in order to be considered from a more grassroots perspective. Specifically, areas that could be covered under this approach include the following (AcSB, 2007, paragraph 79):

- The greater use of historical cost measurements, rather than fair value
- The amortization of goodwill and other intangible assets with an indefinite useful life
- Related party transactions, disclosures, and measurements from a private enterprise user-needs perspective
- Future income taxes on a basis other than full allocation or taxes payable (for example, partial allocation)
- The simplification of requirements for financial instruments

Such areas would require in-depth accounting standards that could be achieved by identifying and accommodating fresh ideas into an independent Canadian standalone approach for SMEs. This approach is likely to offer a completely fresh look at which accounting standards are appropriate for SMEs and to focus on accounting and reporting issues from a Canadian perspective. On the other hand, it will pose a disadvantage if there are only a few areas warranting differences in standards for publicly accountable enterprises; therefore, a strong linkage to those standards (i.e., GAAP or the IFRS) is needed. Also, this approach will bring a lack of comparability and the need for continuous education and training in two different sets of standards (AcSB, 2007). Thus, this approach will be based on the dual-standard concept, but, unlike the other approaches, it might have specific characteristics from the perspective of the approaches to standards setting. Because it focuses on developing standards for SMEs in the context of Canadian circumstances at a more grassroots level, the standards might be partly set without GAAP. In this study, the approach that focuses on incorporating the context of SMEs' circumstances in the standards for SMEs, rather than setting the standards within GAAP or the IFRS, is 'the bottom-up approach'.

7.2.1 Analysis categories of this study

The discussion about the single-standard concept and the dual-standard concept is similar to one that has been going on since the 1990s, namely, Big GAAP versus Little GAAP. Here, whether the standards for SMEs should be individually developed or not is the core issue (AICPA, 1976, 1983). On the other hand, the discussion on the top-down approach and the bottom-up approach is similar to recent arguments on whether the standards should be set by using GAAP or non-GAAP on the assumption of the Little GAAP or the dual-standard approach (AcSB, 2007; AICPA, 2013; Roth, 2013).

First, the concepts of a standards model signify the extent to which the standards should be applied in a standalone document. The single-standard concept suggests that similar transactions or circumstances should be treated the same, regardless of companies' sizes, and therefore, the standards for SMEs should not be set separately. Consequently, the concept will require whether a simplification regulation for SMEs is set in each accounting standard for large or publicly accountable entities or the standards of which gathered a simplification regulation for SMEs is set in the system of standards for large or publicly accountable entities. Under the single-standard concept, the standards for SMEs should exclude some accounting topics which are included in the standards for large or publicly accountable entities because typical SMEs are not likely to encounter such transactions or circumstances. When SMEs do encounter such transactions or circumstances, they should refer to particular standards for large or publicly accountable entities. Also, when the standards for large or publicly accountable entities provide an accounting policy option, SMEs should be permitted to have the same option by cross-referencing the standards for large or publicly accountable entities. Conversely, the dual-standard concept suggests that the standards for SMEs should be constituted aside from the standards for large or publicly accountable entities and be a self-contained, standalone set of financial accounting and reporting standards. As a result, the standards for SMEs should be published in a separate volume, and all cross-references to the standards for large or publicly accountable entities should not be provided.

Second, the approaches to standards setting in developing the standards for SMEs examine whether the standards for large or publicly accountable entities should form the basis of standards for SMEs. This is done because there are differences between SMEs and large or publicly accountable entities with regard to the effectiveness of business, economic efficiency, deficiency in accounting knowledge, and its underteaching. Therefore, assuming the dual-standards concept, the top-down approach requires that the standards for SMEs be simplified or modified versions of the standards for large or publicly accountable entities within GAAP. The bottom-up approach, however, requires that standards be enacted in accordance with tax acts, corporate acts, etc., which SMEs must comply with (i.e., the nonapplications of GAAP basis, cash basis, modified cash basis, income tax basis, contractual basis standards, etc.). If a matrix is created, using these concepts and approaches as an index that analyzes the positioning of the standards for SMEs in Japan and the Philippines, it can be charted as in Figure 7.1.

	Single-Standard Concept	Dual-Standard Concept
Top-Down Approach	A	C
Bottom-Up Approach	B*	D

Figure 7.1 Analysis categories of the position of accounting standards for SMEs in accounting systems

*The B category does not exist because the bottom-up approach is based on the dual-standard concept.

Source: Yamashita (2012).

7.3   The case of Japan

7.3.1   *The Japanese accounting system*

In Japan, the accounting system consists mainly of three governing laws: the Financial Instruments and Exchange Act (FIEA), the Companies Act, and the Corporation Tax Act. The FIEA, which applies to companies trading publicly, protects investors and expects the main function of accounting to establish the comparability of net income for a defined period. Companies subject to the act must prepare financial statements and submit the statements audited by a certified public accountant (CPA) or an audit firm to the prime minister. Next, the Companies Act applies to all companies and protects creditors and investors. Under the act, the key accounting function calculates distributable amounts, and all companies must prepare financial statements and submit them to a shareholders' meeting. Moreover, the objective of the Corporation Tax Act is the fair imposition of taxes and across all companies. They must prepare tax returns in accordance with accounting standards generally accepted as fair and appropriate. Accounting plays the important role here of calculating economically disposable profits. Calculating taxable income is based on the final accounts with return adjustments, known as *kakutei kessan shugi* in Japanese (Kawasaki and Sakamoto, 2014).

The determination of the accounting standards generally accepted as fair and appropriate depends on whether the company involved is subject to the FIEA or the Companies Act. The listed companies that must follow the FIEA rules can use one of four sets of accounting standards in their consolidated financial statements, namely, the Japanese IFRS, IFRS (issued by the IASB), Japanese GAAP, or US GAAP. The others, with the exception of SMEs, are required to use Japanese GAAP under the Companies Act. Figure 7.2 shows the applicable accounting standards under the FIEA and the Companies Act depending upon the company formation and whether or not an audit is required.

Japanese GAAP currently includes accounting standards and implementation guidance on the accounting standards or practical solutions issued by the Accounting Standards Board of Japan (ASBJ), the accounting standards set by the Business Accounting Council[2] (BAC) and practical guidelines issued by the Japanese

Category		Financial Statements		Audited by CPA
		Consolidated	Non consolidated	or audit firm
A	Listed companies	Voluntary application of the IFRS	Japanese GAAP	Audit required
B	Companies disclosing under the FIEA other than ones in category A	Japanese GAAP		
C	Large companies under the Companies Act with stated capital $\geqq$ JPY 500M or total liabilities $\geqq$ JPY 20B: excluding category A or B companies	Not required to prepare		
D	All others: Corporations that are not in categories A, B, or C		ASBJ Guidelines (2005)	Audit not required
			General Standards (2012)	

Figure 7.2 Financial accounting standards and companies subject to the standards in Japan

Source: Kawasaki and Sakamoto (2014: 12), Figure 1.3 (partly revised by the author).

Institute of Certified Public Accountants (JICPA). The ASBJ was established in 2001 as the private-sector Japanese accounting standards-setting body. All accounting standards set by the ASBJ are subject to endorsement by the Financial Services Agency (FSA), a Japanese government agency. Under an agreement between the ASBJ and the IASB in August 2007, known as the Tokyo Agreement, the ASBJ had been working towards converging the Japanese GAAP with the IFRS, but it continues to be inconsistent with the IFRS. Currently, the IFRS is voluntarily adopted when listed companies prepare consolidated financial statements, except in the case of separate financial statements (Urasaki, 2014).

7.3.2 Accounting standards for SMEs in Japan

In Japan, the necessity of accounting standards for SMEs, including auditing matters, has been discussed in the 1990s, along with the progress of accounting standards converging with the IFRS. Unlike listed firms and large or publicly accountable entities, SME management's interest might be mostly focused on how to compute taxable income to as little an amount as possible within the applicable provisions of the Japanese Corporation Tax Act. Since owner-managers of SMEs usually lack sufficient business accounting expertise and the ability to calculate taxable income, Japanese tax accountants advise SMEs and play an inevitable role in preparing and lodging their tax returns to the Japanese tax authorities. Moreover, their managers do not have much incentive to use general-purpose financial reporting due to their debt financing. In general, SMEs have no rigid internal control systems, and so managers can easily override them. Therefore, the owner-managers of SMEs do not have much need to apply GAAP meant for listed firms and large or publicly accountable entities, which apply general-purpose financial reporting and emphasize the transparency and comparability of their accounting information to influence investors' economic decisions. Focusing on such differences, it would be better to set accounting standards appropriate for SMEs rather than to apply standards applicable to larger entities, with the objective of improving the social reliability of the financial statements prepared by SMEs. Currently, SMEs are able to choose between 'The Accounting Guidelines for SMEs' (ASBJ Guidelines), released in 2005, and 'The General Accounting Standards for SMEs' (General Standards), published in 2012 (Kawasaki and Sakamoto, 2014; Urasaki, 2014).

7.3.3   The ASBJ guidelines

Since 2002, each of the three professional bodies, namely, the Small and Medium Enterprise Agency of Japan (SMEAJ), the Japan Federation of Certified Public Tax Accountants' Association (JFCPTA), and JICPA, have developed accounting standards for SMEs for their own political considerations and in order to expand their business opportunities. As a result, some differences among the bodies have brought disorder to the discussion of accounting institutionalization. In the interest of resolving the confusion and suggesting the correct methods to follow for accounting treatment and explanatory notes in preparing financial statements, the ASBJ Guidelines were set forth in August 2005 by the joint initiative of the JICPA, JFCPTA, Japan Chamber of Commerce and Industry (JCCI), and ASBJ. The guidelines state the policy on creating them as follows (ASBJ *et al.*, 2005, paragraph 6):

> In general, the accounting information provided by entities, including SMEs, was originally expected to play a role in contributing to the decision-making of investors and in supporting the interest adjustment of the interested parties. Although SMEs commonly have a few investors and direct businesses, they expect accounting information to play a role as the decision-making function and the interest adjustment function due to the diversification of the financing or the expansion of the business partnership. Therefore, accounting standards should be applied regardless of the size of the entity, in order to match an accounting practice with the actual economic situation of the business.

Such a policy appears to be sourced from the JICPA report, published in 2003, as follows (JICPA, 2003: 4):

*   The recognition and measurement standards of the same business and economic phenomenon should not be a reflection of the scale of the company.

- A financial position and business performance statements that are prepared under different recognition and measurement requirements in accordance with entities' sizes will include not only the difference in scale of the entities but also of the underlying concept (e.g., the accrual basis versus cash accounting, the current price method versus cost price method). Therefore, such information cannot satisfactorily be used for analysis of the management of the actual situation of the entities and for comparison or other purposes between entities.
- If such different accounting standards exist at the same time, the reliability of the financial documents would be lost, the economic society would become confused, and the purposes of the disclosure system of the financial documents would not be satisfied.

After the ASBJ Guidelines were released in 2005, they were revised within a year in response to the influence of the IFRS. As per the revisions, the main arguments were how the ASBJ Guidelines had been globalized for convergence to the IFRS and how the guidelines may be applied by the simplification of accounting standards for listed and large or publicly accountable entities. In addition, they have advocated the approach that the same accounting rules be applied rigidly for similar business practices without considering whether an entity can accept the IFRS or not. However, this guideline is mainly useful for entities employing accounting advisors and that are relatively larger than other entities in terms of revenue and capital size. As a result, the ASBJ Guidelines are not generally adopted by Japanese SMEs (Hirano and Nishikawa, 2008; Kawasaki, 2012). Thus, the ASBJ Guidelines are classified into the A category in Figure 7.1 because their formulating policy is focused on the single standard. Moreover, an argument is presented about the convergence to the IFRS by simplifying the standards for listed and large or publicly accountable entities, which are based on the top-down approach.

7.3.4 The general standards

Under the circumstances where the ASBJ Guidelines had not been adopted, the SMEAJ reorganized the Study Group of Accounting for SMEs in February 2010 and, in September, released a report entitled 'The Interim Report of the Study Group for Accounting for SMEs'. In addition, the ASBJ initiated the Conference for the Accounting Standards for Unlisted Companies in March 2010 and, five months later, issued a report entitled 'The Report of the Conference for the Accounting Standards for Unlisted Companies'. Both these reports recommended that new accounting rules be established for SMEs in Japan (SMEAJ, 2010: 34–38). In February 2011, the SMAJ and the FSA jointly installed the Review Group on SME Accounting and Its Working Group. The Review Group released the exposure draft entitled 'The General Accounting Standards for SMEs', collected public feedback, and subsequently released 'The General Accounting Standards for SMEs' (General Standards) in January 2012 (Review Group on SME Accounting, 2012).

The General Standards are mainly useful for comparatively smaller SMEs such as micro-entities. The premise of these guidelines can be summarized in the four following points (SMEAJ, 2010: 22–3):

1   It shall provide SME managers with understandable rules in order to properly control their businesses (i.e., accounting useful for management).
2   It shall produce accounting information that has necessary and sufficient content to influence the credit decisions made by financial institutions and the business trade (i.e., accounting that offers business opportunities to stakeholders).
3   It shall sustain accounting that is compatible with the tax accounting practices that are common among Japanese SMEs (i.e., accounting that reflects practices).
4   It shall suggest appropriate accounting that does not require undue costs for SMEs (i.e., accounting that is feasible for SMEs).

In addition, the SMEAJ outlined the following four basic policies for creating accounting rules for SMEs (SMEAJ, 2010: 35–6):

1   The rules shall reflect accounting treatments made in the SMEs' accounting practices as conventions that include Corporate Income Tax Act and the BAC's Accounting Principles for Business Enterprises.
2   The rules shall include accounting standards that reflect the broad differences in the current accounting practices of SMEs.
3   The rules shall be easy to understand and simplified for the benefit of SME managers.
4   The rules shall require SMEs to keep accounting records.

As mentioned earlier, in order to help in the clarification of the management situations of SMEs, improve proprietors' accountability for their operations, and enhance financing capabilities, the General Standards were published with the objective of setting up accounting arrangements suited to the unique circumstances of SMEs. Therefore, the General Standards will be classified into the D category of the bottom-up approach in Figure 7.1 because it focuses on developing standards for SMEs in the context of Japanese circumstances from a more grassroots perspective, but does not focus on setting the standards that consider inclusion of the Japanese GAAP.

7.4   The case of the Philippines

7.4.1   Accounting standards and the standards-setting body

The Accountancy Act enacted by the Sixth Legislature in 1923 created the Board of Accountancy (BOA) and gave it the authority to issue CPA certificates. In 1929, the Philippine Institute of Certified Public Accountants (PICPA) was established in the private sector for issuing accounting standards. To begin with, the PICPA started to issue them as accounting bulletins for voluntary adoption. In order to solve the then problems of financial accounting standards and standards setting in the Philippines, the PICPA created the Accounting Standards Council (ASC) in 1981 as an independent accounting standards-setting body. The ASC issued the Philippine Statement of Financial Accounting Standards (PSFAS) from 1983 through 1996, established mainly on US-based accounting standards. However, the council started the move towards the adoption of the International Accounting Standards (IAS) issued by the IASC as early as 1996 and decided to base PSFAS on IAS, rather than update the standards in line with changes in the US GAAP, taking the complex Philippine situation into consideration. In 1997, a decision to move completely to IAS was made. Under the project, the ASC replaced US-based standards and adopted the IAS with no local equivalent and updated previously issued IAS-based standards. In 2005, the ASC completed the adoption of the IFRS and the previously revised IAS. It renamed these accounting standards the Philippine Financial Reporting Standard (PFRS) and Philippine Accounting Standard (PAS) to correspond with the IFRS and IAS, respectively. Currently, accounting standards in the Philippines are promulgated by the Philippine Financial Reporting Standards Council (PFRSC), which became the successor to the ASC in 2006. Once they are approved by the Philippine Securities and Exchange Commission (PSEC) and BOA, the final concurrence of the Professional Regulatory Commission (PRC) gives legal authority to the accounting standards, and CPA compliance is mandatory. After these processes, the standards become the Philippine GAAP (ADB, 2002; Fajardo, 2008).

7.4.2   Requirement to prepare financial statements

There are three forms of business organizations in the Philippines: sole proprietorship, partnership, and corporation. The sole proprietorships register with the Department of Trade and Industry (DTI, 2013), whereas partnerships and corporations are regulated by the PSEC. To a large extent, preparing financial statements is required by the PSEC and Bureau of Internal Revenue (BIR). Their requirements are different depending on the forms of business organization.

The requirement of the Philippine Securities and Exchange Commission

The Corporation Code 1980, implemented by the PSEC, requires corporations and partnerships whose paid-up capital is peso 50,000 and above to submit audited financial statements to the PSEC (sections 75, 141). Under the Securities Regulations Code (SRC) and the special rules on financial reporting, entities, which refer to a juridical person or a corporation registered under the Corporation Code 1980, have to prepare financial statements in accordance with the Philippine GAAP. Currently, based on SRC Rule 68 as amended in December 2011 (PSEC, 2011), the following are examples of the required basic financial statements: balance

Business form		Size criteria		Accounting standards in preparing the financial statements
		Total assets	Total liabilities	
Corporation partnership	Large or publicly accountable entities	More than P350 million	More than P250 million	Full PFRS
	Small and medium-sized entities (SMEs)	Between P3 million and P350 million	Between P3 million and P250 million	PFRS for SMEs
	Micro-entities	Below P3 million	Below P3 million	Income tax basis, PSFAS/PAS, or PFRS for SMEs

Figure 7.3 Financial reporting framework in the Philippines

Sources: SRC Rule 68 as amended in 2011; PSEC (2011), section 2 (A).

sheet, income statement, statement of changes in equity, cash flow statement, and notes to financial statements (accounting policies and explanatory notes). According to the amended SRC Rule 68, the PSEC provides a Financial Reporting Framework for preparing financial statements according to the size of entities: large and publicly accountable entities, SMEs, and micro-entities (Figure 7.3).

First, large or publicly accountable entities are those with total assets of more than peso 350 million or total liabilities of more than peso 250 million, or entities that are in the process of filing their financial statements for the purpose of issuing any class of instruments in a public market. These entities shall be required to prepare financial statements using the PFRS. Next, SMEs are those entities with total assets of between peso 3 million and peso 350 million, total liabilities of between peso 3 million and peso 250 million (if the entity is a parent company, the said amounts shall be based on the consolidated figures), or that are not in the process of filing their financial statements for the purpose of issuing any class of instruments in a public market. The SMEs shall use the PFRS for SMEs.[3] Micro-entities are those entities with total assets and liabilities of less than peso 3 million or that are not in the process of filing their financial statements for the purpose of issuing any class of instruments in a public market. These entities have the option to use as their framework either the income tax basis administered by the BIR, whose accounting standards came into effect as of December 31, 2004, that is, the PSFAS/PAS, or the PFRS for SMEs (PSEC, 2011).

The requirement of the Bureau of Internal Revenue

The Tax Reform Act 1997, also known as the National Internal Revenue Code, implemented by the BIR requires all business entities, that is, sole proprietorships, partnerships, and corporations, whose gross quarterly sales, earnings, receipts, or output exceed peso 150,000 in any given quarter, to submit audited financial statements to the BIR in order to support their annual income tax returns (section 232(A)). Also, the statements for calculating taxable income must be prepared in accordance with the Philippine GAAP (section 43). Under the Revenue

Memorandum Circular (RMC) No. 44–2002 and No. 22–2004, however, in the case of a difference between the application of the Tax Reform Act and Philippine GAAP in calculating taxable income, the former shall prevail. The Revenue Regulations (RR) No. 8–2207 prescribes additional compliance requirements for taxpayers mandated to adopt the PFRS in preparing financial statements. Where differences arise between the PFRS and the tax rules, the taxpayers concerned have to report them as reconciliation items in the filed income tax return.

7.4.3 *Accounting standards for SMEs in the Philippines*

In the Philippines, the PFRS/PAS based on the IFRS/IAS became mandatory in 2004 for all reporting entities that prepared financial statements in conformity with the Philippine GAAP since 2005, under approvals of the ASC (now the FRSC), PSEC, BOA, etc. However, it is difficult for SMEs to use the PFRS/PAS because the standards for large or publicly accountable entities impose a burden on them. In addition, users of the financial statements of SMEs do not have the same requirements as those of equity investors and other users of financial statements in public capital markets, but are focused more on assessing shorter-term cash flows, liquidity, and solvency. Moreover, the IASB made a plan to develop the IFRS for non-publicly accountable entities (NPAEs), now SMEs, with the goals of both meeting user needs and balancing costs and benefits from a preparer's perspective in 2007. In consideration of the significant number of Philippine SMEs and of user needs, the burden of preparing statements, and the IASB's movement, the ASC provided temporary relief to NPAEs in October 2005 by permitting entities that qualified as NPAEs not to use the PFRS/PAS. The temporary relief was provided under PAS 101, 'Financial Reporting Standards for Non-publicly Accountable Entities'. PAS 101 previously permitted NPAEs to apply the applicable financial reporting standards effective as of December 31, 2004, that is, NPAEs were given the option to apply or not to apply any new FRSC pronouncements that became effective after December 31, 2004. In October 2009, the FRSC approved the adoption of the IFRS for SMEs issued by the IASB in July 2009 as the PFRS for SMEs, and therefore, PAS 101 was withdrawn (ASC, 2005, paragraphs 1–3, 16; PSEC, 2005; FRSC, 2009; SEC, 2009, preface, paragraphs 1, 6). PAS 101 is one of the PFRS/PAS, so that the standard number reflects it. This suggests that PAS 101 is located in the financial reporting framework for publicly accountable entities, and therefore, it is set forth under the single-standard concept.

In addition, a qualifying entity under PAS 101 was permitted to not apply the PFRS/PAS that became effective in 2005 in its general-purpose financial statements; however, the entity may still choose to apply any or all of these standards. Therefore, the entity that chooses to avail the option not to apply the PFRS/PAS should apply the relevant financial reporting standards effective as of December 2004 in preparing its general-purpose financial statements. The standards, which were effective as of December 2004, mean the PSFAS is based on the US GAAP. However, some standards for entities with public accountability, such as large or listed entities, banks, or insurance companies, were included in these, and therefore, the following five standards were excluded: PSFAS 19: Summary of GAAP for the Banking Industry, PSFAS 27: Accounting and Reporting for the Nonlife Insurance Industry, PSFAS 29: Earnings Per Share, PSFAS 30: Interim Financial Reporting, and PSFAS 31: Segment Reporting (ASC, 2005, paragraph 14 appendix). That is, PAS 101 was set by simplifying the standards for large or publicly accountable entities and was based on the top-down approach. As a result, PAS 101, which is the old accounting standard for SMEs, can be placed under the A category in Figure 7.1.

As mentioned earlier, the PFRS for SMEs has rearranged most of the IFRS for SMEs issued by the IASB. The IASB intended the IFRS for SMEs to be a stand-alone document for many typical SMEs such as nonpublicly accountable entities. In addition, it is not mandatory for the IFRS for SMEs to add cross-references to the IFRS in consideration of the responses to the exposure draft, *A Proposed IFRS for SMEs*, issued in February 2007 (IASB, 2007, 2009b). Compared to the PFRS/PAS, the PFRS for SMEs contains a number of simplifications: for example, using simplified drafting in writing the standards, making the final document easier to understand and follow, and reducing the number of disclosures to be made when preparing the financial statements (Punongbayan and Araullo, 2010). Thus, because the PFRS for SMEs are similar to the IFRS for SMEs, the two are likely to be set under the dual-standard concept and the top-down approach. As a result, the present standards, the PFRS for SMEs, can be classified into the C category in Figure 7.1.

7.4.4   Problems with accounting standards for SMEs in the Philippines

According to the interview that was held in August 2013 (Inoue, 2014), there are mainly two issues involving the PFRS for SMEs. First, many SMEs use the tax basis, cash basis, or modified cash basis without using the PFRS for SMEs, which they should apply under SRC Rule 68 in preparing their financial statements. Second, compliance with the general guide to financial statements issued by the PSEC is inadequate. As previously mentioned, the PSEC requires entities to submit audited financial statements and does not accept them unless they match the statements that were submitted to the BIR with the income tax returns. Although the BIR also requires audited financial statements to accompany an entity's income tax returns; it is not very particular about the entity's compliance with the PFRS or PFRS for SMEs. Their primary concern is to ensure that entities are paying the right taxes based on the BIR tax rules and regulations. Thus, it is only the PSEC that really reviews whether the entities' financial statements are in compliance with the PFRS or PFRS for SMEs. Due to limited resources, how-ever, the PSEC cannot review all the financial statements submitted to them. Therefore, there is really no strict monitoring of compliance with the accounting standards. Many entities do not actually comply with the requirements of the PFRS for SMEs, and yet they do not get penalized because the likelihood that their statements will be reviewed is remote, especially if the entities are very small. Further, according to Yason (2014), one of the interviewees said that despite the adoption of the PFRS for SMEs four years ago, many SMEs have yet to fully understand the benefits under this standard.

As long as this remains an ongoing problem, many SMEs might informally prepare their financial statement by using the tax basis, cash basis, or modified cash basis without using the PFRS for SMEs. This suggests that the PFRS for SMEs helps a few Philippine SMEs to prepare their statements, but many SMEs need accounting standards under the tax basis, which is likely to be classified into the D category of the bottom-up approach as shown in Figure 7.1.

7.5 Conclusion

By thoroughly comparing the accounting standards for SMEs in Japan and the Philippines from the perspectives of the concepts of a standards model and the approaches to standards setting, this study can clarify the characteristics and homologous points of the two countries with different adoptions of the IFRS and the IFRS for SMEs on the basis of different economic circumstances. In Japan, like other developed countries, the standards for SMEs are individually set, but there are currently two standards with different characteristics (i.e., categories in Figure 7.1): the first one is the ASBJ Guidelines, classified as the A category, and the other is the General Standards, classified as the D category. Both are generally used depending upon SMEs' business circumstances: SMEs with accounting advisors or relatively larger SMEs than other entities in terms of revenue and capital size mainly apply the ASBJ Guidelines, and comparatively smaller SMEs such as micro-entities mainly use the General Standards.

On the other hand, SMEs in the Philippines used PAS 101, the first standard for SMEs, from 2005 to 2009. Since January 1, 2010, the Philippines have adopted the PFRS for SMEs, which has the same contents as the IFRS for SMEs. According to Inoue (2014), the current main problem in the Philippines is that many SMEs do not comply with the PFRS for SMEs. They get away with it because the BIR is concerned only with the taxes and not so much with the entities' compliance with the PFRS for SMEs. As a result, the old standard, PAS 101, was classified under the A category, and the present standards, the PFRS for SMEs, were classified under the C category; however, the standards that comply with the income tax requirements, namely, cash or modified cash basis, were classified under the D category. Currently, in the Philippines, like in other developing countries, the IFRS for SMEs has been adopted, but the other standards for SMEs with attributes of the D category have been properly used informally depending on their circumstances. This implies that it is necessary for the Philippine SMEs, like Japanese SMEs, to be given a choice of two accounting standards, which are classified into the A and D categories, depending on their business circumstances. Figure 7.4 summarizes the positioning of accounting standards for SMEs in Japan and the Philippines.

Thus, both countries are different with respect to the adoption of the IFRS and the IFRS for SMEs, as well as with respect to their economic circumstances.

	Single-standard concept	Dual-standard concept
Top-down approach	**【A】** Japan: ASBJ Guidelines (2005) The Philippines: PAS 101 (2005 to 2009)	**【C】** The Philippines: PFRS for SMEs (2009)
Bottom-up approach	**【B】*** N/A	**【D】** Japan: General Standards (2012) The Philippines: Many SMEs informally use the tax basis standards

Figure 7.4 Positioning of accounting standards for SMEs in Japan and the Philippines

*The B category does not exist because the bottom-up approach is based on the dual-standard concept.

However, they probably have similar features with regard to the status of their standards for SMEs, whether the applications are formal or informal. This calls for the necessity of using an appropriate accounting standard for each situation, for example, the revenue, capital size, management goals, etc., of SMEs.

Notes

1 For consistency, the term 'SMEs' has been used throughout this study. For this purpose, it is a synonym for 'private enterprise', 'private company', 'nonpublicly accountable enterprise' and any similar term (AcSB, 2007, paragraph 1).
2 The BAC is one of the councils set up by the FSA. It consists of a Planning and Coordination Committee, an Internal Control Committee, and an Audit Committee. The council has played a major role in setting accounting standards and has issued auditing and internal control standards since 2001 (Urasaki, 2014:53).
3 However, some SMEs shall be exempt from the mandatory adoption of the PFRS for SMEs and may instead apply it, at their discretion (PSEC, 2011).

References

AcSB (2007) *Discussion Paper, Financial Reporting by Private Enterprises*, Toronto: Accounting Standards Board.
ADB (2002) *Diagnostic Study of Accounting and Auditing Practices, the Philippines*, Asian Development Bank. Available from: www.adb.org/Documents/Books/Diagnostic_Study_Accounting_Auditing/PHI [Accessed: 22 September 2015].
AICPA (1976) Report of the Committee on Generally Accepted Accounting Principles for Smaller and/or Closely Held Business, Accounting Standards Division, New York: American Institute of Certified Public Accountants.
AICPA (1983) Report of the Special Committee on Accounting Standards Overload, Special Committee on Accounting Standards Overload, New York: American Institute of Certified Public Accountants.

AICPA (2013) *Financial Reporting Framework for Small- and Medium- Sized Entities*, New York: American Institute of Certified Public Accountants.

ASBJ, JICPA, JFCPTA, and JCCI (2005) *The Accounting Guidelines for Small- and Medium-sized Entities*, Tokyo: ASBJ Guidelines, Accounting Standards Board of Japan, Japanese Institute of Certified Public Accountants, Japan Federation of Certified Public Tax Accountants' Association and Japan Chamber of Commerce and Industry and the Accounting Standards Board of Japan.

ASC (2005) *Philippine Accounting Standard PAS 101, Financial Reporting Standards for Non-publicly Accountable Entities*, Makati City, Philippines: Accounting Standard Council.

DTI (2013) *A Guide to Registering Your Business*, Bureau of Micro, Small and Medium Enterprise Development (BMSMED), Makati City, Philippines: Department of Trade and Industry.

Fajardo C.L. (2008) The Evolution of Financial Accounting Standards in the Philippines, *8th Global Conference on Business & Economics*, October 18–19th 2008, Florence, Italy.

FRSC (2009) *Preface to Philippine Financial Reporting Standard for Small and Medium-sized Entities*, Makati City, Philippines: Financial Reporting Standards Council.

Hirano M. and Nishikawa N. (2008) Significance and Issues of the Japanese Accounting Guide for Private Entities, *The Review of Economics and Commerce*, The Kanagawa University, 43(3–4), pp. 1–34.

IASB (2004) *Preliminary Views on Accounting Standards for Small and Medium-sized Entities: Discussion Paper*, London: International Accounting Standard Board.

IASB (2007) *Exposure Draft of a Proposed International Financial Reporting Standards for Small and Medium-sized Entities*, London: International Accounting Standard Board.

IASB (2009a) *International Financial Reporting Standard for Small and Medium-sized Entities*, London: International Accounting Standard Board.

IASB (2009b) *International Financial Reporting Standard for Small and Medium-sized Entities: Basis for Conclusions*, London: International Accounting Standard Board.

IASB (2013) *IFRS for SMEs Fact Sheet*, IFRS Foundation, London: International Accounting Standard Board, July 2013.

IASC (1989) *Framework for the Preparation and Presentation of Financial Statements*, London: International Accounting Standards Committee.

Inoue S. (2014) *Interview Investigation about the Adoption Current State of the IFRS and IFRS for SMEs in the Philippines*, Kobe, Japan: Institute of Marketing and Distribution Sciences Research Notes, The University of Marketing and Distribution Sciences, 28, pp. 1–16.

JICPA (2003) *Research Report on Ideal SME Accounting*, Accounting System Committee Research Report, 8, Tokyo, Japan: Japanese Institute of Certified Public Accountants.

Kawasaki T. (2012) Current State and Issues of Accounting for SMEs (Small and Medium-sized Entities) in Japan, *Konan Accounting Review*, 6, pp. 1–9.

Kawasaki T. and Sakamoto T. (2014) *General Accounting Standard for Small- and Medium-sized Entities in Japan*, Tokyo, Japan: Wiley.

PSEC (2005) *Rule 68.1: Special Rule on Financial Statements of Reporting Companies under Section 17.2 of the Securities Regulation Code*, Mandaluyong City, Philippines: Philippine Securities and Exchange Commission.

PSEC (2009) *Notice: Commission En Banc meeting dated 3 December 2009, Department of Trade and Industry, Republic of the Philippines*, Mandaluyong City, Philippines: Philippine Securities and Exchange Commission.

PSEC (2011) *Securities Regulation Code Rule 68, as Amended*, Mandaluyong City, Philippines: Philippine Securities and Exchange Commission, December 2011.

Punongbayan & Araullo (2010) *Accounting Alert: Philippine Financial Reporting Standard for Small and Medium-sized Entities*, Punongbayan & Araullo, Makati City, Philippines. Available from: http://pnagt.punongbayan-araullo.com/pnawebsite/pnagtoutsourcinghome.nsf/369C652AEB7AD4D94825780E00342C14/$file/2010%20Accounting%20Alert%20-%20PFRS%20for%20SMEs.pdf [Accessed: 13 luglio 2015].

Review Group on SME Accounting (2012) *General Accounting Standards for SMEs*, General Standards. Available from: www.chusho.meti.go.jp/zaimu/youryou/about/index.htm#get [Accessed 8 July 2014].

Roth A.E. (2013) *Auditing Standards: Is 'Little GAAP' Finally Here?*, Trends & Developments, Eisner Amper, pp. 5–9. Available from: www.eisneramper.com/Trends_and_Developments/GAAP-Financial-Accounting-1013.aspx [Accessed: 24 July 2014].

SMEAJ (2010) *The Interim Report of the Study Group for Accounting for SMEs*, Tokyo, Japan: Ministry of Trade and Industry, Small and Medium Enterprise Agency Japan.

Urasaki N. (2014) Institutions and Accounting Standard Transformation: Observations from Japan, *China Journal of Accounting*, 7, pp. 51–64.

Yamashita T. (2012) A Study of Accounting Standards for SME's in Japan, *Saga University Economic Review*, 45(4), pp. 49–72.

Yason S.V. (2014) Financial Reporting: A Challenge to SMEs, *Business World Online*. Available from: www.bworldonline.com [Accessed: 17 June 2015].

8 Review of evaluation methods on economic benefits in relation to corporations' environmental sustainability activities

A trial analysis of Toyota Motor Corporation

Ikuo Kato and Tetsuya Takeuchi

8.1 Introduction

Taking advantage of the dissolution of the House of Representatives on November 16, 2012, the Japanese stock market went on an upward trend. It was observed that the main buyers were overseas investors and, among them, institutional investors like pension funds, etc., played a key role in buying up Japanese shares.

Since 2006,[1] Western institutional investors have become signatories to the UN-supported Principles for Responsible Investment (PRI). These investors take into consideration not only corporate financial information, but also environmental, social and corporate governance (ESG)–related information in conducting corporate valuations. There are analyses showing that taking into account sustainability-related activities such as corporate social responsibility (CSR), etc., when making stock investments is beneficial to investment performance.[2] In Japan, socially responsible investment or sustainable and responsible investing (SRI) funds that take into account sustainability information when investing have appeared.[3] Starting with global warming, the current tide of global concern in relation to sustainability cannot be pushed back.

Moving forward, if sustained growth of the Japanese SRI market is to be desired, there is a need to raise awareness that corporate sustainability activities indeed bring benefits to shareholders, fund beneficiaries, etc. This chapter explores the relationship between corporate sustainability activities and corporate profit (economic benefit) and aims to develop information useful in making stock investment decisions.[4]

8.2 Sustainability and corporate evaluation

8.2.1 Stock price forecasting using accounting information

With the huge size of stock assets managed by institutional investors, it is inevitable that various portfolio-based management styles are used. In portfolio management, shares of stock arranged by market value are incorporated into a portfolio and are matched against a benchmark stock price index. Future stock prices are customarily predicted using accounting information, and the inclusion ratios for each stock are adjusted.

The utility of accounting information in stock investing was demonstrated by Ball and Brown (1968). They focused on year-end financial results and showed that there was a relationship between abnormal returns and unexpected profit information. Further developing this theory, Ohlson (1995), using the dividend discount model (DDM) as a starting point and applying the proposition of Miller and Modigliani (1961), concluded that dividend policy is irrelevant and that abnormal returns were related to abnormal earnings with random risk involved (Ohlson, 1995: 667–8).

Next, the study examines what kind of relationship exists between accounting information and sustainability activities.

8.2.2 *Accounting information and sustainability activities*

With regard to corporate ESG activities, the majority fall under nonfinancial information headings. Because only environment-related items are disclosed as environmental accounting information, the study's focus will be on the environment hereafter.

Investment methods taking the environment into account are becoming popular in the West. For example, the California Public Employees' Retirement Fund (CalPERS) already became a signatory to Principles for Responsible Investment (PRI) in 2006. With regard to global warming brought about by climate change, CalPERS ties the influence of climate change to the global rise in demand for food and resources[5] and is concerned about its potential influence on long-term risk-adjusted returns. Over the next 20 years, CalPERS predicts that due to the influence of climate change, about 10 percent of portfolios under fiduciary management will be affected (CalPERS, 2012: 22). This prediction was test-calculated based on the Stern Review.[6]

In Japan as well, the Government Pension Investment Fund (GPIF), the largest investment fund in Japan, also became a signatory to the PRI in September 2015 following the movements in the West. Many Japanese companies publish information about the environment through media such as environmental reports, websites, etc. Among them, environmental accounting information is also released in conformity with the Ministry of the Environment guidelines (Ministry of the Environment, 2005). The elements in environmental accounting are composed of the following: environmental conservation costs, environmental conservation benefits and economic benefits associated with environmental conservation activities (Ministry of the Environment, 2005). Economic benefits are divided into actual benefits and estimated benefits (Ministry of the Environment, 2005: 27–30). The data not only deal with monetary value but also include physical units (Ministry of the Environment, 2005: 2). For example, on the subject of global warming, carbon dioxide (CO_2) emissions volumes and reduction volumes are nonmonetary and voluminous information, whereas the cost incurred to attain such reduction and the amount of reduction are monetary information. Generally speaking, the more a firm reduces its CO_2 emissions, the better its corporate image. This means there are concerns for companies with large CO_2 emissions. In the future when CO_2

emissions volume restrictions are enforced, these companies will be at great risk, and the effects on corporate profitability are unpredictable. The value created by CSR management that pre-emptively prevents and avoids risk is a useful estimated economic benefit for institutional investors who invest in the long term.

In the Ministry of the Environment guidelines (2005), a concrete calculation method for the estimated economic benefits is not actually specified. So, what kind of estimated economic benefits do companies publish? An analysis is conducted based on the companies in the first section of the Tokyo Stock Exchange, ranked according to market value as of August 12, 2013. The situation of the top ten companies is shown in Table 8.1.

Table 8.1 Companies in the Tokyo Stock Exchange first section ranked by market value as of August 12, 2013, and environmental accounting information

Rank	Name Code	Company name	Name of Report	Environmental Accounting	Estimated Economic Benefit
1	7203	Toyota Motor Corporation	• Sustainability Report 2013 • Respect for the Planet (Toyota's Environmental Initiatives)	yes	Customer benefits (reduction in gasoline consumption due to a switch to hybrid vehicles)
2	8306	Mitsubishi UFJ Financial Group, Inc.	CSR Report 2013	yes	Using finance to reduce the burden on the environment
3	9984	SoftBank Corp.	no	No	no
4	7267	Honda Motor Co., Ltd.	Honda CSR Report Honda Environment Annual Report 2013	yes	no
5	9432	Nippon Telegraph and Telephone Corporation (NTT)	NTT Group CSR Report 2013	yes	no
6	9437	NTT DOCOMO, Inc.	NTT DOCOMO Group CSR Report 2013	yes	no
7	2914	Japan Tobacco, Inc.	JT Group CSR Report 2013	yes	no
8	8316	Sumitomo Mitsui Financial Group, Inc.	CSR Report 2013	yes	no
9	8411	Mizuho Financial Group, Inc.	CSR Report 2013	yes	no
10	7201	Nissan Motor Co., Ltd.	Sustainability Report 2013	yes	no

Sources: The Nikkei and the environmental accounting information and websites of the respective companies.

Apart from the previously mentioned companies, companies in the 10 to 100 range that report estimated economic benefits are the following: Canon, Inc. (#12), Denso Corp. (#13), Hitachi, Ltd. (#21), Komatsu, Ltd. (#32), Mitsubishi Electric Corp. (#33), Mitsubishi Heavy Industries, Ltd. (#39), Toshiba Corp. (#46), MS&AD Insurance Group Holdings, Inc. (#48), and Fujifilm Holdings Corp. (#75). Like Toyota Motor Corp., these companies report the monetized value of the achieved reduction in CO_2 emissions when customers use their products. This is called a customer benefit. The environmental load reduction through financing by the Mitsubishi UFJ Financial Group is also a reduction effect occurring on the customer side.

Therefore, if the scope of the study is limited to the top-ranking companies by market value, customer benefit is calculated as an estimated economic benefit.

This customer benefit relates to the companies raising the profile of their products in the current fiscal year, but this benefit is not really directly associated to the evaluation of the value created by managing risk that the companies could be facing in the future due to the advance of global warming. Thus, in the next section, the study considers what the estimated economic benefits (including customer benefits) are likely to be and where the CO_2 emissions volume reduction becomes more useful information to the long-term investor.

8.2.3   Estimated economic benefits useful to the investor

In this section, the study discusses uncertainties pertaining to global warming. If global warming increases, governments will probably regulate companies to reduce their CO_2 emissions volumes. When that happens, companies will probably suffer economic damage. To reduce CO_2 emissions volumes, the immediately available solution is to reduce energy consumption. In other words, there is a risk for companies to be forced to scale down their production activities. In order to find a solution to this problem, the study turns its focus to firms' projects and examines those that integrate CO_2 emissions reduction into their projects.

When forecasting cash flow for capital investments, the net present value (NPV) method, which generally also conforms to investors' investment analysis methods, is used. The NPV method calculates the investment profit and loss for each individual capital investment project; then it compares the project's superiority and inferiority with other alternative investment plans and casts its vote on whether to adopt or reject the project.

Because the NPV method does not conduct probabilistic evaluations, there is a possibility that the calculation of the opportunity cost of unrealized gains from environmental protection is underestimated (Schaltegger and Burritt, 2000: 143). Regarding this point, if, by giving extra consideration to the environment in investment decisions, investors could add choices that make it possible to undertake other investments, then it could be possible to calculate that influence as a project's strategic value (call option) (Schaltegger and Burritt, 2000: 144).[7]

In a strategic management decision to conduct environment conservation measures, there is the possibility to calculate the estimated economic benefit as an option value. This option value will only be an estimated value because it arises from flexible strategic decisions made by a manager. In the next section, the study will examine an analysis and evaluation method of the estimated economic benefits as an option value.

8.3 Examining a method of analysis and evaluation of estimated economic benefits from sustainability activities

8.3.1 Financial information and sustainability information

Here the research will study the example of Toyota Motor Corporation (hereinafter referred to as Toyota), which has the largest market cap stock in the Tokyo Stock Exchange (TSE), based on their published reports. Toyota's main business is the automobile business. In 2012, the world automobile market showed a stable growth led by the United States and the emerging Asian nations. Toyota's automobile sales revenue was 22,064,100 million yen; operating income was 1,320,800 million yen; and net income was 962,100 million yen, an increase in profits. The following were cited as the main factors for the increase in profits: sales (650,000 million yen); cost improvement efforts (450,000 million yen); and foreign exchange fluctuations (150,000 million yen) (Toyota Motor Corporation, 2013a: 74).

Toyota's global vision is entitled "Rewarded with a smile by exceeding your expectations". By contributing towards making a "better car" that exceeds customer expectations and building "better towns/better societies", it receives smiles from customers and society, leading to a "stable base of business" that generates virtuous cycles and achieves sustainable growth (Toyota Motor Corporation, 2013a: 5).

Also, Toyota is aware that it is exposed to various event risks. The following risks are cited: natural calamities; political and economic instabilities; fuel shortages; interruptions in infrastructures like power, transportation functions, gas, water, communications, etc., due to natural disasters; wars; terrorism; labor strikes; and interruption of operations (Toyota Motor Corporation, 2013a: 41).

At Toyota, addressing environmental issues is considered one of management's most important tasks. Based on the thinking that promoting the widespread use of the eco-car contributes to the environment, Toyota is working towards the popularization of the hybrid vehicle (Toyota Motor Corporation, 2013a: 14). In the future, as the company aims for sustainable growth, investment in next-generation environmental technology for fuel-cell vehicles, etc., is a priority (Toyota Motor Corporation, 2013a: 18).

To signal the future direction of environmental activities at Toyota, the company has outlined their fifth "Environmental Action Plan" (Toyota Motor Corporation, 2013b: 34). It is a series of five-year segmented plans that includes operations and environmental initiatives expected of the company during the decade from 2020 to 2030. The priority themes have been determined: "Contribution to a Low Carbon Society", "Contribution to a Recycle-Based Society", and "Environmental Protection and Contribution to a Harmony with Nature Society".

Thus, in the case of Toyota, it can be said that the company's future strategic value can be estimated through its development project of the ultimate eco-car.

8.3.2   A trial calculation of estimated economic benefits from sustainability activities

In Kato (2013), the "Model for Measuring and Evaluating Economic Benefits Stemming from Climate Change Measures" examines the risks related to climate change combined with firms' short- and middle-term business planning (Kato, 2013: 65, Fig. 7). Using that method, the analysis and evaluation model of the estimated economic benefits brought about by Toyota's sustainability activities is shown in Figure 8.1.

In Figure 8.1, the study starts by forecasting cash flow sequentially as a normal capital budget (①). V_0 is the present value of the expected cash flow. Next, from the strategic decision to implement global warming measures, the study assumes a desired future involving the project, and a backcast of future cash flows is made (②). An inference on the gap between ① and ② is made (③). The gap becomes positive, and estimated economic benefits arise when it is inferred that the shaded areas in Figure 8.1 are pushed up due to sustainability activities. This gap constitutes estimated economic effects arising from making decisions that include managing CSR-related risk.

For Toyota, priority ranking in the sustainability report is placed on automobile CO_2 emissions volume reduction. Therefore, looking only at projected normal vehicle sales revenue, growth rates become negative as global warming progresses; but, in the future, eco-cars such as electric vehicles, fuel-cell vehicles, etc., will contribute to sales. In other words, the company forecasts its impact on global warming, invests in research and development to counteract the problem, and expands businesses positively.

Next, the study explains the short- and middle-term (five-year) forecast method by using hypothetical figures. Assume a cash flow of 1,300 billion yen operating income. Then, let the interest rate be 5 percent. A prediction of the growth rate of operating income is needed (the expansion coefficient in Table 8.2). In the same way, predictions of future sustainability-related costs (the expansion cost in Table 8.2) and of volatility (σ in Table 8.2), which follows from their degree of uncertainty, are necessary. What greatly influences the result is volatility. The higher the volatility, the greater the profit that could be earned; but conversely, it could also result in huge losses. If sustainability operations are promoted to avoid or alleviate losses, the sustainability costs incurred in the future would increase, but it is predicted that volatility would decrease.

Here, the study assumes the following: Toyota's future strategic value is in the option to expand, and the underlying model does not pay dividends. Toyota's future operating income growth rate (expansion coefficient) is 10 percent per year; the additional sustainability-related projects cost is 200 billion yen; and volatility is predicted to be at 15 percent.[8]

A trial calculation of estimated economic benefits from sustainability activities is tried with a method using real-options techniques, as shown in Table 8.2, as an example of an analysis method. The option valuation model used is the binomial model.[9]

In Table 8.2, the initial cash flow forecast ("A") is shown. For example, the values after the first period are $130 \times u = 151.04$ and $130 \times d = 111.89$. "A" multiplied

Toyota's Sustainability Activities (2013)

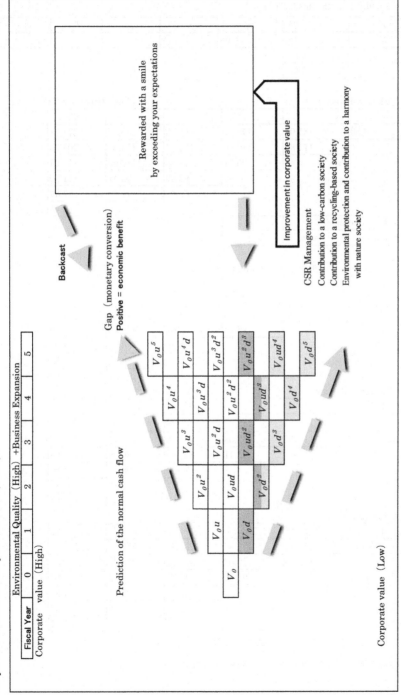

Figure 8.1 A model for analyzing and evaluating the estimated economic benefits stemming from Toyota's sustainability activities (2013)

References: Kato (2013) and Toyota Motor Corporation (2013b).

Table 8.2 An example of trial recalculation of estimated economic benefits from sustainability activities (2013)

r	1.05	*rf*	σ	*t*	*T*	δ*t*
u	1.16	0.05	0.15	5	5	1
d	0.86					
p	0.63					

A : Cash flow Forecast   (Unit:10billion Yen)

0	1	2	3	4	5
130.00	151.04	175.48	203.88	236.88	275.21
	111.89	130.00	151.04	175.48	203.88
		96.31	111.89	130.00	151.04
			82.89	96.31	111.89
				71.35	82.89
					61.41

Expansion Coefficient	1.1
Expansion Cost	20

B : (A×Expansion Coefficient–Expansion Cost)

0	1	2	3	4	5
123.00	146.14	173.03	204.27	240.56	282.73
	103.08	123.00	146.14	173.03	204.27
		85.94	103.08	123.00	146.14
			71.18	85.94	103.08
				58.48	71.18
					47.55

C : Backward induction

0	1	2	3	4	5	
130.68	152.14	177.27	206.77	241.54	282.73	B
	111.94	130.08	151.18	175.72	204.27	B
		96.31	111.89	130.00	151.04	A
			82.89	96.31	111.89	A
				71.35	82.89	A
					61.41	A

D : *MAX(A,B,C)*

0	1	2	3	4	5
130.68	152.14	177.27	206.77	241.54	282.73
	111.94	130.08	151.18	175.72	204.27
		96.31	111.89	130.00	151.04
			82.89	96.31	111.89
				71.35	82.89
					61.41

D–A =   0.68

Created by Kato with reference to Mun (2003: 182, Fig. 7.7).

by the expansion coefficient 1.10, with the resulting product reduced by the expansion cost of 20 (in 10-billion-yen units) is "B". For example, the figure 282.73 (in 10-billion-yen units) in the fifth period can be calculated by 275.21 × 1.1 − 20 = 282.73. In "C", first of all, the figures in the fifth period only compare A with B, and the larger number will be chosen. Therefore, 282.73 (in 10-billion-yen units) is chosen. In the same way, all the figures are calculated for the fifth period in "C"; then from the fifth period, the figures are discounted backwards to arrive at the fourth-period numbers and so on. For example, the figure 241.54 (in 10-billion-yen units) in the topmost cell of the fourth period is calculated as:

$$(p' \times 282.73 + (1-p)' \times e^{(-rf*dt)} = 241.54 \text{ (in 10-billion-yen units)}$$

As a result, the estimated economic benefit comes out as 0.68 (in 10-billion-yen units) and is calculated as a positive effect in this test calculation.

8.4 Updating information in 2015

Since the beginning of 2015, Toyota's stock has been performing quite impressively, maintaining its position as the largest in terms of market cap in the Tokyo Stock Exchange.[10]

On October 14, 2015, Toyota made a surprising announcement, the so-called "Environmental Challenge 2050".[11] It was surprising because they set a long-term target up to 2050 for the first time and also because its first goal is the "New Vehicles Zero CO_2 Emissions Challenge". As mentioned previously, Toyota used to set management plans every five years. The concept of a sustainability-related plan in this study is to set long-term goals, backcast the impact of countermeasures against long-term global warming and put these into a viable short-term plan, which Toyota seems to have undertaken. Their plan is also unique because the idea of making an automobile, which was traditionally a gasoline-driven vehicle, with zero CO_2 emissions is quite innovative.

In Europe some companies such as Volkswagen have been promoting diesel automobiles as a countermeasure against global warming. However, on September 18, 2015, the US Environmental Protection Agency issued a notice of violation (NOV) of the Clean Air Act (CAA) to Volkswagen AG, Audi AG and Volkswagen Group of America, Inc. The scandalous event[12] caused by Volkswagen is expected to cause huge damage, not only to Volkswagen and its associated companies, but also to the German economy. In response to this event, Toyota seems to have started differentiating themselves from other companies that focus on and strategically expand sales of diesel automobiles. The fact that Toyota has set such a long-term goal will affect not only the automobile industry, but also Japanese companies in general.

Figure 8.2 illustrates where the elements of the new "Environmental Challenge 2050" fit into the CSR management concept model shown in Figure 8.1.

In 2013, Toyota's sales growth was greater than expected, and a volatility figure of 0.37 (=ln (1/2) * (2,750,564 / 1,320,800)) is arrived at when calculated based on

Toyota's Sustainability Activities (2015)

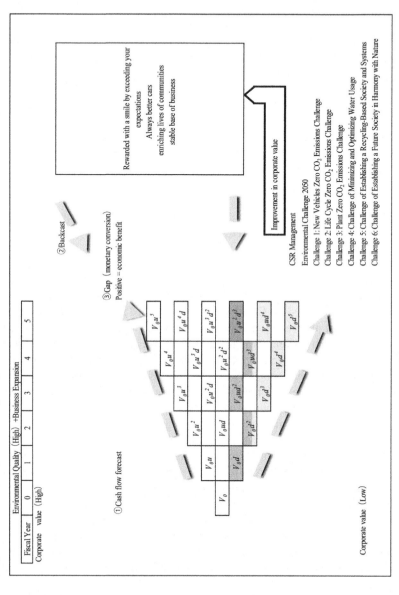

Figure 8.2 A model for analyzing and evaluating the estimated economic benefits stemming from Toyota's sustainability activities (2015)

References: Kato (2013) and Toyota Motor Corporation (2015).

Table 8.3 An example of trial calculation of estimated economic benefits from sustainability activities (2015)

r	1.05	rf	σ	t	T	δt
u	1.45	0.05	0.37	5	5	1
d	0.69					
p	0.48					

Step A: Lattice Evoluion of the Underlying (Cash flow Forecast) (Unit:10 billion Yen)

0	1	2	3	4	5
130.00	188.21	272.47	394.47	571.08	826.78
	89.80	130.00	188.21	272.47	394.47
		62.02	89.80	130.00	188.21
			42.84	62.02	89.80
				29.59	42.84
					20.44

Expansion Coefficient	1.1
Expansion Cost	35

Step B : (A×Expansion Coefficient–Expansion Cost)

0	1	2	3	4	5
108.00	172.03	264.72	398.91	593.19	874.45
	63.78	108.00	172.03	264.72	398.91
		33.23	63.78	108.00	172.03
			12.13	33.23	63.78
				-2.45	12.13
					-12.52

Step C : Backward induction

0	1	2	3	4	5	
131.38	191.04	278.27	406.26	594.90	874.45	B
	89.98	130.41	189.12	274.49	398.91	B
		62.02	89.80	130.00	188.21	A
			42.84	62.02	89.80	A
				29.59	42.84	A
					20.44	A

Step D : Option Valuation Lattice (MAX(A,B,C))

0	1	2	3	4	5
131.38	191.04	278.27	406.26	594.90	874.45
	89.98	130.41	189.12	274.49	398.91
		62.02	89.80	130.00	188.21
			42.84	62.02	89.80
				29.59	42.84
					20.44

D–A = 1.38

Created by Kato with reference to Mun (2003: 182, Fig. 7.7).

2013 and 2015 numbers.[13] Looking at Toyota's environmental accounting, research and development costs were 353.5 billion yen in 2013. Based on these numbers, while discounting volatilities and assuming other conditions are the same as in the Figure 8.1, Toyota's estimated economic benefits through its activities for sustainability can be recalculated. The number obtained is 63.74 (in 10-billion-yen units) and is calculated as a positive effect in this test calculation.

8.5   In conclusion

Using environmental accounting information, this study has examined a method of analyzing and evaluating estimated economic benefits stemming from a firm's sustainability activities. It also shows that environmental accounting information is useful to long-term investors and that there are estimable economic benefits when future climate change is taken into consideration. The use of real-options valuation methods is valid in calculating the value of such benefits. That value can be found in a firm's projects. Taking the example of Toyota, the researchers conducted a trial calculation of the economic benefits from its sustainability activities.

As in the case of Toyota, based only on sustainability reports, it can be predicted that companies that combine sustainability with their main business will have estimable economic benefits coming from the positive influence of sustainability activities on their performances. The example of the current global warming countermeasures undertaken by Toyota is an extension of conventional CSR management. If arising from such sustainability activities a new opportunity like the fuel-cell vehicle comes into being and is sold in the market, the economic benefits may exceed expectations. These estimated economic benefits from sustainability activities, if represented as an option value, would be useful information to investors.

However, because the estimated economic effects were originally intended to be used only internally as strategic accounting numbers, it is not possible to disclose the option value externally as it is. Therefore, how one represents the estimated economic effects as external information will be an issue in the future. For instance, expressing the gap as the amount of carbon dioxide and using that number could be a solution.

In the future, the variable that must be studied continuously is volatility, and the challenge is in increasing the forecast accuracy of this number. To that end, there is a need for positive analysis, but the current situation is that there is almost no disclosure of quantitative information on profit targets, etc., for 50 years in the future. Therefore, it is hoped that companies would examine, as is shown in this study, calculation methods for estimating economic benefits with a limitation use to corporate management use and disclose in the future quantitative predictive information on the possibility that opportunities will arise from the advance of climate change and also on the possibility of the negative risks that follow it.

Notes

1   The UN Principles for Responsible Investment (PRI) were launched in 2006.
2   The Forum for Sustainable and Responsible Investment.

3 In Japan, the 'Eco Fund' was launched by Nikko Asset Management Co. Ltd. in 1999. This fund is considered to be the first SRI fund in Japan.

4 Although this chapter was originally written in 2013, it was updated in 2015 to take the current situation into account.

5 Oil, natural gas, and water.

6 According to the Stern Review on the Economics of Climate Change, CO_2 emissions per capita are strongly correlated with GDP per capita (Stern *et al.*, 2006:11). The review has focused on the feasibility and costs of stabilization of greenhouse gas concentrations in the atmosphere in the range of 450 to 550 ppm CO_2 (Stern *et al.*, 2006:11). And the stabilization of greenhouse gases at levels of 500 to 550 ppm CO_2 is expected to cost, on average, around 1 percent of annual global GDP by 2050. (Stern *et al.*, 2006:13). Therefore, a large-scale uptake of a range of clean power, heat and transport technologies is required for radical emissions cuts in the medium- to long-term. (Stern *et al.*, 2006:13).

7 This option is called a real option. Real options are defined as "the right (but not an obligation) to undertake certain actions (deferring, expanding, contracting, abandoning, etc.) at a pre-determined cost (exercise price) and within a pre-determined period (exercise period)." (Copeland and Antikarov, 2001: 5–6). The option value will use option pricing models. Among the typical option pricing theories, there is the continuous Black and Scholes (1973) model and the discrete Cox *et al.* (1979) binomial lattice-based model.

8 There is the method to use the management estimates (Copeland and Antikarov, 2001).

9 The price of the call option *(C)* using the binomial lattice-based model is as follows: *u* means "move up", *d* means "move down" and *p* is the risk-neutral probability (Hull, 2003: 200–215).

$$C = e^{-rT}[pC_u + (1-p)C_d]$$

$$p = \frac{e^{rT} - d}{u - d}, u = e^{\sigma\sqrt{\delta t}}, d = e^{-\sigma\sqrt{\delta t}} = \frac{1}{u}$$

10 March 2015 results were as follows: automobile sales revenue was 27,234,521 million yen, operating income was 2,750,564 million yen and net income was 2,173,338 million yen.

11 Toyota Motor Corporation, 2015.

12 Volkswagen admitted to manipulating CO_2 emissions test data on its diesel cars globally in 2015.

13 Referring to the calculation method of Amram and Kulatilaka (1999: 212–214).

References

Amram M. and Kulatilaka N. (1999) *Real Options: Managing Strategic Investment in an Uncertain World*, Harvard Business School Press, Boston.

Ball R. and Brown P. (1968) An Empirical Evaluation of Accounting Income Numbers, *Journal of Accounting Research*, 6(2), pp. 159–178.

Black F. and Scholes M.S. (1973) The Pricing of Options and Corporate Liabilities, *Journal of Political Economy*, 27, pp. 637–654.

CalPERS (2012) *Towards Sustainable Investment – Taking Responsibility*, Sacramento: California Public Employees' Retirement System.

Copeland T. and Antikarov V. (2001) *Real Options*, Cengage Learning, New York.

Cox J.C., Ross S.A. and Rubinstein M. (1979) Option Pricing: A Simplified Approach, *Journal of Financial Economics*, 7, pp. 229–263.

Hull J.C. (2003) *Options, Futures, and Other Derivatives*, 5th edition, Prentice Hall, Upper Saddle River, NJ.

Kato I. (2013) A Study on the Model for Measuring and Evaluating the Economic Benefit Associated with Climate Change Measures in the Company: Analyses for the Tokyo Electric Power Co. Ltd., *Association of Yokohama International Social Science Studies*, 17(4–5), pp. 53–72.

Ministry of the Environment (2005) *Environmental Accounting Guidelines 2005*, Tokyo: Ministry of the Environment Government of Japan.

Miller M.H. and Modigliani F. (1961) Dividend Policy, Growth and the Valuation of Shares, *Journal of Business* 34(4), pp. 411–433.

Mun J. (2003) *Real Option Analysis: Tools and Techniques for Valuing Strategic Investments and Decision*, John Wiley & Sons, Hoboken, NJ.

Ohlson J.A. (1995) Earning, Book Values, and Dividends in Equity Valuation, *Contemporary Accounting Research*, 11(2), pp. 661–687.

Schaltegger S. and Burritt R. (2000) *Contemporary Environmental Accounting: Issues, Concepts and Practice*, Greenleaf Publishing Limited, Sheffield.

Stern, N. H., S. Peters, V. Bakhshi, A. Bowen, C. Cameron, S. Catovsky, D. Crane, S. Cruickshank, S. Dietz, N. Edmonson, S.-L. Garbett, L. Hamid, G. Hoffman, D. Ingram, B. Jones, N. Patmore, H. Radcliffe, R. Sathiyarajah, M. Stock, C. Taylor, T. Vernon, H. Wanjie, and D. Zenghelis. (2006) *Stern Review: The Economics of Climate Change*, HM Treasury, London.

Toyota Motor Corporation (2013a) *Annual Report 2013*, Toyota Motor Corporation, Toyota City, Aichi.

Toyota Motor Corporation (2013b) *Sustainability Report 2013*, Toyota Motor Corporation, Toyota City, Aichi.

Toyota Motor Corporation (2015) *Respect for the Planet-Toyota's Environmental Initiatives-2015*, Toyota Motor Corporation, Toyota City, Aichi.

9 Cultural differences towards business ethics

Implications for French and American investors in Vietnam

Marc Valax and Jérôme Rive

9.1 Introduction

The economy is global, and human resources management needs to develop global leadership skills, laying down the business ethics perspectives that must be integrated to meet the globalization challenge (Black and Morisson, 2014). From an international business viewpoint, the subject of business ethics involves people participating in economic transactions and, at the same time, serving their own as well as others' interests. In relation to business ethics, entrepreneurs and managers agree that even if one individual acts according to the law, ethical and moral values are relevant to the success of the firms and are not just for public relations purposes. Competitive pressures can affect sound ethical decisions (Henry, 2011). Improving the community's quality of life also assists the long-run profitability of a firm, and socially responsible behavior is in the best interest of all stakeholders (Sorge, 2005).

Cultural adjustment, health and ethics dilemmas are really important when considering pharmaceutical businesses on an international basis. Proper health coverage ensures that all people obtain the health services they need without suffering financial hardship when paying for them. This requires a strong, efficient, well-run health system; a system for financing health services; access to essential medicines and technologies; a sufficient supply of well-trained, motivated health workers; and, above all, ethical rules, especially in developing countries (Forster, 1997). In pharmaceutical labs, ethical rules to protect participants in drug trials in Vietnam are one area of concern. For the pharmaceutical industry, the attraction of labs in Vietnam are the lower costs of doing drug trials and development activities so as to enter Southeast Asian markets and a less stringent environmental legislation (waste production and emissions, for example). The main incentive for Vietnam is a promise of advanced medical science and immediate access to the latest medications. However, the process of putting in place a legal and ethical framework to protect participants is not advancing at the same pace in Vietnam as in other countries (Nguyen and Wertheim, 2013). One of the problems is how to implement guidelines between the people taking part in the drug trials and the international pharmaceutical labs in a code of conduct. The research analyzes cultural adjustment and ethics practices of the managers from different perspectives in the pharmaceutical labs. The researchers recently had the opportunity to collect primary data using semistructured, in-depth and group interviews of managers.

Exclusive in-depth interviews were undertaken, and articles, public databases and company websites were also researched for additional information to collaborate, triangulate and validate the interview results. The following sections describe the theoretical framework, the research setting and the scope of the study's qualitative methodology. Then, previous explanations of ethical dilemmas in the Vietnamese context are discussed.

9.2   Theoretical framework and research methods

Ethical and cultural considerations are important in the study. It is necessary to consider the consequences of international business ethics within a theoretical framework. The reasons for conducting drug trials in Vietnam are not only because Vietnam has fewer regulations. Anticipatory and in-country variables related to work, interaction and general repatriation adjustment have to be examined with a focus on different expatriates. Cultural distance can hinder general adjustment.

A qualitative methodology has been selected that could go beyond the surface of management rhetoric, and the research will explore different dimensions: responsibility, human rights and cultural aspects.

Ethical business and responsibility

In international business, the cultural context may well affect the shared understanding of what *ethical* actually means (Harzing and Noorderhaven, 2006). Ethics defines the elements essential to human well-being and proposes guiding principles to generate an ethical culture. Ethics also refers to the specific values, standards, rules and agreements that people adopt for conducting their lives. Ethics are not merely social conventions, like table manners. Rather, ethics define the social conditions necessary for human beings to thrive. For the purposes of this study, ethics is defined as "[t]he philosophical study of the moral value of human conduct and the rules and principles that ought to govern it" (Wooten, 2001). This study distinguishes two levels of ethics: 'macro-ethics' (concerned with the collective social responsibility of the manager and societal decisions) and 'micro-ethics' (concerned with individuals and the internal relations of their commitment). Hellriegel *et al.* (2012) note that business ethics involves how a company integrates core values such as honesty, trust, respect and fairness into its policies, practices and decision making. Business ethics are the standards used to judge the rightness or wrongness of a business' relations to others (Smith, 2007). Rossouw and Van Vuuren (2004) point out that business ethics is about identifying and implementing standards of conduct that will ensure that, at a minimal level, business does not detrimentally affect the interests of its stakeholders. The study identifies the scope of business ethics under five headings:

1   Behavior towards customers, suppliers, distributors and competitors (marketing and selling, fair competition, intelligence gathering, inducements and incentives)

2   Treatment of employees (recruitment, rewards, training, promotion, dismissal, employee and employer rights and duties)
3   Treatment of the other stakeholder groups (local communities, government, interest groups)
4   Effects on the natural environment (pollution, recycling, sustainability)
5   Conduct in international business (use of power, respect for human rights and delocalization of operations to lower-cost environments)

Vogel (2005) has defined three categories of ethical issues: *hope* (teleology): utilitarianism, particular ends with a self-actualization; *faith* (deontology): universal principles, particular duties with a case-by-case approach; and *charity* (caring): love for humanity, personal relationships and codes of conduct.

Ethical responsibility involves more than leading a decent, honest, truthful life, as important as such lives certainly remain. And it involves

> something much more than making wise choices when such choices suddenly, unexpectedly present themselves. Our moral obligations must . . . include a willingness to engage others in the difficult work of defining what the crucial choices are that confront management and society and how intelligently to confront them.
>
> (Scherer and Palazzo, 2007: 1105)

Ethical responsibility means taking account of an organization's impact socially, environmentally, economically and in terms of human rights.

Health, human rights and intercultural aspects
Health and human rights investigations raise complex ethical and theoretical challenges. Key questions have emerged about the roles of human rights in the pharmaceutical lab business on an international basis. Human rights may follow ethical codes and well-being norms. Local employees, as well international managers, may exert their influence to limit the scope of or impede investigations into human rights abuses.

Since the original UN Universal Declaration of Human Rights, the rights of a person include having access to a standard of living adequate for the health and well-being of himself and of his family, including food, clothing, housing and medical care and necessary social services. For a society to honor these rights involves specific choices with regard to its social and cultural content. From a cultural point of view, ethically conscious people feel engaged and committed to society, and society is protected from the risks associated with misconduct and lurking ethical issues in an intercultural perspective.

Cultural adjustment
Black, Mendenhall and Oddou (1991) put forth a general model of the dimensions and determinants of adjustment to international assignments. Research on

expatriate adjustment leads to the conclusion that cultures more different or distant from the expatriate's culture of origin present bigger challenges and result in greater adjustment difficulties (Zhou and Qin, 2009).

Black, Mendenhall and Oddou (1991) found that US expatriates tend to experience greater cultural barriers in Asia and Africa in the areas of job satisfaction, stress and anxiety and quality-of-life standards such as housing, food and health care. Similarly, Tung (1998) reported that US expatriates express higher levels of dissatisfaction with their expatriation experiences in Africa, the Middle East and Southeast Asia than in other world regions because the cultures in those areas are most dissimilar.

Any change in a person's life entails a requirement to adjust (Stahl and Cerdin, 2004). Adjustment is the outcome of a learning process that enables the individual to be more effective and content in the new circumstances (Tahvanainen, Welch and Worm, 2005).

The term adjustment is adopted rather than adaptation, assimilation or acculturation to describe what is happening to top management expatriates. The literature has used these and related terms in various ways that are sometimes interchangeable and sometimes hierarchical (Black, Mendenhall and Oddou, 1991; Harrison, Shaffer and Bhaskar-Shrinivas, 2004). Berry, Kim and Boski (1988) regard acculturation as including changes by the individual himself or herself and to the immediate environment. They see assimilation as one of several acculturation strategies. Stress theory distinguishes adaptation and adjustment in terms of the individual's magnitude of change and whether or not a crisis precedes the change (Black, Mendenhall and Oddou, 1991)

Black and Stephens (1989) correlated a measure of cultural distance with expatriate adjustment using self-reports from 220 business expatriates, whose results were negative. Later, Black, Mendenhall and Oddou put forth a model of the dimensions and determinants of adjustment to international assignments (1991). According to the model, it is proposed that cultural novelty will be negatively associated with the degree of international adjustment, especially with that of interaction and general adjustment. Researchers could show the two dimensions of adjustment: general and work adjustment (Tempel and Walgenbach, 2007). Others added the adjustment to interactions with host nationals, which separated interactions with host nationals from other aspects of the general environment such as transportation and climate. Black, Mendenhall and Oddou (1991) proposed three related but separate dimensions of expatriate adjustment:

1   Adjustment to the job (work adjustment)
2   Adjustment to interacting with host-country nationals (interaction adjustment)
3   Adjustment to the general nonwork environment (general adjustment)

The model was subsequently expanded and tested by Shaffer, Harrison and Gilley, who also examined two individual factors and three positional factors as moderators of adjustment determinants (Shaffer, Harrison and Gilley, 1999). The model of determinants of expatriate adjustment proposed by Black, Mendenhall and Oddou (1991) and expanded by Shaffer, Harrison and Gilley (1999) can be summarized as follows:

1   Individual factors (achievement and social self-efficacy, relational and perceptual skills, previous assignments and language fluency)
2   Job factors (role clarity, role discretion, role conflict and role novelty)
3   Organizational factors (organizational cultural novelty, social support and logistical support)
4   Positional factors (hierarchical level, functional area and assignment vector)
5   Culture novelty and family factors (culture novelty refers to the perceived distance between host and parent country cultures and has been found to hinder nonwork adjustment)

Sociocultural adjustment can be measured by adopting Black, Mendenhall and Oddou's (1991) 14-item scale with slight modifications. As the most often tested and utilized measurement to assess an expatriate's sociocultural adjustment, it is designed to measure three dimensions: general adjustment (sample item: "living conditions in general"), interaction adjustment (sample item: "interacting with host nationals on a day-to-day basis") and work adjustment (sample item: "specific job responsibilities"). The respondents indicate how well adjusted they are to their respective host locations on a scale ranging from 1 ("very unadjusted") to 5 ("completely adjusted"). The resulting reliability scores of the three variables are acceptable: seven items on general adjustment (alpha = .76), four items on interactions adjustment (alpha = .84) and three items on work adjustment (alpha = .88).

Psychological adjustment can be measured using the General Health Questionnaire (GHQ-12) developed by Goldberg (1972) with some modifications. It contains a number of questions concerning how people have been feeling recently, including sleeping difficulties, feelings of unhappiness and the respondents' ability to enjoy everyday experiences. Respondents are asked to think about how they have been feeling over the past few weeks (sample item: "Have you recently been able to concentrate on what you're doing?"). Responses range from 1 ("more than usual") to 5 ("less than usual"). Reliability coefficients range from .78 to .95 in various studies.

Cultural distance can be measured by the 8-item scale used by Black, Mendenhall and Oddou (1991). On a 5-point Likert scale, the expatriates are asked to indicate how similar or different a number of conditions are in the host country compared with their home country (sample item: "transportations systems used in the country"). The response categories vary from 1 ("extremely different") to 5 ("extremely similar"). For easier interpretation of the results, this scale is reversed to make a higher score represent a greater cultural distance. There is an acceptable reliability score for this scale (alpha = .80).

The levels of behavioral effectiveness, knowledge of the host culture and the degree of emotional well-being are expected naturally to vary among observers and among expatriates themselves. The expatriate may have to assimilate the new culture, integrate home and host cultures or exist in the environmental bubble of an expatriate community (Berry, 1997). The definition of adjustment and, hence, of an adjusted expatriate, can take many different forms, depending on the aspects one wants to stress, especially in the international situations of business ethics.

9.2.1   *Research setting and qualitative data*

Due to the exploratory nature of the study on business ethics, the study relied on qualitative-case research (Yin, 1994) and planned in the future to be oriented on a quantitative research model in order to get authorization from the Vietnamese authorities. The researchers selected a qualitative methodology that could go beyond the surface of management rhetoric. It focuses on standard expatriates and not virtual or off-shore expatriates to prevent the discussion from becoming too diffuse.

In order to do that, the researchers first constructed an initial diagnosis of four major pharmaceutical labs in Vietnam (established for more than five years), based on interviews with 25 top expatriate managers, either individually or in small groups during intercultural management seminars in 2012, 2013 and 2014. This diagnosis generated a broad description of the ethics management and expatriate assignment based on semistructured interviews and observations in Vietnam. Then, the researchers identified and interviewed 20 top-level managers and local middle managers to gain a better understanding of the previously mentioned issues in ethics and cultural adjustment.

For research purposes, the cases study method proved to be appropriate for exploring the characteristics of business ethics and cultural adjustment. The researchers used a field study to understand the multidimensionality of business ethics and cultural adjustment, the relationships between top managers and middle managers and its antecedents and outcomes. The researchers conducted the study in Vietnam in two locations (Hanoi and Ho Chi Minh City) that had formally implemented clinical trials and marketing actions. Verbatim reports, age ranges, management levels, organizational tenure, ways of thinking about health, approach to ethics and cultural adjustment have been essential in defining the sample. The researchers obtained interviews with some difficulty because of overbooked agendas and took into account the need to find fully comprehensible English speakers. The researcher conducted exclusive in-depth interviews with international specialists and searched public databases and company websites for additional information to collaborate, triangulate and validate interview results. For all interviews, the researchers tried to review the notes for accuracy immediately after the interviews and before transcription.

Trustworthiness in interpretative research was ensured by using four criteria: credibility, transferability, dependability and confirmability. The researchers had the opportunity to collect primary data using semistructured, in-depth and group interviews of top managers and middle managers.

The results of the diagnosis generated a broad description of the ethics management and cultural differences during expatriate assignments. The expatriate assignment is an expatriate's opportunity to build career capital and a company's opportunity to generate social and intellectual capital. The extent of the capital gains will depend considerably on the expatriate's adjustment during the assignment.

Based on the analysis of 45 interviews of top-level managers and local middle managers, the researchers defined three main hypotheses on business ethics and cultural adjustment dimensions:

(Hypothesis 1) The American expatriate top managers in Vietnam perceive a larger cultural distance between Vietnam and their home country than the French expatriate top managers, especially in terms of sociocultural adjustment and business ethics conditions.

(Hypothesis 2) The French expatriate top managers working in Vietnam demonstrate higher degrees of adaptability than the American business expatriates in general adjustment and interaction adjustment, but not in fast business model results.

(Hypothesis 3) French expatriates take a prolonged period of time to adjust, exhibit poor performance in the short run and complete their assignment in a low state of effectiveness.

9.3 Cross-cases analysis in the specific context of Vietnam

In 2013, it was estimated that of the 90,000 international clinical trials conducted globally, more than 40 percent took place in poor countries such as Vietnam (Nguyen and Wertheim, 2013). However, only a few of these trials have focused on diseases that primarily affect the poor or the countries where the trials take place, even if Vietnam is one of the fastest-growing pharmaceutical markets in Asia. In 2014, Vietnam's drug market was worth almost $3 billion – about one-third the size of the Indian market. It is expected to grow at a rate of more than 20 percent through 2017 (Nguyen and Wertheim, 2013). Vietnam ranks 13 out of 175 countries for the fastest-growing global markets in drug spending. Drug consumption per capita in Vietnam is also climbing. In 2014, the typical Vietnamese citizen spent $104 annually on pharmaceutical products. This compares to $148 in China and $51 in India. Per capita spending on drugs in Vietnam should have more than doubled by 2015. That increase is fueled by a richer and older society and by an expansion of the country's national health insurance system. In 2014, 65 percent of Vietnam's 89 million people are covered by the national system. By 2020, that number will reach 90 percent.

All of this makes Vietnam an attractive market for foreign pharmaceutical companies, who continue to enter the country in growing numbers, but Vietnam is still in a phase of transition from a centrally planned economy to a market economy with a still socialist orientation.

9.3.1   Specific Vietnamese context for business ethics

Vietnam's efforts to attract foreign investment have led the ruling party to seek to improve the business climate for foreign investors. This involves attempts to combat corruption, which is rampant throughout the country and permeates the activities of the many state companies that still dominate the economy's strategic sectors. The lack of anticorruption standards implementation and weak enforcement mean corruption continues to be cited as one of the most problematic factors for doing business in the country.

However, some developments in relation to ethics, corruption and investment have taken place:

•   Corruption has moved up on the political agenda in Vietnam, and the legal framework for curbing corruption is now well developed.
•   Although the burden of licenses and permits on private companies is still considerable, Vietnam has abolished almost 200 'unnecessary' permits for operating a company.
•   Companies indicate that special relationships with provincial authorities have declined in importance, and fewer companies feel that 'having friends' is important for negotiating with the government.

Bureaucracy, especially in the tax and customs areas, remains a fundamental issue to be tackled in Vietnam. Local pharmaceutical production accounted for nearly half of Vietnam's drug needs in 2012. However, those products were almost all low-cost generics. Imports accounted for more than 70 percent of the pharmaceuticals market by value during the same year. The most sophisticated tablets are imported in Vietnam and not made there. Vietnam's import value of pharmaceutical and medicinal products reached US$1.79 billion in 2012, or a 12.5 percent increase year on year. In 2012, there were about 170 pharmaceutical companies in Vietnam. Almost 10 percent were owned by foreign investors, with another 4 percent operating under joint venture agreements. To boost domestic production of higher-quality drugs, Vietnam has recently encouraged manufacturers to obtain Good Manufacturing Practice (GMP) certification. However, only about one-third of Vietnamese pharmaceutical companies have GMP certification in 2014. Foreign pharmaceutical companies who want their products widely prescribed have to engage in the bidding processes at hospitals. The bidding processes are rife with corruption. A 2010 government inspection found that Vietnamese retail prices were up to eight times higher than the prices for similar drugs in other nations. In Hanoi, an inspection team found that the winning bid prices for many drugs were 130 to 245 percent higher than their original import prices (Henry, 2011). The reason given by the inspection team was hospital corruption. Often, underpaid doctors and hospital procurement committee members receive "commissions" from drug sales within the hospital. Therefore, they have a natural incentive to accept high bids. In the past, pharmaceutical companies that wanted to survive in the Vietnamese market would go along with hospital requests for higher-than-normal bids. This practice is changing, but slowly.

9.3.2   Discussion: research results in relation to business ethics and cultural adjustment

What is commonly known as a clinical trial is a research investigation in which one or more human volunteers are simultaneously tested with newly discovered health treatments. Most clinical trials are initiated with the objective of establishing the effectiveness of new drugs that are being developed. The clinical trials are extremely carefully regulated, and they are also the most effective way to establish the new treatments that can be more beneficial for human health.

Although testing drugs in Vietnam is clearly controversial, additional ethical dilemmas arise when conducting research on treatments to be used locally. One of the main questions is whether such research should use the "best" available drugs or treatments instead of the most practical and available ones. It is important to realize that conducting relevant research in Vietnam might not imply the use of the best and most effective treatments available in Western countries. Realistically, such treatments will not be readily available or will be too expensive for the majority of people in developing countries.

> *The testing of less effective treatments for use in poor countries is justly controversial and deeply troublesome. At the same time, the failure to do so would be even more problematic, essentially barring doctors in poor countries from conducting locally relevant research that might save or improve their patients' lives.*
>
> (Wagstaff, 2007: 87)

Often, the study participants are poor and may not understand that they are taking part in a study and instead may believe that they are merely receiving proper or preferential treatment for a condition.

Clinical trials must be conducted under conditions of respect for fundamental human rights and for the ethical principles affecting biomedical research involving human subjects, following for this purpose the contents of the Declaration of Helsinki, that is, the settings configured in Helsinki (1964) and updated in Tokyo (1975), Venice (1983), Hong Kong (1989), Somerset West (1996) and Edinburgh (2000). The declaration says that

> In any research on human beings, each potential subject must be informed of the aims, methods, anticipated benefits and potential hazards of the study and the discomfort it may entail. He or she must be informed that he [or she] is free to abstain from participation in the study and they are free to withdraw your consent to participate at any time. The investigator must obtain informed consent freely and preferably in writing.

Considering these principles, the study researchers asked American and European top pharmaceutical managers to describe their viewpoint and their way of conducting clinical trials in Vietnam.

The American viewpoint on clinical trials: "high level of marketing effectiveness in knowing how and knowing why!"
Clinical trials on issues relevant to the US health care system have been conducted in Vietnam by pharmaceutical firms since 2008. In fact, more than 100 clinical trials have been managed in Vietnam on drugs intended for American use. Many drugs intended for use in the United States were still tested in Vietnam in 2014. The drug patient enrollment engagement lasts years, usually between two and five.

The researchers had the opportunity to get interviews inside two American plants focused on technologies that can identify promising vaccine treatments and refine them before they enter costly and time-consuming clinical trials. They also invest in research to better understand the health factors that affect susceptibility to infectious diseases and vaccine efficacy, such as malnutrition and co-infections. Furthermore, they seek more effective models of collaboration with major vaccine manufacturers to better identify and pursue mutually beneficial opportunities.

Their vaccine discovery efforts focus on developing vaccine technologies and closing the knowledge gaps to facilitate the eradication of polio.

These two American subsidiaries in Vietnam work to speed up the identification of the best drug treatments, and, as they do with vaccine discovery, they look for opportunities to collaborate with local pharmaceutical companies because of their unique resources and expertise. They also seek to develop new technologies and approaches to slow the evolution and spread of drug-resistant illnesses, including alternative formulations and drug-delivery technologies.

They support efforts to create a new generation of more effective and less toxic drugs to treat malaria, tuberculosis (TB) and lymphatic filariasis (elephantiasis) and to control severe diarrhea. To take advantage of major advances in materials science, biology and chemistry, they invest in developing new contraceptive technologies, including nonhormonal contraceptive drugs.

Being transparent and efficient with nonmaleficence is the key point
The principle of transparency is a pointed one with an emphasis on Vietnamese people who must be treated with consideration and respect, in a nondiscriminatory manner, and with special protection for the disadvantaged. It is necessary to contribute to the benefits and risks of research fairly.

The principle of efficiency with nonmaleficence accords with no harmful practices, even if the patient acquiesces to such practices. Maleficence is conducting a clinical trial that will not be scientifically valid, either because the working assumption is not plausible or because the design is not methodologically correct.

> With our clinical trial, data helps to improve patient care. It also goes and helps ensure the important contribution made by people who take part in clinical trials is used to maximum effect in the creation of knowledge and

understanding. We are committed to public disclosure of all our clinical research, irrespective of whether the results are positive or negative for our medicines. We believe this is fundamental to the advancement of medical science. It is also the best way to tell patients about scientific findings relating to our medicines.

(Nathan, United States, expatriate in Vietnam
in pharmaceutical firm no. 1)

From theory to practices

From an American point of view, in theory, clinical trials are governed by strict regulation. There are always at least three phases to clinical trials.

Phase A

The first time a new treatment or vaccine is tested on humans, it will usually be given to a small group of healthy volunteers. However, in some cases, such as when a new medicine is being tested, it may be tested on volunteers who have the condition.

Phase B

If Phase A is successful, approval will be sought for a trial involving a larger group of people. Phase B trials will usually (but not always) include patients who have the condition the potential medicine is targeting and aims to establish:

*   Its effectiveness in treating the condition
*   Its effectiveness in preventing the condition (if the volunteer does not already have it)
*   Appropriate dosing levels

Phase C

If the results from Phase B are encouraging, the firm will seek to start a Phase C trial. This will be a much larger trial, often involving hundreds, possibly thousands, of participants coming from a range of different countries.

In practice,

> *The main reason we do it in Vietnam and not in India or in South Africa is firstly the lower costs and then the availability of "treatment open-minded" patients, who accept authority without so many questions . . . Regarding local authorities, the main incentive for Vietnam is the promise of advanced medical science and access to the latest medications.*

(Brian, American expatriate top manager
in pharmaceutical firm no. 1)

It is also important to mention that cultural factors in Vietnam seem to create a barrier to complying with the substantive ethical standard of informed consent, with the manner of how voluntary participation can be ensured in settings in which community leaders may exert pressure on the entire community to enroll in a proposed clinical trial. The verbatim report that follows provides a different viewpoint of the close link between economic status and clinical trials from the theoretical point of view and highlights the relevancy of two more aspects of drug testing: cost and marketing.

> *The cost of development of a new drug has been estimated by the US pharmaceutical firm at 350 million dollars. In addition to this initial cost, once this budget is approved, the marketing and advertising involved in the mentioned development are very costly activities that will raise the overall price of the operations. Therefore, those drugs that have reached the marketing authorization [phase] have to raise funds for the development of many other drugs which have not done so. It is estimated within the industry that the true cost of launching a new drug on the market, including failures, exceeds 650 million dollars.*
>
> (Sheila, American expatriate top manager
> in pharmaceutical firm no. 2)

So it is very important from an American point of view not only to ensure that those drugs placed on the Vietnamese market comply with sales expectations, but also to ensure that the pharmaceutical company's clinical programs can provide high-quality information to support regulatory arrangements, and also information to support business objectives before and after the launch of the drug on the market.

The challenge for the clinical and marketing teams, therefore, is to ensure the best interaction as quickly and effectively as possible once the product has entered into clinical development. The objective of almost all clinical studies is to ensure a quick registration through a process of rational development in order to be able to compensate for the big cost of the clinical research. In the past, most pharmaceutical companies tried to deal separately with the development of commercial teams and regulation teams. The team responsible for the regulatory package usually had no contact with the sales department. Better communication between the clinical and commercial departments, in addition to action-oriented organizational structures and project teams and integrated medical marketing, can give rise to the need for an integrated strategy.

> *The US business strategy in Vietnam can become an operational plan through the profile of a particular product in which the clinical and marketing departments have agreed to collaborate. The marketing department can provide valuable information to determine what information is needed for a particular study and why, and to finance the labelling and advertising. After that, the clinical and regulatory departments may indicate how and when it should be done.*
>
> (Brian, American expatriate top manager
> in pharmaceutical firm no. 1)

The clinical team creates the clinical trials, and once the outline of the study is decided, they will define the treatment, the population and the primary and secondary objectives. The marketing department can advise the most suitable marketing options given the Vietnam-centric nature of the drug development, advising on competition essays that could hinder the recruitment of pharmaceutical personnel and provide a global context for the research.

The research has found that in Vietnam in particular the medical visit has a strong influence on the doctor's prescriptions. A great deal of evidence in research studies. has shown that the attitudes of many doctors on drug promotion in Vietnam can vary to a large extent. Some doctors usually suggest that they should be trained in order to better interact with pharmaceutical companies' sales representatives, whereas others reject this idea. Many doctors strongly believe that the information usually provided to them about drugs by pharmaceutical companies in terms of promotion is useful; however, most doctors think the information is biased. There is a mixed opinion among doctors about direct-to-consumer promotion of drugs. The truth is that promotion tends to influence doctors' attitude more than they realize because they report that promotion is the most frequent source of information about new drugs after a clinical trial.

> It is the responsibility of a company to provide an extensive training to the Pharmaceutical Representatives about products in [the] promotional phase. The roles and responsibilities of Pharmaceutical Representatives should be clearly defined in order to enable Health Care Professionals to get the best clinical-decision-making. However, it is popularly well known that little is clear about Pharmaceutical Representatives['] attitudes regarding their roles as educators or marketers from an American point of view.
> (Brian, American expatriate top manager
> in pharmaceutical firm no. 1)

> Vietnamese people at work are disorganized, insincere and not disciplined at all. We have to be more focused on controlling the whole process of clinical trials in order to boost the work performance. Otherwise, if we let local people [do] the job we will have a low effectiveness. We need to work fast and oriented to be the first ones to enter the market.
> (Steve, American expatriate top manager
> in pharmaceutical firm no. 2)

Unadjusted expatriates regarding business from an America-centric point of view may focus more on the marketing strategy than on sociocultural aspects of their host country with predispositions on a specific business model. This business model, with its three phases, lets American top managers become more efficient but with an intentional, interpretive and memory orientation that can distort their general adjustment related to knowing how and knowing why, but not so oriented on people at work and delegation.

The French point of view: organizational actors, regulations and more ethical values

The pharmaceutical sector in the European Union is currently governed by several specific directives on the matter of clinical trials and many moral duties rather than marketing ones. They reflect the requirements of monitoring, verification and retention of data files of clinical trials even abroad in Vietnam. In an ethically sound consent process, a French member of the research team provides information to the potential participant, determines that the individual understands the information provided and ensures that the individual voluntarily agrees to participate. Although consent traditionally has been documented by the signing of a consent form, other methods of documentation are often acceptable or even preferable, such as oral consent with a witness signature. In many settings in Vietnam, it is also required that the person obtaining the consent sign the consent form or other related documents and that a witness (or person designated by the participant) attests to the process. It is always essential to make a distinction between the consent *document* and the consent *process* and to not allow the document itself to constitute the process.

In the Vietnamese cultural context, questions also arise regarding the appropriateness of requiring information to be disclosed about the use of a placebo in one arm of a clinical trial, the randomization of participants and any uncertainty that may exist regarding the efficacy of an experimental intervention. From a French point of view, drug investigators sometimes struggled with these barriers, responding in two ways. For example, in one case, investigators who believed that it would be impossible to obtain valid informed consent for a randomized trial abandoned the use of randomization in their research. However, in another case, investigators used placebos, even though they did not believe that the research participants understood the implications of doing so. Despite these barriers, cultural differences do not provide adequate justification for foregoing the requirement to disclose key elements of the nature of the clinical trial, such as the use of a placebo or the randomization of participants into different trial arms in Vietnam.

The French Clinical Research Unit where the interviews were obtained was established in 2006 and is hosted by the National Hospital of Tropical Diseases (NHTD). NHTD is a tertiary-level teaching hospital, receiving infection-related referrals from northern Vietnam, and has close ties to the Ministry of Health (MoH).

Through its partnership with the NHTD, the French Clinical Research Unit also works with other hospitals and institutes in the region, including the National Institute for Hygiene and Epidemiology, the National Paediatric Hospital, the National Center for Veterinary Diagnosis and regional hospitals and health stations for clinical trials. They recently completed a national program (Vietnam Resistance Project [VINARES]) to assess hospital-acquired infections, antibiotic use and antibiotic resistance in 16 hospitals across Vietnam. They had an associated closing meeting in October 2013 in Hanoi with 120 international participants. They are running one of the longest influenza household cohort studies worldwide in Ha Nam, Vietnam.

This cohort study has been going on for six years, leading to new knowledge in the area of influenza transmission and immunology with clinical trials.

The researchers had the opportunity to meet ten top executives in a French company. This French firm will expand its current 4 percent market stake in Vietnam. By 2015, the major French drugs will have invested US$75 million in a production plant. The subsidiary, which will be operational by 2015, is designed to meet the rising demand for pharmaceuticals in fast-growing Asian populations such as China, Indonesia and Vietnam. It will have an initial production capacity of 90 million units per year, which may be later extended to 150 million units, according to the company.

This French firm currently runs two plants in Ho Chi Minh City at full capacity; according to its CEO:

> Asia continues to grow and it seems to be less affected by the European economic difficulty. The rise of income and urbanization in the region will give people more access to health care. Currently sales from Vietnamese plants are growing 25 per cent annually, creating more than US$128m annually in Vietnam alone. The company, which exports just 20 per cent of the drugs manufactured in the country, will now expand its production capacity to create an export platform for the Southeast Asian region.

Theoretically from a European point of view, a clinical trial by a clinical trial by the French has three characteristics has three characteristics:

1 A pilot study carried out on humans, assigned to one of the intervention groups.
2 Trials are always prospective, planned and then carried out, following the evolution of research subjects over time.
3 The experimental nature of the clinical trial requires the researcher to consider three dimensions: methodological or scientific, ethical and regulatory rules because it is necessary to protect the integrity of patients and their rights, and the reliability of the data.

The principle of beneficence is a pointed principle, and Vietnamese people should be treated in accordance with this principle, protecting them from harm and ensuring their welfare, which means no intentional or negligent harm, and maximizing the benefits and minimizing the risks associated with the treatment.

In addition, the principle of autonomy is prioritized by European top pharmaceutical managers in treating Vietnamese people as autonomous beings and protecting those with diminished autonomy. In the application of this principle, consent from potential study participants before inclusion must be obtained. The autonomy is decreased in the case of ignorance, immaturity or mental disability.

> The participation of a human being in a clinical trial generates a potential situation of vulnerability in which their rights should be clearly protected. When a local doctor participates as an investigator in a clinical trial, he acts

simultaneously as a physician and scientist, a situation that can lead to an ethical dilemma. As a physician, he should strictly ensure the individual welfare of his patient, while as a scientist he should try to improve the benefits to society by thinking of the common good. Therefore, it is necessary that any medical research [they] undertake meets the ethical requirements clearly established in the Declaration of Helsinki.

(Claire, French expatriate top manager
in pharmaceutical firm no. 3)

Whether a clinical trial from a French point of view is with healthy volunteers or patients with illnesses, it is important to consider the ethical aspects of the study; therefore, at present, all clinical trial protocols must be evaluated by an independent body responsible for the review of their ethical and methodological content: the Clinical Research Ethics Committee.

The clinical trials undertaken by French firms whose objective is to evaluate the effectiveness of an experimental drug, treatment, device or intervention may be integrated into one of the following four phases (one more phase than American firms).

Phase A of clinical trials is carried out to see if the experimental drug or treatment is really safe. After the treatment has been tested in the lab or also on animals, it enters into a Phase A clinical trial because the trial is now done with humans.

A Phase A clinical trial never involves many subjects, and it is usually carried out on only a small number of people in order to determine if the experimental drug or treatment is safe for human use. It is also used to determine the most effective dose of the drug and how the aforementioned dose should be given (orally or intravenously, etc.). They usually test this new biomedical intervention on a small group of people (20 to 80) for the first time to evaluate its safety. The length of the study is usually a few months.

Phase B clinical trials basically study the behavioral or biomedical intervention on a more numerous group of people (usually involving several hundred patients) to determine the efficacy of the drug or treatment and also to further evaluate its safety. The length of Phase B clinical trials is usually up to two years.

Phase C clinical trials investigate the efficacy of the behavioral or biomedical intervention on large groups of humans (usually involving from several hundred to several thousand patients) by comparing the intervention to other standard or experimental interventions, as well as to monitor the possible adverse effects that might arise from a particular treatment. They also collect information that will allow the new treatment to be used in the safest way possible.

Phase C clinical trials may take several years. Once those trials are finalized, the experimental treatment can be approved for general use in humans and, in the case of drugs, for market release (getting marketing authorization).

Phase D studies are carried out after the intervention or the experimental drug has been marketed or once they have got marketing authorization. These studies are always designed to monitor the effectiveness of the approved drug or intervention while being used by the general population and to collect information about any associated adverse events that might arise during the course of the treatment.

A Phase D post-authorization study is a clinical trial, quasi-experimental study or observational study with the objective of gathering more specific information about a particular drug, biological product, device or procedure that has already got marketing authorization. Post-approval research in Phase D post-authorization studies is usually carried out to better understand the product in real-world situations, with the objective of obtaining evidence for higher remuneration or submission for expanded labeling, meaning that the product could be used to treat different or multiple diseases. Phase D post-authorization studies are also carried out to fulfill a specific requirement of regulatory authorities or to monitor the safety of a drug or device in a larger, nonclinical trial setting.

In everyday practice, European firms argue that regulations and ethical considerations are more important than marketing:

> Typically, the information provided by the industry has to reference clinical trials and marketing authorization where we can find the presented data. We must make a critical reading and make sure that the presented information comes from independent and objective sources. Furthermore, we must wonder: Is this relevant to the purpose of the study in Vietnam? Does the local Vietnamese study population reflect the normal clinical practice? Has it been compared to the best possible alternative and are we using right dose? Are we doing clinical trials or more and more business? Do we have non-neo-colonialist behaviour?
>
> (Patrick, French expatriate top manager
> in pharmaceutical firm no. 4)

9.4 Findings

Following the previously cited verbatim reports, the research highlights that health expenditure and some questionable business behavior occurrences are very high in Vietnam. Researchers have seen products sold in Hanoi where thousands of patients are recruited to take the more expensive drug; however, other equivalent cheaper drugs are sold in the same market and with the same benefits throughout the rest of the country. Unfortunately, if the drug has got marketing authorization, there are valid reasons to keep doing research about the safety of the drug, and because the existence of a study is justifiable to improve the product, it seems difficult to stop these kinds of studies.

In Vietnam, a process of community education acts as a precursor to the process of obtaining individual consent. A physician provided additional information and sought individual informed consent at the monthly vaccination session, and a clinical trial for vaccination was preceded by an intensive publicity campaign involving radio, newspapers and discussions with local leaders.

> When mothers attended the first child health clinic, they received an information sheet about the clinical trial to take home for discussion with their families. When a mother returned for the first vaccination, the trial worker

explained the study again, and, if the mother gave oral consent, the trial worker signed the information sheet.

(Lucas, French top manager in pharmaceutical firm no. 4)

Translation and back-translation of a written consent form is one way of ensuring that information is correctly disclosed; however, this may not always be effective. Because the consent form had to be reviewed by the Vietnamese authorities and the European firm, a translation in English was also required. The back-translation of a consent form

> does not guarantee that volunteers have really understood the objective of the study, the risks and advantages, and their voluntary participation . . . The problem may not lie in the idea that an offer to possibly receive medical care is an inducement, but rather in the difficulty of determining when such an offer, admittedly an inducement, becomes undue.
>
> (George, French expatriate top manager in pharmaceutical firm no. 3)

French top executives who argue that participation in research constitutes an undue inducement for poor people in Vietnam would have to maintain that offering high-quality medical care and treatment that participants would not otherwise receive is unwarranted and inappropriate. However, the provision of medical care or treatment that would not otherwise be available to research participants should not, in principle, be construed as an undue influence to participate.

> The fact that the participants in the clinical trial lack access to other alternative medical care does not sufficiently diminish the voluntariness of their decision to participate in the research in a way that would make their consent ethically invalid.
>
> (George, French expatriate top manager in pharmaceutical firm no. 3)

> Some Vietnamese local workforce is bureaucratic and too much focused on details. At the same time to go against corruption practices, it is better to go slow but far rather than to make business on the short run and then to be boycotted by local authorities. We have a huge responsibility for well-being, not just for say but in the everyday practices. To be a leading pharmaceutical lab for one year is not our priority but to go step by step and to get results in the long run is our main concern.
>
> (Claire, French expatriate top manager in pharmaceutical firm no. 3)

That is the main reason why French firms say that even if regulations can be improved, it is important to make more efforts in the ethical education of health care providers, which is of crucial importance to achieving the best health care with more efficiency. This way, only those products that are more competitive could succeed in the Vietnamese market against aggressive American marketing campaigns.

Since the 2000s there has been an increase in clinical trials and observational studies in Vietnam conducted by American and French firms to develop new treatments and also to improve the effectiveness. However, in some of those activities characteristics are apparent that lead the researchers to believe that there is more marketing from the US companies' point of view than science behind them. The attempts by some US pharmaceutical companies to patent new drugs that are basically copies of older developed ones in order to avoid the expiration of the patent and the marketing practices of the commercial teams with doctors as staff members have not contributed to improve the image of the overseas pharmaceutical industry in Vietnam.

Clinical research from a French point of view is seen as a complex project, costly and a long-term business, where they need to find customers. The key implication for clinicians is that it is not sufficient to manage the ethical issues that those studies might involve and that they should also take into consideration that marketing and sales activities play a significant role within an industry that invests billions in the development of new products.

From a French point of view, it has been pointed out that a fundamental principle of research ethics is the requirement that participation be voluntary – that is, "free of coercion and undue influence". However, among the most difficult requirements to ensure is the voluntariness with which participants consent to enroll in a study. It is obvious that the pressure from a local community leader in Vietnam, the power and authority of the medical professionals who serve as test investigators and the fear of loss of health benefits that people would normally expect to receive may compromise individuals' freedom to refuse to participate in research in Vietnam. The provision of medical care and treatment during a study may constitute an incentive for individuals to enroll in a study, but it should not be construed as a coercive offer that would unduly compromise the voluntariness of participation.

Based on the detailed results of this observatory research, the major findings can be summarized in the following: Perceptions of respondents from the two countries differ mostly with respect to climate and general sociocultural adjustment and then business ethics conditions. They consider that home marketing and human resources orientation differ most from those in Vietnam, and everyday customs and business ethics come next.

Therefore, based on the results from the analysis of cultural distance for the respondents from France and the United States, it is proven that the first hypothesis is accurate and true. Hypothesis 1 was: The American expatriate top managers in Vietnam perceive greater cultural distance between Vietnam and their home country than do the French expatriate top managers, especially in terms of sociocultural adjustment and business ethics conditions.

To verify hypothesis 2 ("The French expatriate top managers working in Vietnam demonstrate a higher degree of adaptability than the American business expatriates in general adjustment and interaction adjustment, but not in fast business model results"), the study looked at different variables (work adjustment, role clarity, relational and perceptual skills and assignment vector). It can be clearly observed that all interaction and general adjustment variables are significantly connected to the better process of adaptability for French expatriate top managers in comparison to American ones. Such finding supports hypothesis 2 only partly, however, because it is necessary to better understand and test the French and American business models.

Based on the first results, it seems that hypothesis 3 ("French expatriates take a prolonged period of time to adjust, exhibit poor performance in the short run and complete their assignment in a low state of effectiveness") could be partly true. A longer period of research will have to be taken to prove it.

The study has significant implications for policy makers on a national and international level, as health care development benefits all of us in society from a French point of view. One limitation of the study lies in the classifications of similar or dissimilar cultures relative to the US and French expatriate top managers' cultures as the parent country' culture. Because the expatriates are working in large multinational pharmaceutical labs, differences in the national culture may be obscured by the corporate culture to some extent.

Ethics is a long-term process, and the pharmaceutical sector needs to put a stop to the negative practices highlighted earlier in this chapter. The study reveals how key health care opinion leaders – that is, health care professionals thought to be especially influential on health care practices or policies – were paid to become marketers for the pharmaceutical sector in Vietnam, presumably without revealing this conflict of interest.

References

Berry J.W. (1997) Immigration, Acculturation, and Adaptation, *Applied Psychology*, 46(1), pp. 5–34.

Berry J.W., Kim U. and Boski P. (1988) Psychological Acculturation of Immigrants, in *Cross-cultural Adaptation: Current Approaches*, (eds) Young Yun Kim and William B., Gudykunst, Sage, Newbury Park, CA, pp. 62–89.

Black J.S. and Morisson A.J. (2014) *The Global Leadership Challenge*, Routledge, New York.

Black J.S. and Stephens G.K. (1989) The Influence of the Spouse on American Expatriate Adjustment and Intent to Stay in Pacific Rim Overseas Assignments, *Journal of Management*, 15(4), pp. 529–544.

Black J.S., Mendenhall M. and Oddou G. (1991) Toward a Comprehensive Model of International Adjustment: An Integration of Multiple Theoretical Perspectives, *The Academy of Management Review*, 16(2), pp. 291–317.

Forster N. (1997) The Persistent Myth of High Expatriate Failure Rates: A Reappraisal, *The International Journal of Human Resource Management*, 8(4), pp. 414–433.

Goldberg D.P. (1972) *The Detection of Psychiatric Illness by Questionnaire: A Technique for the Identification and Assessment of Non-psychotic Psychiatric Illness*, Oxford University Press, London.

Harrison D.A., Shaffer M.A. and Bhaskar-Shrinivas P. (2004) Going Places: Roads More and Less Traveled in Research on Expatriate Experiences, *Research in Personnel and Human Resource Management*, 23, pp. 203–252.

Harzing A.W. and Noorderhaven N. (2006) Geographical Distance and the Role and Management of Subsidiaries: The Case of Subsidiaries Down-under, *Asia Pacific Journal of Management*, 23(2), pp. 167–185.

Hellriegel D., Slocum J., Jackson S., Louw L., Staude G., Amos T., Klopper H.B., Louw M., Oosthuizen T., Perks S. and Zindiye S. (2012) *Management*, 4th edition, Oxford University Press, Southern Africa.

Henry A. (2011) Les traductions vietnamiennes d'un code d'éthique français, *Annales des Mines – Gérer et comprendre*, 104, pp. 48–60.

Nguyen KV T. and Wertheim H.F (2013) Antibiotic Use and Resistance in Emerging Economies: A Situation Analysis for Viet Nam, *BMC Public Health*, 13(1158), pp. 1–10.

Rossouw G.J. and van Vuuren L.J. (2004) *Business Ethics*, 3rd edition, Oxford University Press, Cape Town.

Scherer A.G. and Palazzo G. (2007) Toward a Political Conception of Corporate Social Responsibility: Business and Society Seen from a Habermasian Perspective, *The Academy of Management Review*, 32(4), pp. 1096–1120.

Shaffer M.A., Harrison D.A. and Gilley K.M. (1999) Dimension, Determinants, and Differences in the Expatriate Adjustment Process, *Journal of International Business Studies*, 30(3), pp. 557–581.

Smith T. (2007) *Ayn Rand's Normative Ethics: The Virtuous Egoist*, Cambridge University Press, Cambridge.

Sorge A. (2005) *The Global and the Local: Understanding the Dialectics of Business Systems*, Oxford University Press, Oxford.

Stahl G.K. and Cerdin J.L. (2004) Global Careers in French and German Multinational Corporations, *Journal of Management Development*, 23(9), pp. 885–902.

Tahvanainen M., Welch D. and Worm V. (2005) Implications of Short-term International Assignments, *European Management Journal*, 23(6), pp. 663–673.

Tempel A. and Walgenbach P. (2007) Global Standardization of Organizational Forms and Management Practices? What New Institutionalism and the Business-Systems Approach Can Learn from Each Other, *Journal of Management Studies*, 44(1), pp. 1–24.

Tung R.L. (1998) American Expatriates Abroad: From Neophytes to Cosmopolitans, *Journal of World Business*, 33(2), pp. 125–144.

Vogel D. (2005) *The Market for Virtue: The Potential and Limits of Corporate Social Responsibility*, Brookings Institution Press, Washington, DC.

Wagstaff A. (2007) The Economic Consequences of Health Shocks: Evidence from Vietnam, *Journal of Health Economics*, 26(1), pp. 82–100.

Wooten K. (2001) Ethical Dilemmas in Human Resources Management: An Application of a Multidimensional Framework, a Unifying Taxonomy, and Applicable Codes, *Human Resources Management Review*, 11(1–2), pp. 159–175.

Yin R.K. (1994) *Case Study Research: Design and Methods*, 2nd edition, Sage, Thousand Oaks.

Zhou X. and Qin J. (2009) A Study on Cross-cultural Adjustment of Japanese and American Expatriates in China, *International Journal of Business and Management*, 4(12), pp. 197–206.

10 Synthesis and conclusions

*M. Bruna Zolin, Bernadette Andreosso-
O'Callaghan and Jacques Jaussaud*

A selected number of key issues that most East Asian countries are facing currently, particularly since the global financial crisis (GFC), are explored in this book from both a macroeconomic approach and a business corporation's point of view. Even if the East Asian economies are among the most successful economies in the world, the intensity of concerns increased with the GFC and limits on growth have been dramatically emerging. Among the East Asian countries, China plays a crucial role. With the opening of its markets, China strongly influences the world economy, and its contribution to global trade and output growth has been far bigger than that of any other economy over recent decades. With a GDP growth rate that has slipped well below the yearly average of 10 percent, China faces now more and more questions about how its leadership and policy-making authorities should manage the next phase of the country's economic development in a situation in which China is rapidly becoming one of the most indebted countries in the world.

According to Chapter 1, debt restructuring implies a redefinition of the power relations and respective functions of the central and local governments (Zhao, 2013), as well as the relations between the central government and the state sector. The debts' pyramidal structure is linked to the power structure. The central government is supposed to regulate macroeconomic management, to deal with financial stability, and to bail every one out in case of problems. A situation in which local authorities manage most public expenditures and the central government is supposed to cover all risks is a situation of shared responsibility. However, the central government has the ability to modify it. At the beginning of 2014, it gave local governments the go-ahead to issue bonds as a way of rolling over their debt to avoid defaults. This massive debt-refinancing operation is underway (Rabinovitch, 2014). As a sovereign currency issuer, China has some policy space that dispenses it from fiscal austerity measures, which have been the case in Europe. The danger faced by excessive sovereign government budget deficits is inflation, not insolvency (Randall and Liu, 2014). Although local government debt is sustainable at the 2018 horizon, according to different IMF scenarios, the fragmentation of debts at the local level tends to raise the borrowing costs (Zhang and Barnett, 2014). In addition, local governments might easily hide deficits and debts or engage in short-run policies to obtain financing that are not sound in the long run. For these reasons, some stress that the fiscal reform package should put more of the spending and responsibilities at the central level because of the risk of inflation (Randall and Liu, 2014).

Although national and local government deficits and debt are relatively limited, China's corporate debt stands at a world record as a percentage of GDP (150 percent). If much of this debt has been issued by public companies, the national government will come to the rescue of these firms, and potential liabilities could be as high as 100 percent of GDP, perhaps even more if we take into account the impact of this bailout on banks' policies (Randall and Liu, 2014). Tighter credit and the rise of financing costs will produce a slowdown of real estate transactions, which may affect, along with industrial overcapacity, the public finance resources, at the same time when expenditure is growing, not only to cover the foreseeable losses of the financial system, but also to meet the social targets of the new leadership. Because income redistribution and inclusive development depend largely on the state financial capacity, fiscal policy could be a key structural reform. Structural reforms are essential in the long term, but they necessarily hurt many interests as they imply a redistribution of income in favor of the working population. In the short run, the necessary reduction of investment will put pressure on employment and household income growth, unless there is a significant transfer of resources from the state and real estate sectors to households (Pettis, 2013).

Chapter 2 evaluates whether the financialization concept can meaningfully be applied to China by observing economic developments and bearing in mind the role of political actors in financial governance and regulation. Using a number of macroeconomic indicators, the chapter shows that investment (gross fixed capital formation) has tended to move away from savings before the GFC; that profit rates of SOEs have declined sharply with the crisis; that the growth rate of residential real estate investment has, until very recently, surpassed the growth rate of the economy; that stock market capitalization has soared, in spite of underdeveloped stock exchange markets; that there has been a substantial upward trend in corporate financial investment; and that the size of shadow banking could be as large as the Chinese GDP.

Overall, investments and profits in the financial sector have been growing faster than in other sectors of the economy. Concerning its size as a share of the economy as a whole, all the measures show that regulated and unregulated finance in the past 10 to 15 years have gained in proportion, even if the developments in certain subsectors such as real estate have been unsteady. Whereas the financial sector has been expanding in relative terms, there exists as of yet, no systematic research or evidence showing that financial sources of income have become widely and systematically integrated into the core businesses of nonfinancial firms until 2013, constituting a process of financialization in the nonfinancial corporate sector. More recently, however, firm-level, bottom-up financial 'innovation' has contributed to a surge of shadow banking. Local state entities and mostly state-controlled corporations with access to formal finance, channelling these resources into unregulated financial products, may, in hindsight, prove to be forerunners of a wider trend of corporate financialization.

Finally, the chapter suggests that the politics of regulation in China are not sufficiently described as a cat-and-mouse game between financial innovators regularly
outpacing regulators. Indeed, on the political level, financial developments in the
aftermath of the GFC may be built upon to achieve some wider reform objectives.
A deeper and more systematic role for finance in investment and consumption
patterns would confirm a general pattern of experimental policy making defined
by the relationship of central and local actors and their competing or colluding
interests in China's party-state. In some ways, financialization, as an important
approach to better understand today's political economy in China, has very much
been and is still an ad hoc type or coincidental financialization tied to various crisis
dynamics that are currently observable. This could suggest, therefore, that uncertainty is paramount with regard to the question of how finance can be integrated
systematically, or even sustainably, into a new and reformed growth regime. It will
remain to be seen whether the phenomenon of financialization observable in China
will provide the nuclei of a future fully developed financialized growth regime in
the theoretical sense, of which there is currently no sufficient evidence. Just as
likely, current developments may provide the basis of potential economic (and
political) instability arising from 'disordered' financialization in China.

The question posed by Chapter 3 is why, despite the highest growth achieved
by the East Asian region, some countries in the region could not shift to the
higher income group and stayed instead in the same income group for the last
two decades. Chapter 3 also tries to check whether East Asian economies follow
through their development path the Environmental Kuznets Curves (EKCs) in
terms of CO_2 emissions.

Out of nine middle-income countries in East Asia, four countries (i.e., Papua
New Guinea and the Philippines in the lower-middle-income group and Malaysia and Thailand in the upper-middle-income group) could not graduate into the
higher-income group. According to Chapter 3, only Papua New Guinea and the
Philippines seem to be qualified for the "middle-income trap", failing to graduate
into the upper-middle-income group. Upper-middle-income Malaysia and Thailand, which have higher CO_2–GNI elasticities, can be broadly termed as "middle-income trapped" being unable to rise to a high-income status, although they
had shifted earlier from the lower-middle-income to the upper-middle-income
status. China, the world's largest emitter of CO_2 with a low CO_2–GNI elasticity
and currently classified as a middle-income economy, may not be qualified for
the "middle-income trap" group in its rigorous sense despite its recent economic
slowdown after two decades of a 10 percent average annual growth rate. China's
middle-income-trap myth, if it exists, may largely be due to noneconomic factors
such as air pollution and social problems, rather than to economic ones, which
could constrain sustainable development.

The results of the chapter show that EKCs can be traceable to some extent,
although their trend lines are still on the rise, seemingly away from the turning
point. Clearly, the East Asian EKC is still on the rising side of the curve rather than
on the declining side, although further income increases may change the shape of
the EKC, and China's case offers some lessons on how an industrial shift from

self-contained economic policies to openness and reforms can be conducive to economic growth.

In 2007–08, new and old forces drove up the prices of agricultural commodities, causing a major food crisis (Von Braun, 2008). The financial crisis stemmed from different causes, but the two crises have fed on each other and are interconnected, especially in terms of the implications for financial stability and speculation phenomenon. At present, Chinese commodity markets are still at a developmental stage, with only the three stock exchange markets trading in a small group of commodities. In the future, the Chinese government will gradually allow more commodity products to be traded along with various related derivatives. Actually, as a major producer and consumer of commodities, China has a large potential for developing its futures market. Among the commodities, the importance of cotton stems from its connection to both the agricultural sector and the textile industry.

The cotton market is governed by a few countries, and China is the leading actor at the global level, being the world's largest producer, consumer, and importer. Indeed, Chinese cotton public policy, based namely on a cotton reserve system and on import quotas, has a strong influence on the world cotton market. The massive concentration of the global cotton buffer supplied in China provides the country with the power to balance the market: when the international cotton price decreases, China stockpiles cotton and buys abroad – then sells it to the domestic market at a higher price – and vice versa. Following the 2008 global crisis, most studies have highlighted causal relationships between price volatility, derivatives, and futures markets. In Chapter 4, the calculations related to the main macroeconomic variables affecting the cotton market reveal that cotton production in China is influenced by the size of the harvested area dedicated to cotton cultivation and land productivity, whereas cotton consumption is strongly correlated with the increase in population and its living standards. Cotton imports and exports strongly depend on exchange rate movements. A negative correlation between cotton prices and cotton production and imports was found. As expected, a result emerging from the analysis is the strong impact of prices and, most of all, of the price of cotton substitutes. Competition with cheaper and technologically advanced manufactured fibers is indeed one of the biggest challenges that the cotton sector is facing. For farmers, prices are the driving force: unstable crop prices, together with bad weather and high fertilizer or seed costs, are capable of wiping out their profits and pushing them to plant other crops. The Chinese, and consequently the world cotton market, are facing a number of challenges due to the influence of economic, social, and environmental issues. Among the economic issues, the small size of farms prevents the achievement of economies of scale. The survival of small and marginal farms is highly linked to government support and, in the absence of the latter, these farms could disappear. Among the environmental concerns to be considered are the high water requirements of the crop, the abundant use of chemical inputs, the conflicting results of the effects on the soil and on human health of genetically modified organisms (GMOs), the treatment of waste materials (plastic residues), and the limitation of the most important factor of production (land). Concerning social issues, the extreme dependence on income derived from the cultivation of cotton, in particular its importance to rural and poor people in China, has to be mentioned. Considering all these elements, it is very likely that in the future there could be a shift, if not in cotton production, at least in cotton consumption and, consequently, in the textile industry from China to countries with economies characterized by lower labor costs and fewer environmental restrictions, and where future projections forecast increasing income per capita and population growth rates.

The four chapters of Part I clearly set out the macroeconomic background within which East Asian economies and the business entities therein have been evolving particularly since the GFC. The second part of this book is dedicated to a firm's analysis trying to identify the strategies (new or revised) that companies are implementing so as to adapt to different circumstances. These strategies revolve essentially around issues of sustainability, including, for example, corporate and social responsibility (CSR) and ethical considerations.

Chapter 5 focuses on a neoinstitutional approach (DiMaggio and Powell, 1991a, 1991b; Meyer and Rowan, 1991), according to which firms from different countries often adopt different management styles, implement different organizational choices, and even weigh differently main business objectives, such as profitability, growth, and CSR objectives. Based on such an approach and with the help of a regression analysis, a sample of 125 firms was carefully drawn from France, Japan, and Spain, with relevant data on their social, environmental, and corporate governance performance and on their financial performance. The chapter highlights that companies from different countries, with different institutional backgrounds, have different priorities in terms of social, environmental, and corporate governance performance.

Furthermore, in line with Amann *et al.* (2007), the link between CSR performance and financial performance is moderated by the institutional environment of firms, namely by the country they come from. More specifically, Spanish and French firms achieve higher levels of social and corporate governance performance than Japanese firms do, but the latter are more committed to environmental issues than the former. Besides, financial performance has a greater influence on the three dimensions of CSR performance (social, environmental, and corporate governance) for France and Spain. CSR is more environmentally oriented in Japanese companies. This may result from various national characteristics, such as the high concentration of the population in Japan in huge urban areas, which led them to become highly sensitive to environmental issues or to the influence of Confucian and Buddhist conceptions on the relationship between mankind and nature, which contrasts to some extent with the Christian one (Ortas *et al.*, 2015). One may also wonder why CSR is less governance and even less socially oriented in Japanese companies than in French and Spanish companies. In broad terms, a stronger inclination in the case of Japan to informal and undisclosed arrangements may partly explain this outcome, among other institutional reasons.

In Chapter 6, the relationship between CSR assessment and the international transfer of environmental management by Japanese firms in Vietnam is analyzed. If the existing literature did not sufficiently focus on the transfer of environmental practices to overseas operations, the results of the analysis reveal that CSR assessment of parent firms promotes this transfer even to overseas operations. Therefore, for sustainability in the global sense, the environmental strategy and management systems in MNEs are important and effective in the transmission to developing countries. Social consciousness for sustainability promotes good firm behavior. Besides, the research provides useful findings and contributes to the development of new research issues (such as greenhouse gas emissions management and more proactive corporate strategies). For that purpose, the acceptance by firms of a strong social philosophy helps improve the practices of the firms globally. For multinational enterprises, it is important to promote the transfer of environmental management practices and, at the same time, to implement CSR.

Comparing the accounting standards for small and medium-sized enterprises (SMEs) in Japan and the Philippines from the perspectives of a standards model and standards setting, Chapter 7 clarifies the characteristics and homologous points of the two countries with different adoptions of the accounting system for SMEs on the basis of different economic circumstances. Both countries show differences in their approaches to adopting the International Financial Reporting Standards (IFRS) for SMEs, but they display similarities in their approaches to SMEs standards. In Japan, like many other developed countries, the standards for SMEs are individually set, but there are currently two standards with different characteristics which are generally used in accordance with SMEs' business situations. Since January 2010, the Philippines have adopted the IFRS for SMEs. However, many SMEs in the Philippines do not comply correctly, because there is no strict monitoring of compliance with the accounting standards, given that the authorities are mainly concerned with tax revenue. By comparing the cases of Japan and the Philippines, Chapter 7 calls for the use of an appropriate accounting standard for each situation, namely taking into account the limited revenues and capital size of SMEs.

Using environmental accounting information, Chapter 8 examines a method of analysis and evaluation of estimated economic benefits stemming from a firm's sustainability activities. It also states that environmental accounting information would be useful to long-term investors; an example is to estimate economic benefits when future climate change is taken into consideration. The use of real-option valuation methods is shown as valid in calculating the value of such benefits. That value can be found in a firm's projects.

A trial calculation of the economic benefits from sustainability activities was conducted using Toyota as a case study. Based on sustainability reports, the chapter concludes that companies combining sustainability operations with their main business have an estimated economic benefit coming from the positive influence of sustainability operations on their performance. The example of the current global warming measures conducted by Toyota is found in the extension line of conventional CSR management. From there, if a new opportunity such as the fuel-cell vehicle comes into being and can be sold in the market, the economic benefits would be beyond expectation. And that is the estimated economic benefit arising from sustainability activities. If it could be represented as an option value, then it would be useful information to investors. However, because the estimated economic effects are originally intended to be used only internally as strategic accounting numbers, it is not possible to disclose the option value externally as it is. Therefore, how one represents the estimated economic effects as external information will be an issue in the future

Comparing American and French firms operating in the pharmaceutical sector in Vietnam, Chapter 9 focuses on health expenditures and highlights that expenditures and some questionable business behavior practices are very high. Since the 2000s there has been an increase in clinical trials and in observational studies in Vietnam conducted by American and French firms aiming at developing new treatments and also at improving the effectiveness of other treatments. In some of those activities, some characteristics are visible that lead to the belief that there is more marketing from the US companies' point of view than science behind them. The attempts by some US pharmaceutical companies to patent new drugs that are copies of older developed ones in order to avoid the expiration of patents and the marketing practices of the commercial teams with doctors as staff members have not contributed to improve the image of the overseas pharmaceutical industry in Vietnam. Clinical research from a French point of view is seen as a complex project and as a costly and a long-term business for which they need to find customers. The key implication for clinicians is that it is not sufficient to manage the ethical issues that those studies might involve; they should also take into consideration that marketing and sales activities play a significant role within an industry that invests heavily in the development of new products.

From a French point of view, a fundamental principle of research ethics is the requirement that participation be voluntary. However, among the most difficult requirements to ensure is the voluntariness with which participants consent to enroll in a study. It is obvious that the pressure from a local community leader in Vietnam, the power and authority of the medical professionals who serve as test investigators, and the fear of loss of health benefits that people would normally expect to receive may all compromise individuals' freedom to refuse participating in research studies. The provision of medical care and treatment during a study may constitute an incentive for individuals to enroll in a project, but it should not be construed as a coercive offer.

Based on detailed results, the major findings of this last chapter may be summarized as follows. As far as cultural distance is concerned, it was found that the American expatriate top managers in Vietnam perceive greater cultural distance between Vietnam and their home country than do the French expatriate top managers, especially in terms of sociocultural adjustment and business ethics conditions. The French expatriate top managers working in Vietnam demonstrate a higher degree of adaptability than do the American business expatriates in general adjustment and interaction adjustment, but not in fast business model results. Moreover, French expatriates take a prolonged period to adjust, exhibit poor performance in the short run, and complete their assignment in a low state of effectiveness. However, because the expatriates are working in large multinational pharmaceutical labs, differences in the national culture may be obscured by the corporate culture to some extent. Finally, ethics is a long-term process, and the pharmaceutical sector needs to put a stop to some negative practices highlighted in the chapter. The study reveals how key health care opinion leaders – that is, health care professionals thought to be especially influential in terms of health care practices or policies – were paid to become marketers for the pharmaceutical sector, presumably without revealing this conflict of interest.

References

Amann B., Caby J., Jaussaud J. and Piniero J. (2007) Shareholder Activism for Corporate Social Responsibility: Law, and Practices in the United States, Japan, France and Spain, in *The New Corporate Accountability, Corporate Social Responsibility and the Law*, (eds) McBarnet D., Voiculescu A. and Campbell T., Cambridge University Press, Cambridge, pp. 336–364.

DiMaggio P.J. and Powell W.W. (1991a) Introduction, in (eds.) DiMaggio P.J. and Powell W.W., *The New Institutionalism in Organizational Analysis*, The University of Chicago Press, Chicago and London, p. 1–38.

DiMaggio P.J. and Powell W.W. (1991b) The Iron Cage Revisited: Institutional Isomorphism and Collective Rationality in Organizational Fields, in (eds.) DiMaggio P.J. and Powell W.W., *The New Institutionalism in Organizational Analysis*, The University of Chicago Press, Chicago and London, p. 63–82.

Meyer J.W. and Rowan B. (1991) Institutionalized Organizations: Formal Structure as Myth and Ceremony, in (eds.) DiMaggio P.J. and Powell W.W., *The New Institutionalism in Organizational Analysis*, The University of Chicago Press, Chicago and London, p. 41–62.

Ortas E., Alvarez I., Jaussaud J. and Garayar A. (2015) The Impact of Institutional and Social Context on Corporate Environmental, Social and Governance Performance of Companies Committed to Voluntary Corporate Social Responsibility Initiatives, *Journal of Cleaner Production*, 108(A), pp. 673–684.

Pettis M. (2013) *China Financial Markets: The Urbanization Fallacy*, 16 August 2013. Available from: http://blog.mpettis.com/2013/08/the-Urbanization-Fallacy/ [Accessed: 3 November 2015].

Rabinovitch S. (2014) China Gives Local Governments Go-ahead to Roll over Debt, *Financial Times*, 2 January 2014. Available from: www.ft.com/intl/cms/s/0/055e48f8–7371–11e3-a0c0–00144feabdc0.html#axzz42PsOSphz [Accessed: 27 August 2015].

Randall W.L. and Liu X. (2014) *Options for China in a Dollar Standard World: A Sovereign Currency Approach*, Working Paper No.783, Levy Economics Institute of Bard College.

Von Braun J. (2008) *Food and Financial Crises: Implications for Agriculture and the Poor*, International Food Policy Research Institute, Washington, DC.

Zhang Y.S. and Barnett S. (2014) *Fiscal Vulnerabilities and Risks from Local Governement Finance in China*, International Monetary Fund (IMF) Working Paper, No.14/4, January 2014.

Zhao S. (2013) *Zhongxing jieding zhongyang difang quanli guanxi* (Let Us Define the Power Relations between the Central and the Local Governments), Zhongguo jingji baogao (China Economic Report), n°9, Beijing: State Council Development Research Centre.

Index

Note: Italicized page numbers indicate a figure on the corresponding page. Page numbers in bold indicate a table on the corresponding page.